THE
HORSE
IN THE
MIDDLE AGES

THE HORSE
IN THE
MIDDLE AGES

ANN HYLAND

FOREWORD BY
JOAN THIRSK

SUTTON PUBLISHING

First published in the United Kingdom in 1999 by
Sutton Publishing Limited · Phoenix Mill
Thrupp · Stroud · Gloucestershire · GL5 2BU

British Library Cataloguing in Publication Data
A catalogue record for this book is available from the British Library

ISBN 0 7509 1067 4

 ™ ALAN SUTTON™ and SUTTON™ are the
trade marks of Sutton Publishing Limited

Typeset in 10/11pt Ehrhardt.
Typesetting and origination by
Sutton Publishing Limited.
Printed in Great Britain by
Redwood, Trowbridge, Wiltshire.

Contents

List of Illustrations   vii

Acknowledgements   ix

Foreword by Joan Thirsk   xi

Introduction   1

  1 *Domesday and Before*   3

  2 *Supply and Demand*   11

  3 *Everyman's Horse*   27

  4 *Farming and Commerce*   39

  5 *Trades and Crafts*   51

  6 *The Black Prince's* Register*:*

      The Horse in Estate Management 71

  7 *Hunting*   83

  8 *Tournaments*   99

  9 *Medieval Postal Services*   117

10 *Travel*   123

11 *Warhorse Territory: The Geographical Canvas*   139

Conclusion   153

Glossary   155

Notes   157

Bibliography   169

Index of Horse-related Subjects   175

General Index   177

List of Illustrations

The Aberlemno churchyard cross (Historical Monuments of Scotland)   5

A packpony from the Bayeux Tapestry (The Bayeux Tapestry – 11th century. By special permission of the City of Bayeux)   7

Great Seal of King Stephen (J. Hewitt, *Ancient Armour and Weapons in Europe* (1855))   16

Second Great Seal of King Henry III (J. Hewitt, *Ancient Armour and Weapons in Europe* (1855))   16

Seal of the Earl of Winchester (J. Hewitt, *Ancient Armour and Weapons in Europe* (1855))   16

An Italian noble's horse, by Mantegna (By permission of Ministero per i Beni Culturali e Ambientali, Mantua)   20

Woodcut by Dürer of a horse lacking breeding (© The British Museum)   23

Woodcut by Dürer of a well-bred horse (© The British Museum)   23

Muscovite cavalry (© The British Museum)   24

Chinese tribute horses (© The British Museum)   25

Crusaders and pilgrims (Illustration from the Maciejowski Bible, The Pierpont Morgan Library, New York. M.638, f. 10ᵛ; © The Pierpont Morgan Library)   29

Medieval trick horse (1) (© Bodleian Library, Oxford)   37

Medieval trick horse (2) (© Bodleian Library, Oxford)   37

Cart horses in tandem (in *Heures Dites de la Duchesse de Bourgogne*; Musée Condé/Giraudon)   40

Hercarius from the Bayeux Tapestry (The Bayeux Tapestry – 11th century. By special permission of the City of Bayeux)   44

Illustration of a mule by Pisanello (Photo: R.M.N.; reproduced by courtesy of Louvre Departement des Arts Graphiques)   48

The Sigurd saga carving (H. Faith/ATA, Stockholm)   52

Ornamental riding saddle (© The Wallace Collection)   59

War saddle (from the *Encyclopedie Medievale* by Viollet le Duc)   60

Henry V's war saddle (by courtesy of the Dean and Chapter of Westminster)   61

A fifteenth-century medieval spur (from the *Encyclopedie Medievale* by Viollet le Duc)   62

Winklepicker sabaton and shaped footplate (from the *Encyclopedie Medievale* by Viollet le Duc)   63

Stirrup with anti-slip treads (from the *Encyclopedie Medievale* by Viollet le Duc)   64

The bit found in Pergamon (from an article by Wolfgang Gaitzsch, published in *ISTMITT*, 37 (1987))   65

Reconstruction of the bit inside a horse's mouth (from an article by Wolfgang Gaitzsch, published in *ISTMITT*, 37 (1987))   66

Reconstruction of the exterior of the bit (from an article by Wolfgang Gaitzsch, published in *ISTMITT*, 37 (1987))   66

Early mêlée before horses were armoured (J. Hewitt, *Ancient Armour and Weapons in Europe* (1855))   67

Horse with protective armour (© Historisches Museum der Stadt Wien)   68
Elaborate armour (© The Wallace Collection)   69
St Hubert's vision by Dürer (Graphische Sammlung Albertina)   83
A Persian hunt (© The British Library)   88
Lassoing a horse (© The British Museum)   89
Medieval 'hunt servants' from *Livre de la Chasse* by Gaston Phébus (© Bibliothèque
    Nationale, Paris)   93
Three stages of falconry (© The British Museum)   94
A town square mêlée by Lucas Cranach (© The British Museum)   102
Another mêlée crush in a town square by Lucas Cranach (© The British Museum)   102
The Warwick chamfron (Photo: author)   109
Totally encasing jousting saddle (Photo: author)   113
The reality of the joust (© The British Museum)   115
A Persian drawing – Oriental traveller (© The British Library)   124
The battle of Anghiari by Pierre Paul Rubens, copy of a fresco painted by Leonardo
    da Vinci for the Palazzo Vecchio, Florence (Photo: R.M.N.; reproduced by
    courtesy of Louvre Departement des Arts Graphiques)   144
The battle of Pavia as recreated by Leeds Armoury (Photo: author)   145
Two Mamluk horsemen (© The British Library, Add. MS 18866, f. 97a)   147
A Mamluk horseman with a shield (© The British Library, Add. MS 18866, f. 129b)   148
A Mamluk horseman with a sword in his hand (© The British Library, Add. MS
    18866, f. 122b)   149

Acknowledgements

I would like to thank Dr Joan Thirsk for reading my manuscript, making helpful suggestions and for writing the foreword. Thanks are also due to Russell Lyon MRCVS for discussions over various equine and bovine diseases; Professor Frank Walbank and Frank Brudenell for loans of hard to locate contemporary source material; to the Royal Armouries for the chance to take detailed measurements of medieval armour; to staff at Wisbech Library for acquiring other reference material; to my publishers for being always helpful and, unlike some others, completely straight with me. Lastly, appreciation is due to a succession of horses, particularly Magnet Regent, Jacobite, Nizzolan and Katchina, that through the years have shown what is and is not possible on the practical level. This has allowed a better interpretation of medieval equestrianism.

Ann Hyland
Leverington, Cambridgeshire
February 1999

Foreword

A knight jousting at a tournament is one of our thoroughly familiar representations of the medieval world: it shows us a rider and horse, both richly bedecked and bejewelled; the colours are brilliant, and we gaze with wonder at a spectacle. But the image is static, capturing one moment and one circumstance only. Horses performed a host of other duties in the workaday world of the Middle Ages, cultivating the fields, carrying goods, carrying people and complying with needs that demanded the highest versatility; some horses were required to move over long distances at a steady pace, others to fly like the wind as urgent messengers. Yet horses are not mechanical objects; they are living creatures, and if they do not roam wild, someone must daily see that they are fed and watered, brushed and combed, tended through sickness. Then through their constant contact with people, they become companions, sometimes developing a relationship as close and interdependent as that of members of a family.

These universal facts of life are all somewhere embedded in our medieval documents about horses. But it takes the seeing eye to gather from such matter-of-fact statements as expense accounts and books of instruction the precious insights that show the day-to-day routines by which horses and people lived and toiled together, travelled, made war, and disported themselves. Some horses lived in expensive stables: an archbishop in Edward III's reign (1327–77) claimed that one Great Horse cost as much to keep as three or four poor people. In different circumstances entirely, the horse which carried the husbandman's wife to market survived on little beyond common grazings and hay. It is intriguing to reflect that everyone in the Middle Ages, as a matter of course, must have been able to guess the social rank of every horse that came in sight, just as they recognized ranks of people. Horses and people intermingled everywhere, locked in a relationship that made them indispensable to each other.

We no longer live in that world, for the car has driven the horse from everyday life. So when we turn to our documents, we need a discerning eye to perceive the significance of all the clues they offer, and cannot fail to admire those with long practical experience in horsemanship who bring special gifts to that task. Ann Hyland is one such author. She has a stable of horses, she has bred them, trained them and competed with them, sometimes at an international level. From a solid foundation of practical knowledge, she can illuminate much of the detail in our documents that eludes the rest of us. Here, then, is a precious work of history, offering special insights.

The documents, in their turn, undergo appraisal under circumstances that are, in one respect, especially sympathetic in our present-day world. They shed a flood of light on the vigorous mixing of cultures that occurred in the High Middle Ages, and, in that regard, the world was remarkably similar to the one in which we live today. Horses, like human beings, were moving with more than usual freedom and frequency across the whole of the known world. From the Middle East into Western Europe came Berber and Arabian horses, moving readily into Spain; Oriental horses were brought into Europe by the Ottomans; from Western Europe the Crusaders took their homebred horses eastwards. And, as a matter of course, discerning breeders and dealers scoured the horse marts of both East and West. Horses interbred, lived on many different sorts of fodder, submitted to many different styles of management, and at each contact horsekeepers observed and learned new lessons from each other. In short, horses and people lived in a global world in the High Middle Ages, absorbing the influences and mingling the cultures and genetic inheritance of very different civilizations.

Hence, our present age has a strong empathy with that past, and historians explore this story at just the right moment; we are more than ordinarily sensitized to some of the nuances of the experience. It is not surprising, then, that in the last two decades scholars have revived their interest in the study of horses, and Ann Hyland, as a distinguished member of that circle, pulls back yet another revealing curtain in this book. Her rich experience opens up more fresh views of the equestrian world we have lost, and past and present meet here in a most satisfying and stimulating encounter.

Joan Thirsk CBE, FBA
Hadlow, Kent

Introduction

Although this exploration of the medieval horse is centred on England, it would be unbalanced without a wider view. The mental picture of medieval Europe usually conjures up the 'Age of Chivalry' of the High Middle Ages, but a fuller canvas spans the era from the late fifth to the end of the fifteenth century. European equestrianism was influenced by diverse sources – the Levant, North Africa, Egypt, Anatolia and Persia – and was opened up by wars and the intrepid traveller.

Horses for society's wealthy were usually classified as destrier, great horse, courser and palfrey, although the latter was also found among those people in the middle income bracket. Rouncies, sumpters, hackneys, pads and hobbies served in the middle income sector. Carthorses, not the modern stamp, were used by all social classes in the haulage trade. All types of horse were also either owned and/or used by the wealthy in mundane chores. (Stots and affers were low-value animals, especially affers, usually aged farmhorses worth virtually nothing in money terms, but valued for the chores they did for those lucky enough to own one.)

Apart from class horses used by high society in war, the hunt, the tournament and great social gatherings, humbler saddlehorses performed numerous duties in carrying men-at-arms, couriers, pilgrims and merchants. Other horses also had carrying duties, such as keeping royal households equipped as they moved from palace to hunting lodge, and even across the channel; the *Records of the Wardrobe and Household 1285–86* shows that Edward I (1272–1307) shipped 1,000 horses from Dover to Wissant for his sojourn in France.[1] Droves of carthorses hauled household effects in peacetime and supplies and munitions in wartime. Farmhorses initially performed lighter duties, but gradually horsepower began to work with, and then eventually replaced, oxpower. Horses hauled harvested grain and hay to the barn, and carried grain to, and flour back from, the lord's mill. In England, Ireland, Scotland and Wales native ponies were essential to the economy, particularly the larger Fell and Dales types.

The great entrepôt for quality European bloodstock was Spain. Charlemagne (768–814) made reciprocal gifts to the Persian king (Haroun el Raschid), sending him Spanish horses and mules.[2] One of the three horses ridden by Bastard William at Hastings was brought out of Spain for William by Walter Giffard, according to Wace's *Roman de la Rou*.[3]

We can usually only surmise by price and usage what type of horse is recorded in historical sources. Fortunately some old breeds have remained true to type – the Andalusian, Arabian, Friesian, Fell and Turcoman, to name but a handful. Others were adulterated by indiscriminate breeding, a complaint voiced by Prospero d'Osma, Queen Elizabeth I's studmaster. His criticisms give clues as to how medieval studs had long been run, much of which he condemned.

Adventurous souls travelled on their own 'Grand Tours', while ambassadors, even if they lacked the spur of adventure, went where directed, often into very hazardous situations. Many left illuminating accounts of regions as far away as Persia and Samarkand, and for those with a thirst for foreign parts there was no answer but to travel by horse. The following chapters outline the diversity of medieval equestrianism.

CHAPTER 1

Domesday and Before

WHERE DID THEY COME FROM?

Britain today has eight native pony breeds; in the past there were others, now disappeared, which added to the pool of smaller equines that was the backbone of medieval commercial transport. A 1950s study by Professor J.G. Speed, MRCVS, of the Royal Veterinary College of Edinburgh University showed that at least two types of pony were present in Britain well before the Ice Age, and before *Homo sapiens* arrived. They are the Exmoor pony, of approximately 12 to 12.2 hands (hh), and a larger animal termed 'the pack horse type' of approximately 13.2 hh. Fossil remains of both types are found in many locations throughout Great Britain, especially in the Mendips in Somerset, where remains were present in twenty-one out of twenty-seven excavations at the Barrington site (10–8,000BC), the Exmoor in the early and latest strata, the larger pony in the later strata only.

Speed's research supports a migration route for the smaller animal starting in North America and traversing Asia, the eastern Mediterranean, North Africa, Spain, France and thence to Britain – all of which were land-linked. The general westwards spread had a northwards and southwards movement and supports the belief that pony types found along latitude 40° north all come from the same ancestral stock. The only pure survivor of this stock in Britain is the Exmoor pony. The larger 13.2 hh animal, which Speed considers to have survived in the Fell pony, followed a more northerly route of latitude 65° north and reached Britain by way of France from an initial Siberian/Mongolian route through the great lowland plain of Europe. At Solutre, in the province of Saone-et-Loire, a massive concentration of bones from more than 40,000 horses were found which had been used as a protective wall to a Paleolithic encampment.[1]

With the arrival of humans in Britain changes slowly took place in these early horses. Once Britain became seagirt natural ingress was impossible and all further introductions of *equidae* were by man, who realized eventually that they had a more varied role than just filling his larder. No doubt the first of these roles was to carry his other hunting kills, or to drag them; then later to be harnessed to light, wheeled vehicles; and finally to be ridden. The advent of the mount-size horse was important; man improved on what we can now refer to as indigenous stock by crossbreeding. From the scientific point of view, and the ability always to cope with its natural environment, Speed thought crossbreeding a retrograde step, but almost all saddle breeds, heavy warhorses, and draughthorses have been arrived at by crossbreeding. Rare examples of 'pure', as far as can be traced, are the Arabian; the Turkmene, which incorporates regional differences according to tribal pasturelands, which in turn have an influence on stock generated by soil, minerals and quality of herbage; the Caspian of Iran; the Andalusian; and the Mongol pony, which belongs to the same ancestral group as the Exmoor. These breeds have remained virtually unchanged from at least the High Medieval Period. Before then I doubt absolute purity was enforceable. When man needed the horse for war, and the inevitable looting and/or tribute that ensued, crossbreeding was inevitable. Hot-blooded oriental stock reached

Mongolia as tribute payments; whether they and their offspring survived the harsh environment is another matter!

EPONA

The Gallic/British cult of Epona, the Earth Mother, is always associated with a horse. She was essentially a breeder's goddess and a general equestrian deity.[2] The typical Roman funerary cavalry monument of half-rearing horse trampling the enemy is a direct descendant of the Gallic pre-Roman representation where horseman and mount symbolized light trampling darkness, and show a horse considerably larger and more robust than the average, suggesting stock of larger size was available well before the Christian era.[3]

With the heavier Germanic horses noted by Speed,[4] it appears that much European heavy blood was available for breeding into horses of the medieval period. This earlier heavy blood is not to be confused with the carthorse of the eighteenth century onwards, although given that breed evolution can span centuries it did have some influence. The Germanic and Gallic input is borne out by Julius Caesar's remarks that the Gauls took the 'keenest delight' in draught horses which they imported at great expense. Unfortunately he does not say where from. The 'immense statured' German Suebi rode 'inferior and ill favoured' homebred animals, but by training and exercise turned them into superior cavalry mounts.[5] Tacitus described the Tencteri, harassed by the Suebi, as sharing in 'the general military distinction' and excelling 'in skilful horsemanship'.[6] From this it can be deduced that the Suebi's horses were of considerable size, but smaller than the Gallic draught imports.

From Roman times onwards we also have records mentioning horses coming into Britain. Dio Cassius and Caesar refer to the Britons' chariotry and cavalry which used indigenous equines. Roman cavalry *alae* were initially recruited from provinces bearing their title name. The most important equines to land with them came from Frisia, Spain, Thrace and Pannonia. The Frisian and Spanish injections continued in the Middle Ages (see ch.2). Roman records show the mix of *alae* mounts in Britain: Housesteads had a *Cuneus Frisiorum*, as did Abballava (Burgh by Sands); Haltonchesters had *Ala I Pannoniorum Sabiniana*; Netherby *Coh. I Aelia Hispanorum Milliaria Equitata*; Benwell *Ala I Asturum*; Brecon Gaer *Ala Hispanorum Vettonum*; Chester *Ala II Asturum*; and Ribchester *Cuneus Sarmatorum Brementenraco*.

Among the Sarmatian people involved with Rome, sometimes fighting for and sometimes against her, were the Roxolani and Iazyges. The Iazyges settled in the Hungarian plains (part of the province of Pannonia) around AD20, basing themselves there for 400 years. From AD166–175 they were in repeated conflict with Rome, and when peace was concluded in AD175 the price to the Iazyges was the supply of 8,000 cavalrymen and mounts to Rome, of which 5,500 were sent to Britain. The Sarmatian steppe stock would have interbred with indigenous Hungarian stock.[7]

Following the influx of many breeds and types interbreeding took place with native British stock, aiding the diversification of the island's equine population, although much of the indigenous pony population would have remained unaffected on the wilder reaches of mountain and moorland. It is significant that some of Britain's larger native ponies are bred today in or near regions where some of the *Alae* were stationed, in particular the Fell and Dales ponies which clearly have Frisian ancestors.

ANGLO-SAXON CHRONICLE

Until Bastard William's disastrous usurpation we have only spasmodic references to specific and general equestrian matters. Athelstan (924–40) received 300 fine coursers from Hugh, son of Robert of France,[8] and we can be sure many were stallions, rendering service in pomp, hunting, etc., and at stud. This would not have been an isolated import, others of lesser grandeur were overlooked by the chroniclers.

Throughout the Viking inroads, England abounded in horses. The *Anglo-Saxon Chronicle* refers to the 'Force' being horsed on landing under the years 866, 868, 869, 870, 871 and 893. In 892 the Danes brought horses from Normandy in their fleet of 250 ships.[9] An earlier Viking burial on the island of Colonsay, off the West Highland coast, contained human and equine remains of a 'strongly built northern type of stallion'; Speed considered this to be a pointer to the origin of the dun Highland Garrons, and the old type of Orkney or Shetland work pony, as opposed to the better known little Shetland pony.[10]

From the tenth and eleventh centuries a clearer picture emerges from the collection of *Anglo-Saxon Wills*, Hywel Dda's *Welsh Medieval Law* and the Domesday Book. The first two show how important horses of all categories were, especially to the wealthy. From the Domesday Book a picture emerges of the agricultural levels of English society where the horse filled a small but diverse role in rural life.

The reverse of the eighth-century Aberlemno churchyard cross, believed to depict the battle of Nechtansmere in 685 between the Picts and the Anglian warriors of Northumbria (wearing helmets). It shows fine equestrian detail and is a good representation of horse conformation and action.

THE ANGLO-SAXON WILLS

Five of the sixteen wills with an equine content definitely refer to sizeable studs, either as a stud or in the number of horses, mares or foals which are bequeathed. These five are the wills of Wynflaed *c*.950; Aelfhelm, between 975 and 1016; Wulfric between 1002 and 1004; Wulfgeat, undated but usually ascribed to 1006; and Thurstan, between 1043 and 1045.[11] Thirteen of the sixteen include heriot (death duties) due to the overlord on an heir assuming his inheritance. Some, because of the heir's rank, included up to eight horses. The others were those of Wynflaed; Aethelflaed, second wife of King Edmund (940–46); and the Aethling Aethelstan, dated to 1015. The latter's will included a major bequest to his father, King Ethelred II (979–1016), of several estates, armour, weapons, and two special horses which had been gifts to Aethelstan from Thurbrand and Leofwine, two of his friends/retainers. Other beneficiaries were Bishop Aelfsige (a black stallion), Chaplain Aelfwine (a horse), Seneschal Aelfmaer (a pied stallion and eight hides) and Sifirth (a horse). Where land was bequeathed it is almost certain it included any livestock running thereon, some of which would undoubtedly have been mares, foals and herd stallions. We know the horses singled out were all stallions, because in all documents relating to equines they are specified as geldings (rarely), mares, colts (foals of both sexes), and *wilde weorf* (unbroken youngsters), or horses.

The wills indicate that pre-Domesday England was a horsebreeding nation. Horses for heriot surrender would have been upmarket types, with the large studs also containing many ordinary pony-sized horses. The Venerable Bede crystallized this when he recorded that Bishop Aidan had given a well-bred horse to a beggar, which was a gift to him from King Oswine. Much annoyed the king exclaimed that a common horse, of which there were plenty, was more suitable for a beggar.[12] It is doubtful if a beggar got more than a sniff of a horse in the Conqueror's England – possibly as a Norman lordling rode by!

THE WELSH LAWS OF HYWEL DDA

This code of laws, drafted during Hywel's reign (910–50), remained the core of Welsh law but was modified and amplified during the next three and a half centuries.[13] In the royal household twenty-four people were entitled to a mount including the steward, the judge, and all the hunt and stable staff, even down to minor posts, including the cook, brewer and chambermaid, probably the only female servant to be so entitled in medieval times. The twelve *Gwestwa*, a sort of entertainment tax gatherer, were also provided with mounts.[14]

At the general level, laws governed the worth of a working draught or pack horse or mare.[15] Saddle-galling a borrowed horse incurred a hefty fine, escalating according to the degree of damage done to its back.[16] The sale of a horse or mare had to be accompanied by the equivalent of a modern veterinary certificate. The animal was required to be free of staggers (encephalitis) for three nights, glanders for three months, and farcy for a year (see ch.5). An outward blemish came under *caveat emptor*.[17] When someone died intestate the deceased's household received most of the smaller livestock; the king appropriated any gold and silver, the horses, oxen and large cattle.[18]

Welsh laws governed just about every aspect of equestrian and equine life. These extrapolations, plus those on stud management (see ch.2), show that medieval Wales possessed a rich harvest of homebred stock which held a value far higher than the pecuniary.

DOMESDAY 1086

Twenty years after laying England in thrall, Bastard William had a survey made of thirty-four English counties. The Durham and Northumberland surveys were not transcribed,

From the Bayeux Tapestry, a packpony obviously commandeered by Norman foragers; possibly one of the many indigenous ponies of England.

and most of Cumberland and Westmorland were not yet part of England, so were not surveyed. The brief to the commissioners was to tally every particular regarding: land ownership; animal- and manpower; the division of land into arable, pasture and woodland; and resources such as livestock, mills and fishponds. Two time periods were to be noted: that prior to 1066, when William allocated land and all its perquisites to his incoming Normans as rewards for service; and 'now' (or 1086). This early 'Inland Revenue Assessment' was made to see if more taxes could be forced out of the population. The completed tax returns were collated, abridged and copied at Winchester, the major reductions being omission of livestock and human numbers. William died before the task was completed, and several East Anglian returns still have the livestock numbers intact which allow us to view the position of the agriculturally based horse in English farming and rural life at the two periods.

Several items had an eventual connection to equestrianism; some were the foundations on which later kings could raise men and/or cash for their interminable wars. Abbeys and bishoprics prospered under William – his guilt payments – holding land in many 'hundreds' in each county. They sub-let to tenants, notably the men-at-arms of their military households. In Huntingdonshire, small in comparison to Norfolk, the Abbot of Ramsey granted land to men-at-arms in Stukely, St Ives, Hemingford Grey and Bythorn. The Bishop of Lincoln held land in Lincolnshire and had men-at-arms at Leighton in Huntingdonshire. On the Abbot of Peterborough's lands in Northamptonshire a similar pattern showed, with men-at-arms holding land from the abbey in several villages – e.g. at Caster, Milton, Ailsworth, Southorpe, Glinton, Werrington and many others (much of this land now lies in Cambridgeshire). Men-at-arms needed mounts so they would have raised sufficient horses on their land allocations, or had recourse to a dealer's yard. On baronial and episcopal estates, stock of a quality commensurate with their owner's social and fiscal standing would have been raised. Unfortunately, this element is largely absent from the Domesday Book, but some information can be culled.

Sheriff Eustace of Huntingdon had parcels of land in many villages in the hundreds of Normancross, Hurstingstone, Kimbolton, Toseland and Leightonstone, settling his men, including men-at-arms, on several. The returns show Eustace was a hard, grasping man, often unjustly appropriating land, and we can be certain his men-at-arms were a ready threat against any angered peasantry.

Sheriff Picot of Cambridgeshire was another greedy Norman who imposed new duties on ox and horsepower. Prior to 1066 the burgesses of the Borough of Cambridge *lent* their plough to the Sheriff three times a year; Picot *demanded* it nine times a year. A similar situation pertained to horsedrawn carts; from being a courtesy to the sheriff it became an imposition. Prior to 1066 when Aelric Godricson was sheriff, he levied a £1 heriot on a lawman, one of the twenty-four burgesses of Cambridge, who sat in the Borough Court. Picot *demanded* £8, a riding horse and arms for one man-at-arms, as if he were the man's tenurial overlord. The cash alone would have bought a quality warhorse judging by prices paid in William's own Normandy: Roger I of Montgomery received a horse worth 30 livres (approx. £7.50) and a hauberk worth 7 livres from the monastery at Jumièges in settlement of a land deal. Purchase of land at the founding of Fécamp's priory of St Gabriel near Caen was paid for with £312 2s and seven horses valued in total at £39 4s 6d.[19] Medieval European currency was measured in marks and pounds, but the various pounds used in France were worth about a quarter to a fifth of an English pound, and it is possible the Domesday pound was measured on the Norman/French basis. Nevertheless Picot's levy was still excessive. Another Picotian exaction is from Fulbourn where twenty-six freemen paid an annual total of £8 in tax and provided twelve horses and twelve escorts if the king visited Cambridgeshire. If he did not visit they paid cash of one shilling for a ridden escort and eightpence for horse haulage. Prior to 1086 they only paid the sheriff for escort and/or cartage. Here we see a double imposition if the wording in the Domesday Book reflects the actuality. Not only were freemen obliged to keep riding and draught horses, but if they were not used by the sheriff they paid cash too, creating a double burden with fodder, oats, pasture and capital investment plus the cash levy. Throughout the Cambridgeshire Domesday Book freemen are shown as liable for escort and cartage, implying many horses were owned.

Count Alan of Brittany, William's son-in-law, held extensive lands in Cambridgeshire, amounting to 157 hides and 48.5 acres of ploughland, not counting meadow, pasture and woodlands. This land was held previously by an English noblewoman, Edeva the Fair, many of whose tenants were freemen owing escort and cartage. Very few freemen remained on Count Alan's lands and it suggests their livestock, including riding/draught horses, disappeared into the Norman maw.

From the unabridged returns for Norfolk much more information is available. Norfolk appears to have been a much wealthier county, and in many villages there were several rouncies. The terminology used was 'always', 'then' and 'now', and before 1066. Horses were nearly always stated as 'at the hall', indicating a possibly superior type of rouncy.

Parks for beasts of the chase were sited at Costessy, and there is mention of William hunting at Fotheringhay where the woodlands were worth 10s – when stocked when the king was not hunting. At Burrough Green in Cambridgeshire, Count Alan had a park for woodland beasts, while another at Kirtling in Chevely Hundred was held by Countess Judith.

From the extant wills we know studs were widespread, but from the Norfolk returns it seems they were either dispersed and/or run down and that whatever horsebreeding survived on the old lines was taken out of the taxable agricultural bracket, remaining only with the wealthier strata of society. From studs, identified as such by note of 'wild mares' at fourteen Norfolk locations, a total of 381 mares were recorded under 'when acquired' or 'then'; by the 1086 survey there were only 111. Only two studs had foals noted: Great Bellingham's six mares all had foals, and the twenty-eight mares of the Wereham Stud had twenty-five, which is an exceptional fertility rate. At Holkham 'then' with 220 mares, all had gone by 1086.

The *Inquisitio Comitatus Cantabrigiensis* shows animal numbers and can serve as a broad base for other abridged surveys, bearing in mind that actual numbers will differ. Whereas Cambridgeshire shows no instance of a recognizable stud there were counties that would have had considerable numbers of breeding stock on Norfolk's pattern, especially in areas such as Exmoor and Dartmoor where ponies ran on the moors but were owned, as they are today, by several individuals and were not wild in the sense of belonging to no one. The breakdown in the *ICC* is 132 horses, six mares, twenty-four donkeys, one mule, seven horse and two donkey foals. The Fulbourn exaction of twelve horses for twelve escorts is not calculated in these horse numbers, and this confirms that many other horses were available and those shown were only the top of the iceberg. Only one horse in the *ICC* had its use noted – a *hercarius* – for harrowing. Most of the horses would have been in the rouncy category.

These admittedly incomplete records do, however, give an idea of the equine situation in eleventh-century England. The overall impression from the Domesday Book is one of mass dispersion of freemen's lands, a tightening of the tax screw, and on the equestrian level the disinherited class that previously had bred many horses were no longer able to do so. Those who maintained studs at their former level were few; the major exception in the Norfolk returns being Reynold, son of Ivo Tallboys, who maintained the stud at Wereham and started one at Cleythorpe.[20]

The Norman invasion was the start of a major change in the equine population among the wealthier and military classes, who can be bracketed together for equestrian purposes (as an impecunious man-at-arms looked to his lord to provide a horse). The abbeys were heavily into horsebreeding (see ch.2), and many would have imported their farming and stud practices along with their bevy of Norman monks.

CHAPTER 2
Supply and Demand

Two main threads of equestrian life were the studs, large and small, and the middlemen – horsedealers, copers, corsers, local dealers, traders at big English horse marts and prestigious international dealers who scoured Europe for class horses on behalf of wealthy patrons.

THE DRAIN ON EQUINE RESOURCES

Demand often outran supply. Among medieval horses mortality and hardships were high. Added to natural wastage, animals' working lives were often cut short by war, injury, starvation in harsh campaigning conditions, inadequate veterinary care and a rudimentary pharmacopoeia unable to deal with many diseases and traumas.

Epidemics killed horses in droves; a chronicle for the year 791 recorded Charlemagne's war against the Avars in Pannonia, saying 'the campaign was accomplished without any misfortune, except that in the army under the king's command such a pestilence broke out among the horses that of so many thousands of them hardly the tenth part is said to have survived'.[1] As Charlemagne was said to have raised between 15,000 and 20,000 horses for a campaign only five years later[2] this was some understatement! In the interminable Russo–Mongolian conflicts pestilence hit hard. In the mid-1500s the Nogays lost droves of horses and cattle; the Crimean Tartars lost 10,000 horses. Cold, too, killed many.[3] English records often refer to murrain killing horses, cattle, sheep, etc. One reason Edward III reduced his studs after 1360 was that murrain broke out regularly and indiscriminately. In 1299 Dumfries Castle lost several carthorses. At Heacham Manor in Norfolk, in thirteen of a twenty-six year period, and in ten of Richard II's twenty-two years reign, horses, cattle, and especially sheep, were lost.

What were these pestilences? It is impossible to positively name them, but, in consultation with Russell Lyon, MRCVS, it is thought likely that where only horses were concerned the disease could have been strangles; where the disease was non-selective it may have been anthrax, which lies in the soil for an extensive period.

Lower value horses were expendable, especially those for hire (a hirer's interest being to reach destinations expeditiously). The Black Prince was hard on horses, expecting the same of his servants, and several horses were killed or rendered permanently unfit by overriding (see below, p. 78). If a harvest was lean, men and animals suffered. Among equine war resources *carectarii* and oxen would have suffered before the cavalry horses, which were owned by the royals, nobles and their retinues who expected leaders to secure adequate rations. In 1306 Edward I complained about the impressed draught animals supplied by county sheriffs and monasteries (see p. 41). Debility among farm animals must have been common; purveyors took the best, but when crops failed, or hay mouldered and rotted from excessive rains, then all paid the price. There were bad harvests from 1310 to 1314; crops failed in 1315–16; 1317–18 saw a temporary improvement, with mediocre crops in 1321; in 1325–26 drought struck, followed by floods in 1327. Concurrently sheep murrain broke out with flock mortality ranging from 25 to 70 per cent. Hard on murrain's heels came cattle plague, probably rinderpest, with up to 50 per cent mortality.[5] Although horses were not as susceptible to murrain, oxen mortality meant land lay fallow and more horses with fewer provisions for maintenance were used for heavier commercial draught. Dearth of oxen may have been a factor in accelerating the use of horses to plough. Many peasants died through famine and related disease, but the wealthier could procure produce from areas less badly hit; although the 1315–16 crop failures were widespread, other failures were only sporadic,[6] so while the horses of the wealthy would have had at least some corn, the affers, stots, and *hercarii* used in day-to-day farming would have been sorry specimens indeed.

MEDIEVAL STUDS AND BREEDING PRACTICES

Evidence about studs comes mostly from the wealthier strata of society, but some comes from other sources. Early information derives from the sophisticated Byzantine Empire. The Logothete of the Herds was in overall charge of herds on the imperial estates in Cappadocia and Phrygia. Adult horses were sent to army remount depots and imperial stables at Malagina, some onto Constantinople. Byzantium also drew on the imperial herds in Thrace.[7]

Gregory of Tours occasionally hints at stud and stable occupations in the Frankish kingdoms. His nephew Attalus was taken hostage, enslaved and set to mind his master's horse herds. King Charibert's wife, Marcowefa, made a man called Leudast master of her stables, and King Guntram appointed a man named Leudesgisel his Count of the Stables.[8]

THE FRANKS

The late eighth-century *De Villis Capitulary* gives an excellent outline of royal stud organization in continental Europe. Noblemen's studs would have been run on similar, if less extravagant, lines. Fifteen rules directly or indirectly concerning stud management appear in the *De Villis*.[9] Stud management was under the steward, assisted by stablemen and grooms. Stewards decided on stable size and the number of horses allocated to each, with inmates' cleanliness a prime consideration. Stallions were herded together, except when each went into his mare band for the covering season. As weanling foals were sent to the king at his winter palace on St Martin's day, 11 November, the Carolingian covering season (and other systems that used pasture breeding) began in late April/early May, when grazing was good and lengthening days, sunlight and warmth brought mares into regular oestrus. Foals would have been about six to eight months old at weaning. (Some systems ran offspring on the dam till its second year, but the translation of the *De Villis* says foals, and an eighteen- or twenty-month old cannot be considered a foal.) Good land management was practised: pasture rotation prevented paddocks spoiling through overgrazing, parasite infestation and souring from a dung burden; perimeter fencing was maintained where animals were emparked; and at appropriate times a watch was kept on open meadows, implying a herder during the breeding season. Another task was to catch predatory wolves by poison, pits, or hounds.

Stewards' duties included separating colts from mares before they became a nuisance (some colts are precocious as weanlings and capable at a year). New mare bands were formed from excess fillies; colts were future war and hunting horses. Pruning studs was done regularly, marketable animals sold and old and/or worn out stock eaten provided they were healthy and mange-free. The *De Villis* recommendations help our understanding of how other European studs operated.

ANGLO-SAXON ENGLAND AND WALES

An early reference to *organized* horsebreeding in England comes from the seventh-century Kentish chronicles in which Stodmarsh on the Great Stour is noted ('*Stod*' meaning 'herd' or 'stud' of horses.[10]). Guided by this, horsebreeding centres can be plotted on a map of Anglo-Saxon England. The laws of King Ine (688–726) refer to the 'Horse Wealh' who stood in high regard and had charge of the king's stud. The 'Horse Weard' appears in Ine's and Aethelbert's (860–66) laws; he watched over the king's horses, being responsible for protecting the herds, preventing straying, abstraction of mares by unauthorized stallions, and general care of free-range stock.[11] These references imply breeding was done in self-contained studs, and on open range.

Foremost in Anglo-Saxon wills were the heriots, with horses heading the bequests, followed by arms, armour, gold, etc. The higher the rank the more horses due – from earls it was eight, from barons four, and from vavassours one.[12] Heriots indicated that nobles needed their own studs – which in an agrarian economy were cheap to run because labour was a feudal obligation from tenants. Some studs were extensive, and some were run on a herd system.

The will of Wynflaed 'grants to Aelfwold . . . a horse . . . and she bequeaths to Cynelefu her share of the untamed horses which are with Edmaer's . . . and Eadwold and his sister are to have her tame horses in common . . .'. From this we can surmise that Wynflaed appears to have been wealthy with a substantial herd running with Eadmaer's stock as well as having a string of saddle horses.

In another will, Wulfric left his lord the requisite four horses, but the monastery at Burton gained a huge stud of 100 wild (unbroken) horses and sixteen saddle geldings. Wulfgeat included in his heriot a small stud of ten mares and ten colts, their total value 43 mancuses of gold, a little short of the normal cash of 50 mancuses. He left Brun, not identified but obviously someone he felt he owed a hefty debt of gratitude, six mares and colts. His wife and daughter were to share the remaining herd. Wulfgeat was clearly 'horse poor' – too many animals, too little cash.[13]

Hywel Dda's lawcode, referred to earlier, shows the stud system and the high value of breeding herds. Welsh involvement with the horse was of long standing with an early Spanish input in the second century when Brecon Gaer was base for the *Ala Hispanorum Vettonum*.[14] Writing in the twelfth century, Giraldus Cambrensis noted the main interest of the Welsh 'consists of caring for their horses and keeping their weapons in good order'. He also recorded that Robert de Bellême, one of the Conqueror's harshest knights, had imported prepotent Spanish stallions to his new Welsh appanage.[15]

A stud of horses was the king's second most valuable asset, the first was his household; among noblemen's assets studs stood first. Fifty mares constituted a legal herd, implying breeding was regulated by law. Any studs on territory he conquered became the king's property. Other laws governed the covering process. Prior to the stud season stallions were stabled and fed high for six weeks, after which the value of each horse was doubled to £1. His *teithi*, or his worth as a breeding stallion, exceeded his legal value because 'if he was lost the breed was lost'. The *teithi* was assessed as 'a horse which can cover with a mare before him and another behind him', i.e. coping with two mares in quick succession. If a stallion 'ran loose at grass' it lost its status. These laws indicate in-hand covering of selected mares, and that unmonitored coverings by an escaped stallion running with lesser quality mares resulted in inferior offspring. The onus of producing quality therefore rested on the stallion not the mare, an erroneous idea still somewhat prevalent today. During the covering season, if a stallion savaged another animal there was no legal redress, but if he bit a person outside the season he could be claimed as *sarhad*, or injury money.[16] Many stallions are aggressive which is why they were so useful in military clean-up operations relishing the harrying.

The earliest surviving reference to English royal stud operations comes from an 1130 pipe roll. Henry I's scutifer received 30*s* for taking the king's stallion to Gillingham, Dorset, to cover his mares.[17] Doubtless there were many entries that had they survived would show equine movements, purchases, maintenance costs and a general outline of early stud management.

NORMANDY AND SPAIN

Between infesting and subsequently giving their name to Normandy where they permanently settled, before ravaging England again in 1066, the Northmen (Normans) became noted cavalry and either rejuvenated the Frankish studs they had ransacked and/or raised new establishments. Normandy had ideal horsebreeding conditions with limestone-rich soil and plenty of pasturage and forestland for herds in the plethora of wealthy ducal, noble and ecclesiastic estates.

Prior to invading England, William and his wealthy vassals improved their studs. William of Poitiers stated that in the 1040s Auvergne, Gascony and Spain sent gifts of horses to William. Normans campaigned in the Spanish wars against the Moors on many occasions[18] and would certainly have returned with Spanish horses and some booty horses from the Moorish enemy. Although the Moors initially availed themselves of the larger Spanish horses, they had imported huge numbers of Barbs, and there would also have been Syrian strains and some purebred Arabians as Moorish officers came from the Damascus Caliphate. The Moors, no less than the Spanish, were great horsebreeders. Ibn al Amir, known as Al Mansur, was chamberlain to the weak Ummayad Caliph Al Hishamm, acting as virtual ruler from 978 until 1002. He established many studs around Córdoba, importing Berber foundation stock.[19]

ENGLAND AND SPAIN

During the Plantagenet era stud work was inextricably linked with imports, which were in the most expensive categories: warhorses, coursers and palfreys. Spain was the greatest exporter, sending large consignments to England and to England's French possessions. Most, but not all, were destined for royal circles.

The dubbing (knighting) of Geoffrey Plantagenet (Count of Anjou and husband of Queen Matilda) in 1128 was followed by lengthy festivities, including a tournament for which Geoffrey was mounted on 'a Spanish horse . . . reputed to outstrip many birds as it ran . . . wonderfully fleet and poised, and graceful in his speed'.[20]

In England Geoffrey and Matilda's descendants were at the forefront of stud expansion, importing on many occasions from Spain, Flanders, Lombardy, Sicily, Navarre and Normandy. During the civil wars between Matilda and Stephen (1135–54) the Earl of Gloucester supported his half-sister, boosting his forces with 300 horsemen and mounts from Normandy, and added to by judicious purchases of horses while held in free custody at Rochester. When released Gloucester found them 'both serviceable and beneficial'.[21]

Henry II (1154–89), a king on almost permanent campaign, used all means to acquire horses – dealers, tribute, stud farms, gifts and booty. He was a master of the rapid strike, losing many mounts in the process, as shown by his *Blitzkrieg* when Louis of France threatened his rights of overlordship of Normandy, Anjou and Aquitaine. Gifts of horses came to Henry from the Moorish king of Valencia and Murcia in 1162, and when Raymond V did homage for Toulouse in 1173 an annual tribute of forty 'very valuable horses' was demanded,[22] putting a considerable strain on Raymond's stud and pocket.

THE PLANTAGENET ERA: ENGLAND AND FRANCE

The fullest picture of horsebreeding and high-value horsedealing comes from during the reigns of the Plantagenet kings and their dual realms of England and their French possessions.

Although King John (1199–1216) has often been vilified, as a horseman he left England a rich legacy and boosted the size of the by then indispensable warhorse by importing 100 heavy stallions from Flanders, Holland and the River Elbe area.[23] Such a number would have had an enormous and rapid effect on warhorse breeding, which was the main task of royal studs, although other types had their important roles too. If only a portion of those 100 stallions enjoyed stud duties the effect would have been felt on the battlefield within five years.

In 1214 King John sent Thomas Briton to Spain with 200 marks to purchase horses, and a subsequent 1214–15 inventory lists eight Spanish horses in his stables.[24] Equipping themselves for the 1242 conflict over Aquitaine, Henry III of England and Louis IX of France both imported Castilian chargers, with Henry acquiring six destriers. Horses ordered by Louis went by ship to La Rochelle; Henry's went via Navarre. Under James II of Aragon (1291–1327), warhorses and rouncies were exported to Narbonne, Perpignan, Montpellier, Rodez, Foix, Genes, The Pope at Avignon and to Portugal. Edward I sent many times to Castile and Navarre for horses to be used in his French possessions and in England[25] – in 1281 he consigned 1,000 marks for Spanish purchases. The trade increased in Edward II's reign with purchases occurring in seven of the years between 1308 and 1319, not just from Spain but also from France, Germany and Navarre;[26] in 1309, for example, agents purchased twenty destriers and twelve mares in Lombardy.[27] Edward III continued the practice, obtaining horses frequently from the German Landuch (who checked out horses he bought from other dealers) and buying heavily in Spain until the start of the 100 Years War, but when Castile allied with France export licences were hard to obtain,[28] though the Aragonese trade with France and the Avignon papacy continued.[29] Edward III's officers stationed in Gascony circumvented the problem by regularly purchasing Spanish mounts from dealers.[30] From 1330, however, stud costs spiralled and horses from Germany, Spain, Sicily, Belgium, Liège, Luxembourg, Ireland and England were added to those bred in the royal studs.[31]

THE FRAMEWORK

From John to Edward III horsebreeding in royal circles was a big business relying on expert horsemen – agents and officers sent on purchasing missions – and a bevy of reputable horsedealers with royal patronage. Doubtless there were dishonest corsers, but with a martial nobility whose safety depended on sound stock free of vice – to its rider at least – the martial purchaser would have made it his business to have an eye for a horse.

The most important official in royal stud management was variously known: under John as Chief Keeper; and in Henry III's day as King's Farrier, Sergeant or Keeper of the King's Horses; eventually this evolved into Master of Horse. Thomas Landa was John's chief keeper (in charge of other keepers) and his movements indicate stud locations – London, Berkshire, Kent, Yorkshire, Northants, Worcester and Wiltshire. Henry III expanded stud locations; one lay across the channel at La Rochelle. By Edward I's accession, administration was divided between studs north and south of the River Trent, each division controlled by a deputy keeper, under whom each stud master operated. By Edward III's reign there were studs in at least twenty-five English counties, mostly in East Anglia, the South and Southeast and the Midlands.

Stud expansion meant constant building. Eighty stables were built at Freemantle in the Manor of Kingsclere in the mid-1240s; 200 at Clipstone, Notts, in 1282–83; and new

Great Seal of King Stephen.

Second Great Seal of King Henry III.

Seal of the Earl of Winchester.

stabling at Sheen in 1369, an establishment on which Richard II spent heavily. The maintenance of studs fell largely on the local populace, sheriffs being responsible for stable expenses such as shoeing, medicines, staff wages, small tack items, halters, bridles, etc. Purveyors exercised their right of pre-emption when buying feedstuffs, issuing tallies to be exchanged for cash. Abuses proliferated: grains bought by the heaped and paid for by the razed measure; false tallies issued by unauthorized purveyors; purveyors selling excess grain for their own profit. Although the three Edwards tried to curb abuses, they were constant; and although a royal stud gave employment, the peasant farmer did suffer.[32]

Contemporary with Edward I, Philip III of France raised his nation's equestrian profile, his war needs prompting a raft of laws in 1279. Landowners had to keep from between one and six broodmares according to income and acreage; mares and foals were not to be distrained for fines or debts. Prices were regulated: no palfrey was to cost over 60 livres tournois; rouncies were to cost 15–25 livres tournois. Merchants were limited to a string of thirty warhorses per fair; any excess were to be confiscated.[33]

Warhorse buying and selling was subject to politics and restrictions. Prior to his first Welsh War Edward I was able to secure licences to import via France, as well as a batch of horses from Philip himself. He imported 158 warhorses and licensed his barons to bring in another forty-five, using the services of many dealers.[34] These would all have been entires, and some at least would have covered mares prior to mustering at Worcester on 24 July 1277. By 1282 the situation had changed, Philip forbidding purchase from and transit through France, ostensibly because France needed all the available horses,[35] but the real reason was that Edward was prevaricating over doing homage for Gascony. In England itself exports were banned on many occasions, particularly to Scotland where bans were reiterated throughout medieval and Tudor times.

Movements between studs were frequent to ensure close in-breeding was avoided. Colts were sent for breaking and future use, and/or sent to stud at whichever location the king, in consultation with his Master of Horse, decided. Fillies were kept to put into mare bands. The Church had its cut, tithes being a regular drain on the annual foal crop.[36]

ECCLESIASTIC EQUESTRIANISM

Ecclesiastic horsebreeding was of long standing. In the ninth century the Abbey of St Wandrille received an estate at Nojon sur Andelle (now Charleval) and the eight horses the estate was obliged to supply for the postal service. The abbey had a need to breed or purchase replacements long term. Concurrently, abbeys in the Cantabrian Mountains bred horses. In 876 Pope John VIII requested the king of Galicia to send him some 'of the excellent Moorish horses which the Spanish call *al faraces*'.[37] According to Abou Bekr Ibn Bedr, *Faras* stands for purebred Arabian, though the Spanish may have used it in a more general sense.

NORMANDY

Orderic Vitalis, an Englishman at St Evroul, commented on the buying and selling of horses, and as St Evroul also received tithes of mares it probably ran studs at its various houses. In Normandy and England horses featured in exchanges for land: in 1059–60, in return for praying for the soul of the eldest son of Engelnulf de L'Aigle, St Evroul acquired a valuable horse, soon passed to Arnold of Echaffour for an estate at Boquence. The pattern was repeated on several occasions. The abbeys of Jumièges and Fécamp exchanged so many horses for land that their herds must have been extensive.

Tithes of mares supplied regular fresh breeding stock, counteracted sales and natural wastage, and helped supply monastic travel needs. In 1050 William Fitzosbern gave the Abbey of Lyre half the tithe of his mares at Glos La Ferrière, near St Evroul. Raoul Tancarville gave his tithe of his Roumare mares to St Georges de Boscherville, near Rouen. In 1067 the nuns of St Amand in Rouen had Gerold's tithe of Roumare mares, and St Sever, in Lower Normandy, received tithes from Hugh, Earl of Chester.[38] These sites are close together: nearby are the La Perche and Bellême areas, noted medieval (and modern) horseraising centres. (At its modern heart is the French National Stud at Haras du Pin.)

ENGLAND

The Anglo-Saxon bequest to Burton Monastery of 100 wild horses indicates that monastic studs flourished early on. They continued to do so under the Normans. Yorkshire had Fountains, Rievaulx and Jervaulx abbeys, and others. Cistercian abbeys were especially productive. Land was exchanged for cash and often a valuable horse, the monks getting the best of the deal. An 1179 gift to Easby Abbey from Picot de Lascelles was that of grazing rights for sheep and forty broodmares on his hill pasture (see also ch.4). Beaulieu Abbey in the New Forest was the largest southern Cistercian house,[39] its monks burdened, by King John, with maintaining many horses for the eventual use of his young son Henry.[40]

Some prelates kept elaborate equestrian establishments. In 1305 Edward, Prince of Wales, bought Earl Warenne's stud at Ditchling, Sussex, and requested the Archbishop of Canterbury to loan him a good stallion to cover its mares.[41] The Archbishop of Salzburg received an annual tribute of 500 horses, and English bishops commonly stabled up to fifty horses, but some establishments were more modest. The 1335 inventory at the death of the Bishop of Marseilles shows only one great horse (bon cheval), one palfrey, twelve rouncies, two of which were past their best, and two mules. Monastic and lay studs flourished from the thirteenth to the fifteenth centuries in the Dauphiné where Cistercians were the leading monastic breeders. Lay breeders both large and small raised stock for war service, and while rouncies were purchased from local breeders, better stock was often imported from Hungary, Flanders, Lombardy, Spain and Germany.[42] Gascony also had a noted breed for war service, and many Spanish horses imported into Gascony were sold to northern France.[43]

MONASTIC MILITARY ORDERS

The *Rule of the Temple* has more than 100 rules concerning equestrianism. It establishes that Knights Templar bred some warhorses; others were acquired as loot, or by purchase and importing; while some came with recruits. A plan of Acre at the end of the thirteenth century shows two Templar farms used as stables and cow parks. The most telling rule forbade commanders to take away a brother's horse and send it to stud unless sanctioned by the master and the full chapter.[44]

Spain's military orders needed a constant supply of warstock; so too did the Templars, as shown by one of their studs at Montsaunes in Comminges, southern France.[45] Licences were issued to Hospitallers and Templars from the kingdoms of Sicily and southern Italy by Count Charles I of Anjou, a practice continued by Charles II. On 13 April 1277 the Templars were allowed to send to Jerusalem horses and arms belonging to the late son of Charles I. Between 1269 and 1300 nine licences were issued to the Hospitallers for shipping warhorses, palfreys and mules to the Levant. Other licences were issued to non-religious military. Some Hospitaller licences were for large numbers, others for smaller, and others still were for unspecified shipments. The largest was for sixty horses and forty mules.[46]

In eastern Europe the Teutonic Knights had the greatest network of monastic studs. Ever-hungry for land and loot they constantly needed war-, post- and draughthorses. Draught and native-bred lighter stock were often purchased from peasants. Marienburg records for 1412 show villagers sold forty-six horses for 229 marks.[47] Warstock was provided in several ways: direct imports from Germany (each recruit had to bring three horses with him); looting, which provided irregular but substantial additions; and raids into Lithuania, which were both profitable and retaliatory. In 1377 1,000 cattle and 100 horses, and in 1378 531 cattle and 723 horses, were lifted in retaliation for the 1376 raid by Kenstutis, Grand Duke of Lithuania, who had stolen fifty mares and sixty stallions from the Insterburg stud alone.

The order's commanderies were in strategic locations – Riga, Memel, Elbing, Danzig, Königsberg, Tilsit and Ragnit, Marienburg, Graudenz, Torun (Thorn), Tuchel, Osterode, Strassburg, Christaburg, Insterberg, etc. Each had its own studs, and some raised just enough for its own use. Larger commanderies – Königsberg, Brandenburg, Balga, Christaburg and Mewe – had studs in their demesnes. Königsberg had four *Pfleger* (sub-commanders); each ran a stud and smaller establishments. In 1404, at its peak, Königsberg commandery in total had ninety-five great horses, 394 broodmares, 235 stallions and 650 farmhorses, not counting foals; in 1414 Elbing had 154 mares, sixty-six foals, thirty-nine two- and three-year-olds, seventeen aged mares, 121 draught and letter ponies (couriers mounts) and nineteen horses being trained. They were distributed throughout Elbing's studs. In 1428 the total had risen from 429 to 513, which were distributed among seven studs. Other demesnes were not indicated, so records were incomplete or have not survived. In 1410 at the disastrous battle of Grünwald (Tannenberg), where the knights took their worst hammering from the Polish army, the toll in horses and men was high. Significantly, Elbing's stock declined from the 606 in 1404 to 395 in 1412, and between 1406 and 1415 Christaburg's from 1254 to 275. Was this due to Tannenberg, or to the widespread horse sickness prevalent at that period, or a combination of both?[48]

NON-ROYAL STUDS

In 1300 on the death of John Wake of Liddell, Liddesdale, his heirs were disinherited by Sir Simon de Lindesey, Keeper of Liddell, who appropriated Wake's stud of thirty-nine horses for the king. Going by their extremely low values, these were not warhorses but they would have served well enough for pack duty. Cattle, oats from twenty-four acres, salt-meat, wine, and a cart with harness and tools, were also requisitioned.[49]

The 1265 accounts for the Odiham estate of the Countess of Leicester shows a small stud was run in conjunction with the normal estate stable of thirty to thirty-eight horses, which was liable to massive fluctuations when her husband Sir Simon de Montfort visited. Five foals are listed, but no mares appear in the costings as they were probably at spring grass.[50]

Great magnates with scattered estates had large establishments. Those for the Fitzalans, earls of Arundel, were extensive. The accounts for 1313 to 1394 show Shropshire studs at Rednal, Ruyton, Shrawardine, Wroxeter, Withford and Lydly Hays. In 1313 they were visited by twelve travelling stallions, one of which was the earl's destrier, Morel Lestrange. In 1381 the Fitzalan studs were still large. Rednal and Ruyton were stallion headquarters with as many as four senior and fifteen junior covering stallions. Other studs were at Bromhurst (Bromwich Park), Maesbury, and Upper and Lower parks at Oswestry where twenty-two mares and fifty-two colts and fillies were kept.[51] Breeding on this scale was only possible for the wealthiest magnates, but a nationwide stud map would have been very impressive.

A GREAT ITALIAN STUD

The Gonzagan dynasty of Mantua had been breeding exceptional horses since at least 1329. Subsequently they became known throughout Europe, including England, for their excellence. Agents were employed to seek good horses and drew stock from Spain, Frisia, the Barbary States, Sardinia, England, Ireland, France and Italy, and from the Ottoman Empire, and by the 1490s the Mantuan studs held 650 horses. In the sixteenth century England's King Henry VIII (1509–47) imported many Gonzagan mounts.[52]

Although the foregoing outlines Europe's stud framework we lack specifics on size and weight of equines, but from excavations of Roman and Anglo-Saxon sites skeletons have

An Italian noble's horse by Mantegna. Although it depicts a very large horse there are many irregularities in the conformation, unlike Dürer's work, which is accurate.

been found in the range twelve to fifteen hands, though few reached the latter height. In the eleventh century most warhorses would have been stocky fourteen- to fifteen-handers, and palfreys similar but slighter. As cavalry's importance increased so did height and bulk due to assiduous selection.

THE ORIENTAL ASPECT

Although contemporary with European practices, Oriental studs were radically different. In the Levant and in Egypt horsebreeding reached a peak of excellence under the Mamlūk Sultanate (1260–1517) (see p. 147) which had a huge investment in horsebreeding. El Nacer Muhammed ibn Kalouan (1298–1308 and 1309–41) was the prime-mover devoted to all aspects of equestrianism, especially his stud farms. Abou Bekr's comprehensive work on Mamlūk equestrianism and veterinary medicine outlines El Nacer's involvement, giving the names of thousands of broodmares. The Arab historian Makrisi adds other details. El Nacer was fanatical about purebred Arabians, paying huge prices for top specimens and making even the £150 paid by Edward III for a horse he gave to the Earl of Salisbury look paltry. Other breeds were used but Arabians from the Bedu were El Nacer's pride, coming from Arabia, the Persian Gulf, Bahrein, Haca, Katif, the Hejaz, Iraq and parts of Syria over which the nomadic Bedu passed in annual migrations. The Beni Mouhanna, to whom other Bedu brought prize horses, were the most favoured tribe; and in Syria the Anazeh people gave their name to a strain of Arabian that, over time, blended with Turkmene horses. The Mouhanna were well rewarded, gaining monetary and territorial grants from El Nacer. On the Sultan's death his stables contained 4,800 horses and 5,000 racing camels.[53] At one time it is *alleged* he owned 130,000 Arabians, and although this is almost certainly hyperbole it does represent power by possession.

Unlike most occidental stock, we know what El Nacer's Arabians looked like: very much as they do today, because many strains have kept their purity. So distinctive are they that to any knowledgeable horseman an Arabian is immediately recognizable. In the West, although we have many distinct breeds they have largely been arrived at by repeated crossings until a type is fixed and becomes established as a breed. The Andalusian is possibly the only European *horse* (as opposed to pony) breed unchanged in centuries. In the sixteenth century it was in danger of losing its integrity by being crossed, at government orders, with heavier blood imports from Naples and central Europe, but the Carthusian monks of La Cartuja, on the Guadalete River, refused to obey the government's order, kept their herds pure, and even threatened with excommunication any who rode in the imported French fashion – *à la brida* instead of the Spanish *à la gineta*.[54]

HORSEDEALING

Horsetrading was essential to medieval movement. Traders had to cross borders and seas to sell. No doubt *caveat emptor* applied then as now, although quality horses were then more common in a dealer's yard. On the whole a medieval rider was a more knowledgeable buyer, and even wealthy owners had frequent recourse to dealers.

FAIRS AND MARKETS

Fairs are normally held outside towns and markets within; dealers congregated at both. In England between 1200 and 1400 4,680 were chartered.[55] The choice of goods was wide, from luxury imports such as furs, spices and jewellery, to everyday needs, like farm produce and livestock, including horses. Special horse fairs were held at major venues.[56]

Laws dating from the earliest English kings governed horse sales. Under Ine, King of Wessex (688–726), there was a thirty-day period of grace. Any blemish arising within that time (sickness or untoward behaviour) and the seller had to take the horse back or swear he knew nothing of it. Under Alfred (871–99) sales were only permitted at legal markets and had to be witnessed. This law was reiterated under Edward the Elder (899–924), Athelstan (924–40), Edgar (959–75) and Ethelred II[57] (979–1016).

International horsetrading was conducted on a wide web. In the mobile towns which followed medieval armies, the horsecorsers dealt profitably, but it was horse fairs which drew the regular buyer. Among the most prestigious were those of Champagne, Brie, Leipzig and Antwerp.[58] On his four-year 'Grand Tour' which began in 1435, the Spaniard Pero Tafur visited horse fairs at Cologne, Frankfurt, Geneva, Medina del Campo and Antwerp, which he reckoned the largest.[59] In the Orient, Asia and Eastern Europe horses for sale were moved by the drove and information on these comes largely from intrepid travellers, but data on European trading comes via royal and official correspondence, wardrobe books and chroniclers.

ENGLAND AND EUROPE

In 1155 William Fitzstephen described the weekly horse fair at London's Smooth Field. Buyers could choose from palfreys, hackneys, sumpters, warhorses, farmhorses and unbroken colts.[60] The Black Prince purchased horses from Little Watte of Smithfield from 1352 until 1359 at least.[61]

Some interesting details about dealing activity come from Edward I's reign. In 1299 the wardens of the great fairs of Champagne and Brie corresponded with London's Lord Mayor over payment owed by the Florentine dealers Fauberti, then trading in England. They claimed they had paid the debt incurred at Bari in 1292, which had been following them around ever since. The Lord Mayor prevaricated, saying the issue could not be decided as the king was too busy with the war in Scotland.[62]

Other sources tell us that the German dealer Albert de Liaigre, who traded in Avignon, brought a string of eighteen to England in 1373; the famous French merchant Jacques Coeur also dealt in horses, and his agents scoured Sicily for good prospects in the mid-fifteenth century.[63]

LICENCES

In an attempt to prevent any excessive drain on a nation's equine resources, and sales of warhorses that could then be used against an exporting country, bans were frequent and often circumvented by illicit trade, or by applying for a licence which was sometimes met with consent, but more often with denial. At one time the Spanish Inquisition was landed with the task of policing illegal traffic on the Catalan frontier – the so-called *passador de cavalls*.[64] A regular, presumably legal, run was noted by Ramon Muntaner when recording the late thirteenth-century trade of Domingo de la Figuera of Zaragoza who grew wealthy on sales of Castilian horses to Gascony and Navarre, doing particularly well in Toulouse and Bordeaux where he sold strings of twenty or thirty horses.[65]

EASTERN EUROPE

Hungary had an enormous trade in horses. In 1435 Bertrandon de la Brocquière described droves of 3,000–4,000 driven into Zegedin for sale. From there he travelled to Pest, passing huge herds on the plain; at Pest he toured many dealers' yards where horses could be bought in lots of up to 2,000 or in small consignments of ten for a total price of

Woodcut by Dürer of a coarse and rather gross horse which lacks breeding. The man was using what was available in the horse market.

Woodcut by Dürer of a strong and reasonably well-bred horse up to weight, owned and bred by a man of moderate to good means, with a lop-eared nag in the background.

200 florins. Despite their cheapness, quality was high; most horses were raised in Transylvania.[66]

Hungary and Germany were the main suppliers of warhorses, and German dealers were particularly prominent in the latter part of the medieval era. In 1507 Pandolfo Malatesta purchased four Hungarian destriers at 200 ducats each from Hermes Bentivoglio.[67] Moldavia and Wallachia also exported horses, including sales to the Crimean Tatars whose herds were often under strength.[68] After Russia broke its Mongolian yoke it horsetraded with its former masters, the trade developing into one of huge proportions. In the sixteenth century well over 50,000 horses were annually driven to Russia after a deal was struck between Tatars and the tsar.[69]

ORIENTAL HORSETRADING

In addition to horse marts and individual sales, most selling was done en masse. The huge volume of horses entering medieval India from Persia, Arabia and the Turcoman tribes awed almost every traveller.

Ibn Battuta described the Turcoman tribes which made their living raising horses. Horses were more numerous with them than were sheep in his country, the Maghreb. Some breeders had over 10,000 head, counted by a marker flag per 1,000 displayed on their wagons. Worth as little as one silver dinar each, they were regularly driven to northern India in droves of 6,000, traders having batches of 100–200 with an *alqashi*, or

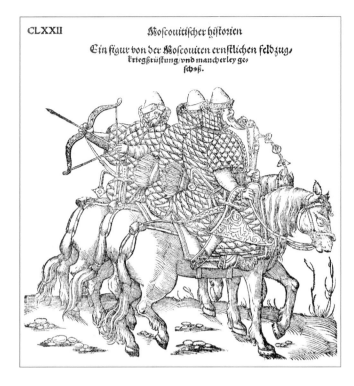

CLXXII

Moſcouitſcher hiſtorien

Ein figur von der Moſcouiten ernſtlichen feldzug/
kriegßrüſtung/vnd mancherley ge-
ſchoß.

Muscovite cavalry, showing Tatar influence.

drover, for each fifty horses, but thousands still perished in transit. Because the horses were destined for war, prices in India rocketed to 100–500-plus dinars, partly a result of customs dues being levied in Sind at Shashnagar and Multan. Racehorses came from Yemen, Oman, and Fars, costing 1,000 to 4,000 dinars.[70]

Ibn Battuta also visited the great Delhi horse mart.[71] At Travancore in southern India, the *Kuderai-Chettis* (horsedealers) had their professional guild HQ, controlling imports to southern ports during the twelfth and thirteenth centuries.[72] India also traded with Yunnan, Assam, Nepal, the Himalayan region, China and Tibet. Jusjaini, an early thirteenth-century chronicler, said 1,500 a day were sold at Krmbt in Tibet, where Bengal bought large quantities of Tamghan horses, considered strong, powerful and comfortable.[73]

Athanasius Nikitin, a Russian travelling extensively during 1468–1474, shipped out of Hormuz with his horses and entered India at Chaoul after hugging the coast from Muscat. In Gujerat he visited a horse fair at a place he Russianized to 'Shikhbaludin Peratyr' which was close to Bedar (Ahmedabad), which itself sent about 20,000 head to the fair each year. Nikitin also commented on the Dabul trade in horses from Khorassan, Turkestan and Heghostan.[74] The huge trade in Arabian and Gulf-Arab (Persian cross-Arabian) horses was noted by Marco Polo in the thirteenth, Ibn Battuta in the fourteenth, and many Portuguese travellers in the fifteenth and sixteenth centuries, including Duarte Barbosa (1518) and Tome Pires (1512–1515).[75]

Ambassador Ambrogio Contarini referred to Tatar horses coming out of the *Lordo* (horde) having seen a herd of 4,000 at the Persian court, and many others in his travels to Persia. From his deprecatory description they were typical Mongolian ponies: 'nags worth between 8 and 10 ducats that come out of Tartarie which the merchants bring at 4 or 5,000 at a clappe . . . being litell and serving only for carriage (pack).'[76]

These Chinese tribute horses are similar to the droves Barbaro saw in his travels.

THE PRIVATE TRADER

Not only agents and dealers horsetraded. The Celys were a fifteenth-century merchant family whose main trade was in wool. They had a branch at the Calais staple, and letters between family members show the factor there, George Cely, was more interested in his horse deals than his wool transactions. Horsecoping was an attractive sideline, provided you could shift your stock fast; George Cely was not always so lucky, but did turn a few pounds profit overall. Clearly he loved horses and the excitement of trade, selling horses on both sides of the English Channel. Having left two horses at London which were not finding ready buyers, his brother, Richard, warned 'they stand you at great cost daily', and George's father was warned that George had five more horses at Calais. Brother Richard assured the father there were only three, and George had earlier stated, 'I purpose never to have past one at once'. But the letters show that, with all good intentions, George could not resist a bargain and periodically became horse-poor. George's sideline must have continually worried his staid father as a considerable portion of the *Cely Letters* which cover the whole business of a family empire are devoted to George and his horses, some of which he traded for in Calais, others in England. When any fell sick, or could find no buyer, there was the additional cost and effort of putting them to pasture in various parks.[77]

CHAPTER 3

Everyman's Horse

The horse was a luxury item and a necessary adjunct to daily country living for almost all classes; ownership divisions were of cost and usage. Details from *The Register of the Black Prince* indicate many levels of equestrianism underpinning much of a rich man's estate management, but the horse also appears in many mundane occupations too.

PILGRIMAGES

Pilgrimages engendered much travel, some made them on foot, but many did so on horseback and, without denigrating the spirituality of many pilgrims, a number of them can be seen treating the experience as the medieval equivalent of a jaunt to the seaside, as did Chaucer's motley group heading to St Thomas' shrine at Canterbury. His travellers' tales, told to while away the dusty miles, show much of contemporary equestrianism through the nine pilgrims' mounts selected. No breeds are named; and conformation and performance are shown by scant comments on gait and type. Illustrations from the fifteenth-century *Ellesmere MS* are useless as guidance, despite some authors' efforts to read into them breed, size and movements. The text conveys the superior mounts' appearance by the knight's 'fine horses', his son's ability to 'sit a horse and ride', and the hunting monk's stable of 'many a dainty horse'. Indeed the monk's horse is the best portrayed – a berry brown palfrey in fine condition. The merchant sat 'high on his horse', suggesting a tall animal; the impoverished student rode a bony beast 'thinner than a rake'; the ploughman had obviously taken his cart mare out of traces for the jaunt; the Dartmouth seasalt novice rider 'rode a farmer's horse as best he could', a common mount suited to a farmer's purse and status, akin to the Reeve's dapple grey trotter cob stallion called Scot; the much-married wife of Bath rode astride on an easy paced ambler enlivened by her spurred heels. The prologue's only other equestrian comment notes the summoner who rode at a trot. The picture is of a mixed group of plebeian animals, choice dictated by means, some owned, some hired from a livery stable.[1]

A look at the horses the knight and his son were used to comes from 'the Knight's Tale' where exotic foreign vistas are peopled with scenes from his own experience; a nobleman rides his high-couraged restless 'courser full of flickering fires', and an Indian king rides a horse armoured in steel overlaid with a diapered cloth of gold housing. The squire likens a mechanical bronze horse to the best horseflesh – Lombard coursers and Apulian steeds, well-proportioned, tall, strong stallions. Lombardy and Apulia had produced quality horses for centuries; the Lombardic stock influenced by heavier Germanic blood from northern Europe, the Apulian horses with a heavy infusion of Greek, Oriental and Spanish blood gained from successive incursions across and adjacent to Apulia. Apulia and Campania were excellent horsebreeding centres from early Roman times.[2]

TRAVEL LICENCES

Not all pilgrims were Sunday trippers. Many went to *real* foreign parts, not the fabled lands of Chaucer's knight and squire. Pilgrims often needed licences to take horses out of England. During periods of peace or truce during the centuries of conflict between England and Scotland licences were always needed and stipulated the numbers of riders and how many horses were permitted. The issue of licences was often strict, but at other times lenient. In 1332 pilgrims to Santiago were allowed to take horses with them, but in 1352 all foreign travel, including pilgrimages, was banned unless under royal licence. By 1356 pilgrims could travel from Easter onwards. A year later licences were again needed. Gradually restrictions eased and pilgrims were allowed their horses; at first 'small horses for their own riding', then hackneys, and finally horses valued at no more than £2 – a fairly good category as many a man-at-arms' horse was valued at £2. After the Treaty of Bretigny in 1360 further relaxations followed with frequent journeys made by all classes of traveller. In the reign of Richard II (1377-99) Scottish pilgrims frequently visited English shrines: in 1381 the Abbot of Holyrood was allowed a dozen mounted attendants.[3] In the 1390s several Scots pilgrims came under safe conducts.[4]

THE TROT, THE AMBLE, THE RACK AND THE PACE

Before leaving Chaucer's saddle-weary pilgrims an examination of a horse's gait is indicated as on these depended the degree of comfort of equestrian travel. Some medieval records differentiate between trotters and amblers. Some contemporary writers mention pacers and a few documents, notably the *Border Papers* from the Tudor era, mention rackers. During the sixteenth century many books on horsemanship were produced; all four gaits were included, but only in some texts. However, some modern authors, and I suspect many of their medieval counterparts, lack comprehensive understanding of all gaits. Ambling has frequently been equated with pacing by modern authors; the mistake has been perpetuated by dictionary and equestrian manual definitions, where the amble is actually described as a pace, as is the rack. Acquaintance with all four gaits shows completely otherwise.

Today we have the benefit of the video camera and the ability to slow down film so that gaits can be analysed. The sound made by each hoofbeat can also be recorded. Accuracy is more desirable than in former centuries as so much modern horsemanship is competitive. Trying to equate medieval illustrations of a horse ambling with two legs on one side moving forward at the same time and calling it a pace is inaccurate, especially as the legs are not shown with the same forward thrust or elevation. The sequence of hoofbeats determines various gaits. The trot is two-time with each *diagonal* pair of legs moving together; the pace is also two-time but with each *lateral* pair moving together. The amble and the rack are four-time, and these are *identical* gaits with the hoofbeat sequence of near hind–near fore–off hind–off fore. Other gaits that also have this sequence are the walk, and the two gaits commonly used in America (and somewhat in South Africa): the running walk and the slow gait. The difference lies in the cadence, length of stride and speed with which these four beat gaits are executed. (India too has the rack and the running walk, but under Indian names.) Before audio and video aids were available, confusion could well have arisen because the sequence of lateral two-beat pace and that of four-beat rack (amble) to the untrained eye and ear can *appear* the same, particularly if gaits are executed on soft going, when the split-second difference in the hoof fall of the near hind and near fore of the rack (or its slower version, the slow gait) can appear to be simultaneous, as it is in the pace, because the actual touchpoint is hidden from both eye and ear by the deep going.[5]

In medieval times, however, there was another reason for confusing the two gaits: true pace and true rack (amble); and the clue lies in George Fleming's *Horseshoes and*

Crusaders and pilgrims.

Horseshoeing.[6] A medieval shoe is described with a point on the toe. Such shoes were put on the hind hooves of a horse being taught to pace. If the horse did not extend sufficiently, i.e., if he racked, he was struck in the forehoof by the point, which of course made him extend. This method ensured the natural four-beat gait was converted to the desired two-beat pace; any reversal to rack was painfully punished. Eventually the ambler would become permanently converted to the pace. Another, less painful, device to force a horse into a pace was by fixing trammels on each pair of legs to induce the horse to pace. The modern equivalent is used on Standardbred racehorses, some of which trot, some pace. Some destined to be raced as pacers have a tendency to break gait to a trot, thus losing speed. To correct this they are worked in hopples (hobbles) to ensure they do not break gait.

The word '*amble*' derives from French. A dictionary of medieval French has it as *marching*, i.e., *a four-beat gait*. English translations have used the word too loosely and very inaccurately. Anyone who has ridden the modern pacer and a horse that racks will immediately feel the difference. The former at high speed is comfortable, but at a slower speed it produces a rolling sensation, whereas the rack is supremely comfortable.

MONASTIC PLEASURE RIDING

The horse and the mule were needed by ordinary monks who had business with the outside world, and by the parish priest who was often better educated in farming and tilling his glebeland than in clerical matters. Not all riding, however, was done for business. The Venerable Bede described a spontaneous horse race between young clerics sparked off by Herebald who owned 'a splendid horse' he wanted to try out.[7]

Monks' favourite pleasure-riding was hunting, which many carried to such extremes, neglecting spiritual duties, that it brought papal and abbatial opprobrium. Pope Innocent III tried to ban monks hunting in 1215, and the need for subsequent bans showed how ineffective they were. The Abbot of Cluny tried the same for his monks in 1310, but excepted monks at monasteries that had 'the right and custom and usage of hunting', but he warned them to participate in moderation.[8] Restrictions never worked. Complaints were loud and frequent, often finding their way into the literary outpourings of clergy whose conduct was on a higher spiritual plane, or who looked at life with a sour visage. Many criticized the damage done to the poor. In *Piers Plowman* (*c*.late fourteenth century) William Langland wrote acidly of clerical corruption and pride. Defining 'reason', Langland used equestrian metaphors, such as he 'set my saddle on Wait Till I Get a Chance'; 'girthed him with good advice, and used a heavy bridle to help control his head'; and 'for he is sure to start neighing before we get there', i.e., give loud unwarranted opinions. To obtain absolution after confession, Langland avers some priests preferred a horseload of wheat than the penitent's sorrow for sins committed; yet other priests took to the highways begging rather than tending to their human flocks, while friars forsaking their customary begging for sustenance turned venal and 'grow rich and ride about on horseback'. The spikiest attack is against the religious orders where 'religion is a rider of horses, a rover through the streets, an arbitrator at days of settlement, and a purchaser of land. He rides like a lord on his palfrey from manor to manor, with a pack of hounds at his heels . . . the nobles should have more sense than to transfer property from their heirs to Religious orders . . .'[9]

For blatant neglect of his spiritual duties at Goodrich parish, Bishop Spofford of Hereford replaced Sir Walter ap Gwillim with Sir William Hanyes. When Sir Walter protested Sir William bought him out with a present of £5. This went into the record books many years later when, in 1490, two witnesses, one a priest, related the incident to Spofford's successor, explaining Sir Walter 'busied himself too much with hunting, so that on the holy day of Good Friday he was a-hunting when he ought to have been in Church and busied with divine service.'[10] In 1512 Thomas Murner, a Franciscan prior and a professor at the University of Paris, wrote *Gild of Rogues*. He castigated the hunting abbot, likening him to the Devil:

> how deem you this a strange tale, even though the Devil himself were Abbot? . . . Spiritual prelates will hunt and blow their horns and howl and kill great game; they will gallop madly, and chase and drive through the poor man's wheat with 20 or 30 or 40 horses: are those fit doings for a spiritual prelate?[11]

The medieval peasant with his few strips of land, and the landowner with a moderate demesne which his tenants farmed, but who lacked enough power to hold the Church liable for damages, had scant hope of the law working to their advantage.

THE LAW

In addition to laws governing horsedealing, noted in Chapter two, other laws governed horse ownership. Under Edgar, stealing livestock became a capital crime and a guilty man was sentenced to 'lose his head'.[12] Previously the punishment had been a hefty fine. Under Alfred, the amount of fines was levelled: 'formerly fines for stealing gold, horses, bees and many other fines were greater than the rest [at 120*s*]',[13] but theft of a cow, or broodmare with a calf or foal, was more leniently assessed. The calf or foal attracted a one shilling fine, and the cow or broodmare was to be assessed according to its value.[14] The further law clarified that theft of a horse meant specifically a stallion. The sum of 120*s* was a huge penalty, when we consider that under the laws of William I *wergild* payments were spelled out: if a stallion was used as part-payment it was valued at 20*s*.[15]

Under Athelstan an attempt was made to standardize stock values: the horse was assessed at 10*s* 'if it be worth as much, if less to be paid according to its appearance and what is approved by the owner'. If the owner could prove a higher value this was awarded.[16] If we consider the low value of the horses noted below in the *Cambridgeshire Gaol Delivery Roll* it indicates that in Anglo-Saxon times horses and horseownership were more valued than at a later date, and that the Cambridgeshire thievings were of scruffy, ill-conformed horses of the cheapest sort.

Under Athelstan the law also required a horseowner to take part in a hue and cry if called on:

> no quest shall be abandoned on north or south boundary until every man who has a horse has ridden out once. He with no horse shall go on working for his lord, when the latter proceeds on horseback or foot in his stead until he (the landlord) comes home unless justice has already been obtained.[17]

CUSTOM

Custom lay heaviest on those who could least afford it. Several customs directly involved horses, others indirectly inasmuch as horses were agricultural tools. Where customs and law did not feature, sometimes the malice of an interloper Norman overlord caused irreparable damage to down trodden tenants.

Heriot and mortuary were the most onerous customs. A wealthy landowner could better afford the heriot due to his overlord, but the heir of the tenant peasant had to surrender his best beast to his lord and the next most valuable to the village priest. He also had to pay merchet for permission from his lord to allow his daughter to marry; and tallage for permission to sell a colt, on the premise that both were sired by the lord's stock, i.e. by his peasant serf and by his stallion. Under William I the heriot of a villein was the 'best animal whether horse, ox, or cow'.[18]

The farm affer or stot had various agricultural duties and needs. It carried grain to and flour back from the lord's mill; when it needed new shoes the peasant had to use the lord's smithy. Failure to do so incurred a fine, or additionally the loss of the horse – and in the case of the mill, also the grain.[19]

Some ecclesiastic overlords were exceptionally greedy. A glaring example comes from *The Customs of Darnel and Over*, concerning the manor of Darnale in the early fourteenth century:

> also when any of them dieth, the lord shall have all the pigs of the deceased, all his goats, all his mares at grass, and his horse also if he has one for his personal use . . . (and a long list of other perquisites including gold and silver) . . . they ought also to keep all the lord's pigs and mares and horses of the woods (silvestres) . . .[20]

The fine of 20s exacted by the Church on its Durham manors for using a mill not the abbot's was far above the value of any packhorse and a peasant would have been hard pushed to find so much cash.[21] If deprived of his horse he was reduced to being his own beast of burden with diminished carrying capacity resulting in multiple carrying journeys.

Deodands (see p. 76) bit heavily into possessions. When John, a servant of William de Brikhulle, accidentally drowned when he fell off a cart into the River Weaver, the monks of Vale Royal claimed a deodand of 'one cart bound with iron, with two horses and other chattels to the value of £4' as the accident happened on their land.[22]

However, not all lords were grasping. Some abbots, although claiming their dues to the hilt, made sure their side of the bargain was kept. When making his will, Richard of Flete freed his tenants' widows of all heriots due to his heirs in perpetuity.[23] Although exacting suit of mill, the Durham prior insisted the millers, to whom Durham Manor mills were farmed out, kept them in working order to ensure tenants had no cause to go elsewhere to grind their grain.[24] No doubt there were many cases of rapacity but other manorial lords must have been, if not as generous as Richard of Flete, not so demanding that they left folk destitute, realizing that to strip them of the means of livelihood meant they would be unable to perform customary services.

ABUSE

Sympathetic monastic chroniclers recorded flagrant abuses. In 1071 Ivo Taillebois, a Norman given lands at Hoyland, ravaged Croyland and drove livestock into the marshes to drown; he broke the backs and legs of beasts of burden and mutilated some in the ears and tails, lamed cattle, oxen and horses, and also impounded and sometimes killed pigs, sheep and poultry.[25] These evil deeds wrecked agriculture and deprived the peasant farmer of his livelihood. He had been far less burdened under Anglo-Saxon rule. A tangential look at the ear and tail mutilation reveals that in much of the later medieval era, and for many centuries thereafter, it was the disgusting and cruel fashion to crop the ears and dock the tails of some horses. From the Croyland chronicler's text it would appear that the customs were unknown in England until after the Norman usurpation.

SUPERSTITIONS

Medieval man was superstitious, partly as a collective relic from pagan times, and many old practices lingered even though nominally the populace was Christian. Some chroniclers were extremely gullible and helped strengthen superstitions. Whenever horses are a component of these they are always black and linked with the Devil.

The unnamed monk responsible for recording the events of 1127 in the *Anglo-Saxon Chronicles*, relates the tale of the pluralist Abbot Henry of Poitou who sought numerous (but short-term) clerical preferments, eventually quitting inhospitable France for England where, as a kinsman of Henry I (1100–35), he acquired the Abbacy of Peterborouogh: 'and there he stayed just as does the drone in the hive. All that the bees draw in is eaten by the drone, and taken out . . . and so he did . . .' stripping his diocese. His coming-in was marked by a 'Black Hunt' that ravaged from Stamford to Peterborough, hunting by night throughout Lent with twenty or thirty horn blowing black hunters on black horses and black he-goats with 'hounds all black and wide eyed and loathly'.[26] This is almost certainly a layover in the national psyche of Hern the Hunter of Celtic myth.

William of Malmesbury, otherwise a credible chronicler, tells a witching tale of devils raising a dead woman from her coffin in the church, upon which she was unwillingly mounted on a loudly neighing black horse with 'iron hooks rising from his back'. Her cries as the horse galloped away with her could be heard for a long distance.[27]

HORSE STEALING

Horse theft is an age-old problem; today's light-fingered fraternity follow their medieval forbears' criminality. Whereas modern thefts cause financial loss, emotional trauma and a hike in insurance premiums, the medieval theft was far more damaging as horses were essential to many trades and occupations.

Periodic thefts were noted in a *Cambridgeshire Gaol Delivery Roll* covering the 1332–34 period. If found guilty the culprit faced the death penalty. Willelmus le Aunblour of Sutton, in Holland, Lincolnshire, remitted to gaol for stealing a mare and a horse worth 10*s*, broke out of prison, was recaptured, and at the Court Sessions at Norstow and Cesterton (Chesterton) sentenced to be hanged. Also at Norstow, Peter Roughe was arrested on suspicion with *mainour* (caught with the goods) of a horse in Histon; because of this he was charged with burgling the grange of Emme de Colne in Histon and stealing 4*s* worth of grain on 26 December 1331. The jurors of Northstow found him not guilty and stated the horse was his, and as no one claimed against him he was acquitted and allowed his horse. John Arneys was also acquitted by the Cambridge jurors on two counts of horse theft in May 1332, but had spent nine months in prison awaiting trial (set for 15 December).

Clerical thievery, however, was blatant. Robert le Fysshere (Fisher) of Swavesey admitted stealing two horses at Barton on 27 April 1332, but turned 'approver and appealed' (meaning he informed and accused) John, son of Thomas, for being his accomplice in stealing another horse worth 7*s* near Puckeridge, Hertfordshire, on 7 May 1332. He also accused Hugo Hynnessone of Bixworth as his accomplice in stealing yet another horse worth 5*s* at Braughing, Hertfordshire. Fisher pleaded 'Benefit of Clergy' and was remitted to the ecclesiastic courts. The other accused pleaded not guilty and were remitted to prison to await trial. After a two-year delay they were acquitted on 27 July 1334. Unfortunately the *Roll* does not relate what punishment Fisher received from his clerical superiors. To his admitted thefts, others were added. Roger, son of Walter of Forysnote, admitted he was a thief and that with Fisher had stolen a horse at Waldingfield, Suffolk, worth 4*s*. He also pleaded benefit of clergy and was remitted to the deacon for the Bishop of Ely where he awaited the king's permission for purgation (the chance to clear himself of the crime).[28] Fisher's 'burglary beat' ranged over a wide area, from Swavesey, about ten miles northwest of Cambridge, to Puckeridge, about twenty-five miles south of Cambridge, and well into Suffolk. It seems there was a well-organized gang led by Fisher who had his 'snouts' on the lookout for likely horses.

BORDER INFRACTIONS, REIVING AND CUSTOMS

Thefts in the border country were usually, but not always, linked with Scottish/English animosities. Some were of significant numbers of horses. (Customary rights of pasturage were fought out in the law courts.)

A complicated matter of alleged theft came before the Sheriff of Cumberland in 1280 concerning Henry Scott who had legally purchased a mare at Carlisle Fair. Scott complained that John of Wynchelas claimed the mare was his and had been 'furtively lifted'; Wynchelas accused Scott, citing the 'law of the March of Scotland' whereby Scott had either to find sureties or pay Wynchelas 'whatever sum he estimated as damages for the theft, at his pleasure, even though he was to place them at £1,000' or undergo judgement as though legally convicted. Scott was prepared to go to trial to prove his innocence, and King Edward I ordered the sheriff to hold the matter over until he came in person, when a jury was to be impanelled.[29]

A straightforward theft in 1302 was due solely to the state of war, much of which was of reciprocal depredations. Sir William Dunolm was awarded 20 marks 'by the king's gift and his own hands' to buy a charger for himself as he had lost his horses and armour when Sir Simon Fraser spearheaded a raid at Werk on joining the Scots against King Edward I.[30] Such raids were endemic throughout the reigns of the three Edwards. In February 1327 or 1328 Roger Maudyt complained that his son, John Story, Adam Read, Simon Davidson and other 'malefactors' raided Redeshead and Erleside. They carried off six prisoners, sixty horses, twenty oxen and twenty cows worth £100, and rescued three prisoners of war worth £20 in ransoms to Maudyt. Edward III appointed William Denum and three others to conduct an inquisition into the raid.[31]

Horses feature in several misdemeanours committed by members of Edward I's army in Scotland. The following cases from the *Placita Roll of the English Army in Scotland* in 1299 were brought before court sessions. Those proved innocent were delivered from gaol; the guilty were imprisoned. Trouble often came from within the English ranks, not from the Scottish enemy.

William of Lodelaw was accused by three other soldiers with concealing a red (chestnut) horse worth 10 marks which they had found when plundering the king's enemies on a manor in Scotland. When arraigned Lodelaw claimed the horse was so weak he could not drive it away. His testimony was accepted, the three soldiers were fined and William delivered from gaol at Roxburgh. Superficially his excuse seems plausible; the other soldiers may have accused him out of jealousy. However, 10 marks meant quite a valuable horse, and it would have had to be almost dead from starvation or crippled to be unable to move, so William probably got away with cheating his fellow soldiers of their share.

The marshal of the army in Scotland, Sir John Lovell, seized two horses worth 10s belonging to Aymer of Rotherford who complained and had his horses restored to him. Others who fell foul of Lovell also felt the force of the law: Ralph of Ireland was accused and found guilty of wounding the charger of Sir John Lovell who had come to pacify a lethal dispute between the English and the Welsh troops in Edward I's army in Scotland. Ralph of Ireland was sentenced to prison at Cluny. Sent to prison at Montrose was Alelinus of Wheltone who had been warned by Lovell not to go in advance of the banner of the constable; Alelinus ignored the warning and at Cluny proceeded to do so, whereupon the marshal arrested him and the two horses he had attempted to 'rescue in the king's contempt and the marshal's damage of 100 marks'. Despite pleading ignorance of the warning Alelinus was found guilty of the 'rescue' and imprisoned. Although couched in contemporary phrasing clearly Alelinus had stolen two horses.

Lastly, in the same document, Hugh Despenser sued John Simpson and Robert Eyr of Presfen because when he sent his 'avers' from Scotland to England, viz: 966 oxen, cows, stirks, stots and heifers, and two chargers in care of his men and under the king's safe conduct, they had seized them and driven them to Werk Castle and there detained them. At the king's request they released 800 beasts, the chargers and Despenser's men. One charger, worth £50, was lost due to the 'duresse of the said defendants' and the men's work for three weeks to a total sum of £100. In his defence John Simpson claimed there had been a hue and cry against Despenser's men so he was duty bound to arrest them and the beasts until the matter had been decided in the king's court. When the beasts were released to Hugh's men they got all except two which they refused (to take). Hugh counterclaimed he had his safe conduct which John Simpson refused to look at, and still detained 166 animals. He demanded an inquisition. Simpson claimed he never saw the safe conduct and also demanded an inquisition. The Sheriff of Northumberland was ordered to assemble twelve jurors 'not holding of the castle and liberty of Werk, to make inquisition'.[32]

These cases reveal much about the era's legal proceedings; that justice was to be seen to be done, and that some accused had the flimsiest excuses for crime, and got away with it!

In 1279 the Abbot of Jedburgh brought a case against William Belingham before the itinerant justices. The abbot demanded that William repair the fences surrounding his 'hays' of Heseliside. The abbot's men and his 'avers' repeatedly entered these 'hays', and upon so doing William had them taken and imparked to the abbot's damage amounting to £20. The matter was agreed between the two men, the abbot paying William half a mark. In return William summoned the abbot to answer why he refused common pasturage for two workmares and their followers of two years (two-year-old colts or fillies). The case was thrown out and William fined. Subsequently an agreement was reached between the abbot and William; William was to keep his fences in good repair, their state to be inspected once a year at Whitsun and any timber necessary for repairs procured; the abbot was to have common pasture for his 'avers' of Evelingham all the year round, and in the 'hays' during open time (i.e., before being set aside for the growing hay crop). William gave up the right of common pasture for his workmares and their offspring in the abbot's parks of Belingham, Wardlawe and Evelingham. The abbot, in turn 'quit claims' (gives up) his right to graze forty mares and their two-year-old offspring in Belingham, Wardlawe and Greenacres, but retained the right to graze forty cows and their yearling offspring, quoting the right given by charter of William's grandfather to the Church of the Blessed Mary of Jedburgh and the canons.[33]

This shows how acrimonious wrangles between laity and Church could be, and gives evidence of the considerable stud of mares and young stock owned by the Abbot of Jedburgh.

SPORT AND RECREATION

The average town and countryman's life could be a harsh grind, so windows of enjoyment were more keenly felt. Markets and fairs were ideal for itinerant entertainers. Medieval manuscripts reveal the existence of performing animals, among which were horses. Some acts exhibited true cleverness, other things we find reprehensible, but in an age which seems cruel to us today they were tolerated and enjoyed by spectators. One manuscript depicts a horse being baited by dogs, illustrating the killer instinct of canine versus grazier whose natural instinct is to flee. Several other 'acts' used a horse's natural instincts and turned them by assiduous training and adept showmanship into spectator delights: a 'joculator' (showman) armed with shield and cudgel is attacked by a rearing horse; another horse strikes a drum with its forefeet; yet another with its hind feet.[34] Rearing and striking is habitually done by stallions fighting over mares and territory. Striking with the hind feet is a natural response by a horse surprised by a sudden movement to its rear. A domesticated horse has these reactions 'trained out', or the horse is 'booted out' (or should be) if it continues to use them against man, but in an era when the warhorse was a weapon, refining natural skills would have been part of a trainer's job, even though a prized warhorse was hardly a fairground exhibit.

By repetitive training and association horses can be trained to perform to music. My experience of this was in a quadrille ridden at the Bath and West County Show. My two horses in the four-pair team definitely keyed into the musical beat and on certain bars performed movements in advance of the rider's direction. Less credible, but reputedly seen, were a horse walking a tightrope, and others being 'ridden' by oxen holding trumpets in their mouths.[35] The latter could be explained; a bulling heifer is a common sight in the country. Some medieval oxen were very small and at certain times mares are amenable to 'being ridden'; the weight of a small, weak ox would not be too burdensome, although hardly what the mare was expecting.

HORSERACING

Although formalized horseracing was very well established in Egypt and Syria during the Mamlūk Sultanate[36] it did not cross to the occident until much later. In England it had to wait until Stuart times. Match racing for fun and a wager, however, is a sport common to all eras. There are scattered references to various forms of horseracing in medieval times, but none that really describe any formality. In Henry II's time Fitzstephen described the customary challenges at Smithfield between owners of 'such chargers that are so powerful to carry and so swift to run'.[37] A sidelight on this shows chargers were not the ultra heavyweights often depicted as warhorses.

An entry in the *1286–89 Wardrobe Book* refers to 'a Bay courser for the king's running £8 13s 4d', a rare note of a courser being specifically for running, which may mean Edward had a love of spontaneous 'flapper'-type racing.[38] We have already seen how Bede's Herebald loved challenging his fellow clerics to an on-the-spot race, and Sir Thomas Gray commented on the sports followed by young bloods in Wales, soon after David, brother of the Welsh prince Llewelyn, was taken near Denbigh. Edward I had:

> bestowed lordships of Wales upon diverse seigneurs of England, on condition they should dwell there, which they did, and led a jolly life and took much delight in hounds and hawks and horseracing and leaping, and especially in killing deer by hunting them on horseback.[39]

At Chester match racing had been 'customary time out of mind'. On Shrove Tuesday the saddlers guild presented to the drapers a wooden ball, embellished with flowers and placed upon the point of a lance. In 1540 this trophy was changed to a silver bell.[40] This dating indicates a medieval forbear for the Chester races, and such racing was probably replicated at major fairs throughout the country between those who had fast horses.

We have more certain information from Italy about racing. In 1115 Laurence of Verona described a festival in which Hugo Viscount of Pisa took part in which were 'games with spears' (a tournament) followed by *cursibus equorum*, which surely indicates Italian 'flapper' racing.[41] We are on more secure ground with the Gonzagas of Mantua who started racing under Luigi Gonzaga at Mantua in 1329, where strains were specifically perfected for racing and the Margonara Italian strain outstripped barbs imported to pit against them.[42]

Perhaps best known is an Italian race that is still performed today. The Palio is run in Siena every July and dates back over 500 years. Each *contada* (district) puts up one horse and jockey who draws for his mount and rides bareback. Dirty tricks are the order of the day, and even if a jockey falls off, or is pushed off, provided the horse finishes carrying his bridle plume he can be declared the winner, or could in days gone by. Today a tourist attraction (and probably a betting furore too), it still has its medieval overtones – being run to honour Our Lady.[43]

achies quen nulles terres / na œualiers meillors
pardieu fait alixand / se nestrai ames mors
dont ne siu re pas nes / de gentis ancessors

Medieval trick horses.

CHAPTER 4
Farming and Commerce

CARTHORSE AND PACKPONY

In the early medieval era horses played only a small part in heavy farm duties; it was more common for the ox to be hitched to a plough. However, draught horses had a considerable part in other duties. They were indispensable for transporting bulky and/or awkwardly shaped items that could not be carried by a pack animal. In commerce the sumpter was more important than the draught horse, especially where speed in carrying perishable foodstuffs such as fish was concerned. They carried produce to market, often with the goodwife aboard, her legs spread wide around her pony's burden, or sitting sideways, maybe with a footrest to ease her balance – the forerunner of the sidesaddle. The pack rather than the draught horse was always preferred when carrying specie to court from the royal mints, or to military camps – cash needed to pay troops, or as a hobelar was suspected of contemplating 'he would take off for want of sustenance'.[1] Specie packhorses appear regularly in Plantagenet accounting. A *hakenei*, probably a faster animal than a common sumpter, was often used. Frequently, and always in war, an armed escort protected the specie. A man-at-arms could lead a sumpter or *hakenei* at the gallop, whereas a draught team would be dead in the water and ripe for capture if attacked. In most cases a specie animal carried 100 lb, a quarter of the upper load limit and half of a normal load.

England's wool wealth – of which the king availed himself via customs dues, with the residue going to the landowners, on whose runs the sheep grazed, and the middlemen, whose fortunes were made in buying and reselling the clip – meant money was available to build the soaring cathedrals that grace the land, the stone-built castles and fortified manors, and the prestigious abbeys and monasteries, which relied on their agricultural produce whether hoofed, horned, or in grain. Working with stone and timber required strong carthorses in the traces. Domestic and foreign wars needed an increasing number of draughthorses, which often put undue burdens on the owners when they were channelled from complaining abbot to the royal war-baggage train.[2]

THE DRAUGHT HORSE IN AGRICULTURE AND WAR

The appearance in Europe towards the end of the tenth century of the horse shoulder collar[3] was one of the most significant advances in harnessing horses to a vehicle. It enabled the horse to maximize on its strength by pushing against the collar, thus increasing the weight which could be drawn. Alone, however, it could not fully affect overall efficiency; improvements in the breeding of the short-statured, chunky draught animal in the fourteenth and fifteenth centuries,[4] and advances in vehicle construction were essential. Provided the animal in the shafts was of sufficient weight combined with strength, and the cart built sturdily, it was possible for one animal to shift a one-ton load. The collar also enabled the horse to back the vehicle and exert braking power going

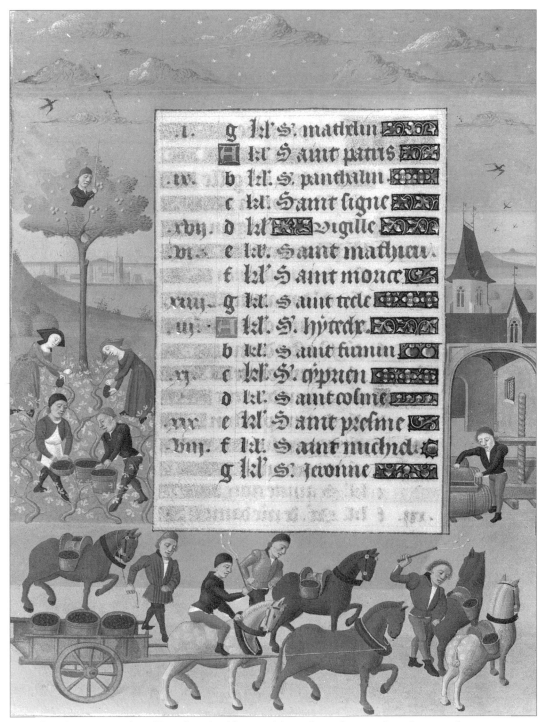

Cart horses in tandem. Note that the rider, not driver, directs horse and carthorse, and packhorse sizes are the same.

downhill. The whippletree (whiffletree, splinter bar or swingletree), a medieval innovation, acted as a shock absorber, protecting the vehicle against the jerkier movements of a horse taking up the strain as it started to shift the load. (The slow plod of an ox put no such sudden strains on a vehicle.) The whippletree equalized strains on the traces in a turn. Its connection to the vehicle by a single hook facilitated changes of direction, but because the bar was subject to frequent breakage (hence the name splinter bar), the iron connecting hook was made weaker so that it broke first. It was easier to change the hook than to fashion a new bar.[5]

Even lacking concrete proof of the actual size and weight of each category of animal, the value of the animal indicates its perceived utility, and to an extent its size. Between 1710 and 1785 the size of animals offered at Smithfield meat market doubled in weight due to better farming methods and nutrition.[6] To an extent the same can be expected of draught horses, and of horses of the less well-off who had sufficient means to feed their stock better. Horses of the wealthy had always fared better when in work, as shown in many household accounts which always had a section for stable expenses. Many royal and noble studs paid great attention to raising the standard of their horses. The medieval broodmare often fared badly, being expected to produce foals without hard feed if we are to be guided by Prospero d'Osma, Queen Elizabeth I's Italian studmaster who was brought in to overhaul practices at her Malmesbury and Tutbury studs. His new diet for broodmares was hay one day and bran and stubble for the next three. In the original manuscript the word for stubble, 'restopio', indicates gleanings, straw and ears of corn, which also had a variety of herbs beneficial to the mares. It was hardly a balanced diet but considerably better than the pre-d'Osma diet of hay only.[7]

As mares and horses were used in draught work, and only (usually) horses as war mounts, it suggests that a great percentage of war stock had for dams horses suitable for draught, barring those in wealthy magnates' studs. Medieval illustrations of draught horses show horses that could just as easily have been used under saddle; what we would term today 'ride/drive' type, chunky but not massive.

Requisitioning of carthorses for war purposes from among the populace was done by local sheriffs, and by levies on monasteries. Levies were frequent and a huge burden on the farming populace, who also had to surrender their harvests to royal purveyors at the king's price. The top grade of draught animal must have been rare, and on occasion unfavourable comments were angrily aired over the animals submitted.

In July 1306 accounts were drawn up concerning oxen, horses and carts supplied for the war effort against Scotland. James de Dalileye, the Carlisle receiver, played down the animals' worth. Most horses were described as of 'small value'; some as 'weak and of little value', one was infected and 'worthless', two were 'totally dried up in mind and body'; twelve oxen were 'small, weak and lean' and forty-two were weak. Of a total of 108 horses only twenty-one, and of sixty-six oxen only twelve, did not have some deleterious remark against them.[8] As these were drawn from a wide agricultural base, and sheriffs and abbots had dared to offer them to the irascible Edward I, it gives an idea of the general condition of farm animals – a fair percentage of them were at the bottom of the strength table: if the king had on occasion to make do with this standard, what went for the rest of the country? and indeed Europe?

In 1299 seventy-nine horses were hired at fourpence each per day, and seven wagons at one shilling each per day to haul provisions from Annan to Lochmaben. An additional six horses were bought by the Sheriff of York to draw the king's carts from York to Carlisle. Prices varied – a black horse at 33s; a bay mare and a white horse 26s 8d; a liard (grey) horse 15s; another black 29s; and a favel (dun) 13s.[9] Prices could have reflected quality, size, and/or difficulty of procurement, but the range is quite startling and I would suggest two types are possible: smaller, weaker ones at the lower prices, more strapping horses at the higher prices. In 1303/4 William de Molecestre, Sheriff of Cumberland, paid £50 for twenty wagons and 124 oxen to transport victuals from Cumberland to the king at Roxburgh; £23 17s 4d was paid for fifty oxen and 120 sheep (for meat) to be driven to the same venue.[10] A district would often be swept clean of all its available animals, some on a long-term basis, others for shorter periods.

Edward I also bought on the open market in Scotland prior to his warring years. It is to be expected that his valet William FitzGlaye did not fear his servants, presumably in royal livery, would be outbid at Stirling fair when ordered to procure avers to be driven to Lindseye and thence, without hindrance, into England.[11]

A valuation of the estates in Kent belonging to the late Isabel, Countess of Athol, was made in 1292 and gives a useful guide to values of different farm animals and two grades of horse. At Chilham: two carthorses each 10s; twelve stots, each 4s; thirty-two cows, each 4s; thirty-two swine, each 1s; two sows, each 1s 4d; ten pigs (presumably piglets), each 6d; forty-one sheep, each 8d; ten lambs, 4d each. At the manor of Kyngestone all animals were similarly valued, except the stots which were only worth 3s each; it was a similar story at Rydelyngwolde, except for the ten weak stots worth a total of 26s 8d.[12] From the valuations shown below the 10s horses would have been plough horses and the stots general purpose animals; it suggests farms usually kept horses for the many chores which arose throughout the farming year.

The Agrarian History of England and Wales has a useful guide to average prices of oxen, plough and carthorses throughout the fourteenth century. Carthorses were always the most expensive, costing about a third more than oxen before the Black Death (1348) then rising to half as much again, till by the end of the century they cost 70 per cent more. Plough horse values had a greater swing, being 80 per cent of ox prices pre-Black Death, then rising to almost as much as oxen, and by the end of the century costing 10 per cent more, before dropping back to only 90 per cent of ox prices, then dropping sharply at the end of the century to well below the price of an ox.[13]

	plough horse	carthorse	oxen
1300–10	11.56	19.75	12.73
1310–20	14.50	23.41	15.99
1320–30	11.81	18.28	15.38
1330–40	10.26	17.51	12.61
1340–47	9.45	14.65	12.14
1350–60	10.34	17.95	13.41
1360–70	13.50	25.58	16.31
1370–80	15.72	25.76	16.15
1380–90	13.54	22.36	13.76

Note: prices in shillings

THE HORSE IN THE PLOUGH

Ploughing with oxen was usually eight to a plough, although it might be as few as six or as many as ten.[14] Integrating horses with oxen was a slow process; it was not until modern times that horses totally superseded oxen.

Plough horses are mentioned in the *Statutes of the Synod of Clermont* in 1095,[15] and ploughing with horses and oxen – a mixed team – began earlier in Europe than in England.[16] A fully horse-powered plough is implied in 1260 in France: the Archbishop of Rouen was out riding on St Matthew's day and found ploughs at work: 'wherefore he caused the horses to be brought to Meulan, seeing that they (the ploughmen) presumed irreverently to labour on the day of so great a saint.' At Meulan the ploughmen had to find guarantors for whatever fine the archbishop should decree. Four years later the same archbishop gave an on-the-spot fine of 10 sous to a man using a three-horse hitch to shift timber on a Sunday.[17]

Horse ploughing in England is first mentioned in a document from the reign of Henry I. This was at Ringstead, Norfolk, a Ramsey Abbey holding where three ploughs each of four oxen and three horses are recorded. Fifteen of Ramsey Abbey's eighteen demesnes used mixed teams by the end of the twelfth century. In the *Pipe Roll* for 1165–66 Keyston in Huntingdonshire showed three teams of eight oxen each, and one of six horses.[18]

As the century progressed, the use of horses expanded. Records are sometimes clear as to plough composition; sometimes the wording is ambiguous: Fairstead, Essex, had a mixed team of six oxen and two horses, and one harrower; but at Wiverton and Stowe Beden in Norfolk each manor had two teams of eight oxen and six horses, which could mean one of oxen and one of horses, or mixed teams of four oxen and three horses. Eastern England, where much of the soil is lighter, led the way in using mixed teams, and occasionally solely horse teams. Twenty-three locations are noted: Norfolk, nine; Huntingdonshire, five; Suffolk, four; Essex, two; and one each in Cambridgeshire, Bedfordshire and Buckinghamshire.[19]

Walter of Henley, author of the late thirteenth-century *Seneschaucie*, a treatise on farming, has much to say about horses and other farm livestock. Oxen were cheaper to feed than horses, and when their working life ended they could be fattened on grass for a summer and sold for meat, with their hide and hooves, when rendered, providing neatsfoot oil. The horse, because of a church ban on eating horsemeat, was only worth its hide for leather and hair for ropes. Between 18 October and 3 May (the feasts of St Luke and Holy Cross) horses and oxen were stall-fed, the rest of the year being spent at grass, either cut daily or at pasture. Winter feed cost 3s 4d for an ox and 9s 2d for a horse, the horse receiving a halfpenny's worth per day of oats and the ox one penny's worth a week of oat sheaves (i.e., oat straw with some grain remaining). Ten sheaves were equivalent to one bushel of oats. Summer grass cost one shilling each. With an estimated 50 lb per bushel[20] the plough horse was adequately fed, the poor ox less so although oat straw provided bulk and some nutrition. Walter also advised keeping work mares in preference to horses as the foals were a bonus. A mare used to steady work could safely continue work until fairly close to foaling. As the normal foaling season was May to June, heavy ploughing was long past so mares could expect an easier time during the foal's first few weeks before haymaking and harvest arrived. The reeve was responsible for managing the manor's stud and if a mare failed to foal annually the cause(s) was to be investigated; e.g., was she barren? overworked? underfed? was a stallion lacking? If the reeve failed to exchange an empty mare 'in time', i.e., before the breeding season was over, he was held liable and fined the value of the foal for this and other failures. This highlights two aspects of farm breeding: it suggests a travelling stallion, maybe the lord's on circuit around his estates, and means the reeve had to know a mare's cycle in order to time the stallion's visit for when the mare was in oestrus; it also reveals that covering could be haphazard, and a failure to do so at the optimum time could result in a failure to conceive, which has nothing to do with barrenness, which is an inability to breed.

Although a horse worked faster and was able to continue for up to two hours longer a day than the ox, the reverse side, according to Walter, was that without adequate supervision the ploughmen would let the mixed team work at the plod of the ox rather than the accelerated speed of the horse.[21]

Of course the *Seneschaucie* was based on the model manorial farm; many plough horses used by impecunious peasants would have been low-value avers, usually old and worth only a few shillings.[22] In 1348/9 accounts for the Bishop of Winchester's demesne at Bishops Waltham, Hampshire, showed a huge crop of heriots; among them were five

Hercarius from the Bayeux Tapestry.

carthorses, forty-four affers (avers) and twenty-four oxen. Those immediately sold averaged as follows: seven oxen, 9s 4d each; five carthorses, 7s 10d each; and thirty-two affers, 2s 6d each.[23] This falls far below the national average shown above and suggests the carthorses were plough horses, and not up to the heavier demands of road haulage, or they were so decrepit the bishop's reeve got shot of them as not worth their feed.

OTHER FARMHORSES

The *hercarius*, or harrower, appears in many documents and illustrations. In the Bayeux tapestry one is pulling a tined harrow harnessed with a shoulder collar directly attached to what looks like a swingletree; immediately behind it comes the seedsower, and behind him a single mule (or donkey) drawing a two-wheeled plough which is attached to the coulter. Presumably these activities should have been in reverse order, the harrow following the plough to break down the clods for the sower. Another scene showing William's men foraging has other farm animals being gathered in: a sheep, a cow kneeling with an axe-wielder (or butcher), a piglet borne on a soldier's shoulder, and a packpony with corn loaded on what appears to be a wooden crosstreed packsaddle. Although only a very rough idea of animal sizes can be gained the packpony is significantly smaller in relation to its handler than the *hercarius*, showing an attempt to represent a difference in equid sizes.[24] Other farm carrying duties performed by horses and/or ponies were: produce to market; manure in panniers to the fields; seed to the field; and corn to the mill. Indeed, some mills were actually horse powered.

CARRYING DUTIES

Carrying duties stretched back to Anglo-Saxon times and were imposed on the Lord's farmer-tenant, the *gebur*, who was required to have a horse to perform them.[25]

After the Norman Conquest and wholesale land confiscation peasants were less likely to own a horse, but nevertheless there were some who did, even riding horses, as shown by tolls paid at Bishops Cleeve and Henbury in Salt Marsh in Gloucestershire.[26]

Carrying duties and other '*works*' are outlined in the peasants' farming year for the small Fenland village of Landbeach, Cambridgeshire. On the Chamberlain Manor five-acre men owed to the lord 164 work days a year, and two and a half-acre men 111 days; on the Bray Manor five-acre men owed 164 days and two and a half-acre men sixty days, plus an assortment of extra dues – chickens, geese, capons, salt and carrying services. At harvest this meant carrying grain from field to barn; on a yearly basis a weekly carrying service was demanded, with the tenant carrying in his cart or on his horse two bushels of wheat, three bushels of barley or dredge corn (mix of oats and barley), or four bushels of oats. In addition, all other 'necessaries' were to be carried – as much as 'he could reasonably carry'. There were other impositions, such as heriots and transporting the lord's wife, or sons, by water to Ely or Wisbech.[27] It is clear the loads carried were by weight and not capacity as barley needs considerably less room than oats.

MURRAIN

This unspecified disease hit all farm animals, but struck sheep the hardest, wiping out whole flocks, with cattle next worst affected. There were some losses among horses, but the numbers were fewer; however, there were seldom many horses on farms where sheep proliferated, so the comparisons do not give a true picture of murrain's malevolence among horses. One guide that it was more serious than records indicate is that this disease was one of the reasons why Edward III disbanded some of his studs, notably those north of the Trent after 1360.[28]

Murrain hit hard in 1316, and again in 1348 – plague year. According to chronicler Knighton, in one place alone 5,000 sheep died and neither 'beast nor bird wuld touch the flesh and fear so great that cattle disposed of for very small prices. A horse of 40*s*, sold for half a mark (6*s* 8*d*), a fat bullock 4*s* and a cow for 12*s*.'[29] Was the plague the reason for so many heriots on the Bishop of Winchester's demesne at Bishops Waltham, and the reason the animals sold for so little - no one to buy them or use them to till the land?

A spin-off at Landbeach in 1349 was that no sheep showed in the reeve's accounts in the list of the lord's livestock. But peasants' flocks and herds were revealed by cases of trespass and cases of failure to put their sheep on the lord's land in order to manure it. In the number of trespass cases brought before the court, horses headed the list, rising to a high in 1372 of fifty-one cases involving 105 horses, one cow and no sheep.[30]

THE RHUDDLAN ACCOUNT ROLL

Rhuddlan Castle accounts for 1282 give a mass of information. The castle was built in 1277 as the base for Edward I's advance into Wales. Cavalry and infantry mustered here and needed massive provisioning. Activity in and around the castle show the stockpiling of supplies for the military push, and bringing in building supplies for Rhuddlan Castle and Macclesfield, which was used as the main residence for the king's family. This peripatetic family also used Caernarvon, Aberconway, Chester, Northwich and Bromburgh. Considerable baggage and provisions went by cart to all these places. Demand for horses and carts was heavy; accounts show that five-, four-, three- and two-horse carts were used. Most used were three-horse hitches, then two-horse carts. Only once was a five-horse cart needed, plus a two-horse cart to shift the queen's gear from Bromburgh to Macclesfield, costing 10s total for the five-day hire. Only occasionally did the queen use a four-horse cart, costing as much as 6s for four days.

Baker Huddle needed horsepower to shift huge quantities of wheat and meal. Some was brought more than a mile from harbour to castle, some from Ruthin and Chester, respectively sixteen miles and twenty-five miles from Rhuddlan. Mostly he used a three-horse hitch costing one shilling and twopence per day; occasionally he used packponies costing fourpence per pony per day for the one-day trip from Ruthin to Rhuddlan. Other packhorses carried luxury items such as almonds, wax for candles, figs and raisins.

Carting hay used the greatest concentration of horses and carts. From cutting to storage took seventy-six days and at various peaks used twenty-three mowers, 160 spreaders, twenty-four rakers and seventy-seven stackers. The king's hay and that of the queen were kept in different barns, but the accounts were totalled together. For the main crop for the castle's horses and those of the 750 cavalry mustered:

Six carts, each with three horses for one day:	6s 10d
Eight carts, each with two horses:	6s 8d
Twenty carts for three days:	£3 0s 4d
Three carts for two days:	6s 4d

For the queen's hay:

One cart with three horses and one cart with two horses for eight days:	2s
Five carts, each with three horses:	5s 2d

The wording varies and costs are confusing; some work out at the daily flat rate of one shilling and twopence per three-horse hitch and tenpence for a two-horse cart. Other entries only state carts and price and do not tally using the flat rate, representing more nearly a daily rate. Discrepancies show that there must have been some leeway for negotiating prices. The total for all stages of haymaking came to £7 13s 4d, which included purchasing a pitchfork and repairing the roadway from hayfield to castle. But the accounts do show how vital draughthorses were; at the carting stage, at its peak, seventy-five horses were on-site hauling hay in before it had a chance to get rained on. That pilfering was liable is shown by the 12s 6d paid to a servant to watch over the crop for the seventy-six days.

Other heavy use of draughthorses was to carry timber; thirty horses were used at one time, followed by another entry showing twenty-six. No oats or other grains for fodder are shown in the accounts but some grain crop, possibly oats, peas or beans, is suggested by the twenty-nine carts hired for three days to take litter (straw bedding) from the field to the castle after twelve mowers had cut the unnamed crop.[31]

PACK PONIES

Agriculture met commerce in areas with scant population, few if any proper roads, and mountain and/or moorland terrain. There, much of the grazing was only suitable for sheep or native ponies: the two were compatible – one grew the wool the other transported it. Carrying mineral ores needed the strong backs of native ponies - lead, coal, iron and alum were the heavy burdens carried by sturdy ponies. Many sheep runs were on monastic lands, especially in the north of England. Jervaulx, Fountains, Rievaulx and many others were responsible for much of the annual wool crop. For this they needed their own strings of pack ponies and from a very early date they ran stock on the moors. In 1200 King John ordered:

> Master Forester, Hugh de Neville, and other powerful men to notify all Cistercians to remove their stud horses, pigs and flocks from the royal forests within the week. At the end of this term any found within the forest are to be taken for the king's use.[32]

A boon for an abbot's tenant was rounding up his mares and foals on the 'waste'; i.e., moorland. The Lake District still retains many old narrow tracks only wide enough for a single-file string of ponies. Where streams were crossed bridges were built with sides raised just high enough to contain a pony that might slip or stumble, but low enough to permit its load to pass over without hindrance or damage. The Fell and Dales ponies were native to these parts. The Scottish Galloways were used by cattle drovers bringing Scottish cattle to fairs and sales held all over the Lake District, and much Galloway blood was infused into the Fell pony. Using old drove roads, these drovers went the whole length of England selling cattle at major towns, such as Manchester, Birmingham and London. This horsetrading meant that Galloway blood was melded with horses in many other parts of the country, but as a distinct breed it had vanished by the 1700s as a Dr Anderson wrote of the Galloway in the past tense.[33]

In the seventh century the king of Northumbria made a huge land grant to Abbess Hilda of Whitby; subsequently the abbots of Whitby expanded their holdings. For eight centuries prior to the Reformation, Whitby Abbey owned the fishery of Whitby and in 1394 they kept sixty-three packhorses to carry fish inland to market. Whitby properties at Hackness, Suffield and Everly ran broodmares, and the abbey's tenants had to 'go to stud' and round up mares and foals several times a year. North of the abbey horsebreeding also occurred in Harwood Dale where the monks ran mares and the stallion, together with dairy cows. In 1231 the abbot of Whitby was engaged in a legal wrangle with Bridlington Priory over grazing rights and after much argument a compromise was reached: the abbot allowed the prior to graze his mares there, but not his stallion, which must have failed to meet Whitby standards. It was not only the Whitby Benedictines who ran horses at pasture. The Cistercians of Rievaulx and the Austin canons of Guisborough also bred horses, relying for land on large grants from local landowners like de Brus of Skelton and de Mauley of Mulgrave. They also gave pasture rights, usually stating how many head were to graze on any run, often with other stipulations such as the removal of three-year-old colts. This helped to avoid deleterious incest breeding. The sturdy Chapman horse standing around 14 hh had its roots in this area. It was one of the ancestors of the Cleveland Bay.[34]

Without the cart and pack animals the court would have ground to a halt at one very smelly location. The accounts for Edward I's huge enterprise – when he shipped his court to France for three years – shows extensive packhorse use. Money was a frequent load: six horses to carry £1,000 from London to Lyndhurst cost a 15s hire fee for three days; five horses with £1,000 from Corfe to Somerton, a one-day trip, cost 5s, 2d more per horse – maybe of a better class for a heavier load? Other entries are fuller: two hackneys, each with 200 lb of specie, at 2s; ropes to secure it, 10d; and a guard, 1s, the cost of a mounted soldier. Hire of a hackney to carry jewels from London to Canterbury cost 11d for two days. Other loads carried by hackneys were figs and raisins at 8d per day per horse, and lampreys with one horse for £2 14s 8d. This last is unusual, for the cost was enough to purchase the horse not hire it. Maybe it was an accountant's error? These entries are from among many in the accounts.[35]

One incident where it may be excusable to guess (estimate) the breed of packhorse is for the troop of 300 which was used to carry supplies for the 200 English cavalrymen setting out for a raid on Stirling in 1298.[36] Were these animals drafted in from the northern counties' indigenous stock as a compulsory purchase, or even as a loan, as happened in Elizabethan days when horses were needed for border warfare?

A COMMERCIAL CAMEO – THE MERCHANT OF PRATO

Ser Francesco Datini's diary, covering the late fourteenth and early fifteenth centuries, shows the web of mercantile contacts he developed over a lifetime (1335–1410). He traded with the Balkans, the Black Sea, Catalonia, Majorca, North Africa, Spain, France, the Balearics, Flanders and England, to name some of the centres. The variety of goods was enormous, including wool, cloth, oil, wine, salt, furs, metals, cattle, wax, sandalwood, alum and slaves.[37] Most imports and exports reached their destinations via the maritime network, but prior to and after shipping the equine element came into operation – strings of mules, donkeys, packhorses, and in the oriental sphere camels too no doubt, were involved.

He imported slaves into Italy from Spain, Africa, the Balkans, Constantinople, Cyprus and Crete, but especially from the Black Sea where horses were an essential part of the slave round-up, as witnessed by another Italian, the Venetian ambassador to Persia, Ambrogio Contarini (see p. 24).

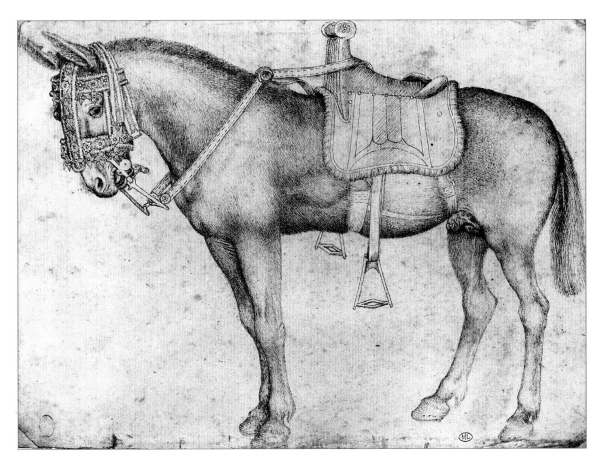

Datini had to search hard for a mule similar to this handsome animal by Pisanello.

Datini was a native of Prato, but his early adult life was spent in Avignon where he set up his first trading companies. He stayed there for three decades, then returned to Italy. Between 1382 and 1392 Datini opened businesses in Pisa, Genoa and Florence, but there was the ever-present menace of the Duke of Milan, Gian Galeazzo Visconti who wanted to extend his power from Lombardy into Tuscany. That Datini's choice fell on Tuscany was mainly due to Florence's ascendancy and her acquisition of the services of the great English condottieri, Sir John Hawkwood.[38]

While resident at Avignon, Datini observed much of the minutiae at the exiled Papal court, the luxury prevalent there, even down to the mules and horses being bitted with gold and with gold upon their trappings. He noted Petrarch's caustic comment: 'soon they would even be shod with gold'. Italian merchants monopolized the trade that flourished at the court, especially the luxury trade in horses, armour and spices.[39] One of Datini's chief imports was Italian armour, especially from the Milanese makers Basciamuolo of Pescina and Danesruolla of Como. His biographer notes that he had no qualms about providing arms to both sides: the 'free companies' who plagued Europe and the various communes who had to rebuff their inroads. All these goods had to be carried on mule back across the Alps via Pavia and Avigliana, arriving at Avignon after a three-week journey.[40] (Comments on transport via muleback occur throughout the diary.)

Datini's international dealings also depended on the horse. His correspondence about purchasing Cotswold wool, using the firm of Orlandini and Vettori in London, notes that Neri Vettori was due to ride to the Cotswolds to purchase 1,000 ducats worth of the 1403 clip. Merchants often rode far greater distances: Ser Lapo Mazzei, Datini's friend and notary, commented on a merchant who rode abroad on his company's business; he praised the horse which did not tire though carrying its master from Barcelona to Paris, and then all around Flanders.[41]

Datini had a considerable stable. At Prato he always kept several horses, plus two mules for himself and his wife, and the pack animals on which his business depended. Prices varied; one bought in 1401 cost 16 florins, while another in 1402 cost 22 florins. He spent much more for a bay palfrey – 28 gold ducats – but his joy was to own a prized Spanish mule, and for this he paid the high sum of 122 florins and 16 soldi in 1396, but not till after a prolonged search of nearly two years. Some years later a cheaper bay mule cost him 48 florins. It seems that these mules were pampered pets. Datini required them to be as mild as a lamb and without vice, and on more than one occasion he was criticized for overfeeding his mule.[42]

CHAPTER 5
Trades and Crafts

Many trades which needed highly skilled craftsmen were centred around the horse. Some crafts, such as the making of rich, flamboyant tack and apparel, catered to the wealthy; while others provided more utilitarian equipment. The crafts of the saddler, loriner, farrier, and of course veterinary care, which included advice on stable care and training, touched the hose more closely. The role of farrier and veterinary practitioner were often indivisible.

THE *MARESCHAL*, FARRIERS AND SHOEING

At first the farrier was called the *mareschal*, or marshal. (In France he is still called the *marechal-ferrant*.) The first recorded marshal was Leudast in the mid-sixth century. An ex-slave, he was the *mariskalk*, promoted to master of Queen Marcowefa's stables.[1] After Charlemagne's reign, the post of marshal carried military responsibilities. The tenth-century Archbishop Hughes I of Besancon's *mareschal* was responsible for his horses and commanded his men-at-arms.[2] In England the marshal held one of the senior offices in a royal or noble household. In Plantagenet times the department over which he presided was the Marshalsea, which was chiefly responsible for transport and baggage horses.[3]

Between 1257 and 1269 Ellis of Rochester appears as King's Farrier, Sergeant or Keeper of the King's Horses, and finally as Marshal of the King's Horses, a title that eventually became Master of Horse.[4] The seal of Walter Marshall, seventh Earl of Pembroke has a horseshoe with a nail within the shoe branches. The seal of Ralph, *Mareschal* of the Bishopric of Durham, had a six-nail horseshoe, a nail outside each branch and a shoeing hammer within, the whole surrounded by the legend:

'S'RADUL MARESCHAL D L'EVECHIE D D'REME'

In the fifteenth century the title and the occupation diverged, with the former becoming a military title, Earl Marshal, which was, after the king, the highest office in the land.[5]

The marshal appointed to a prestigious household would not necessarily do the shoeing himself. In the returns for Edinburgh garrison on 28 February 1299 (1300), Elias the Marshal *and his shoer* were listed.[6]

The term *mareschal* gave way to *ferrator*, smith or blacksmith. Very much later there was the distinction between farrier and blacksmith. The former could (and can) be both, but the blacksmith was not necessarily a farrier.

SHOEING

It still has not been *conclusively* proven whether horses were shod in the Roman period, hipposandals excepted. The difficulty is the inability to *prove* a shoe comes from a Roman archaeological level because shoes from a later period could have reached a Roman strata. Any horseowner is expensively aware that working a horse in heavy going, or suddenly hitting a boggy patch, especially when travelling at speed, can result in one or more hooves coming clear of the mud minus shoe(s). The *Tactica* of the Byzantine Emperor Leo VI (886–911) instructed cavalrymen to carry iron shoes and nails.[7]

Horseshoes started to make their appearance in Europe around the ninth to tenth centuries. This coincided with the start of selective breeding for a heavier horse.[8] Mounted warfare was the catalyst, for horses bred in wetter than steppe and/or desert conditions develop softer, shallower hooves. With the stresses imposed by the weight of a cavalryman and the pounding impact with the ground hooves needed protection from splitting, cracking, laminae deterioration and sole bruising.

By kind permission of John Cherry of the British Museum, I have examined several horseshoes; two were 'era-tagged', one Roman, one Norman. Both were identical in form (wavy rims, hole punches, sizes, web widths), although the 'Roman' one had a very slightly narrower web, smaller calkins and one fiddle-key headed nail still in a hole. Its rim was little-worn, showing it was thrown prematurely.

Later, John Clark of the Museum of London showed me a wide range of shoes from sites in London. Some were Norman, some Plantagenet and others from post-medieval dates. The so-called 'Roman' shoe is so like a Norman shoe that we suggest all are Norman. I cannot believe that no advances had been made in farriery between the Roman

The Sigurd saga, carved on a rock in Sweden, shows some farriers' tools with a contemporary appearance.

and Norman eras. Thereafter the basic style did not change for around three centuries. Some pre-Conquest shoes were found at Cheddar, London, Portchester, Thetford and York. They are approximately 4 in wide, less than a quarter of an inch thick, slightly wavy edged, with six round nail holes, three per branch. Some have calkins. Norman-era shoes have the marked wavy outline caused by punching holes through soft narrow metal: the web is only half an inch and the depth a quarter of an inch. They average about 4 in wide, taken across the widest part of the shoe, and are very light at *c*.3 oz. They have six, occasionally seven, nail holes and calkins are fitted. From the size of these shoes, and from skeletal remains, it has been estimated that most horses were small, at around 13 hh.[9]

Horses of the same breed, height and weight do not always have the same shoe size. An archaeologist measures a horseshoe across the web, branch to branch. A farrier does it from toe to tip of each branch. The difference is approximately half an inch. Many Norman shoes have the last nail close to the branch end which suggests the horse was shod very slightly short. The narrow metal between the outer web and the nail hole indicates that shoes could have been set slightly under. These factors suggest some horses were slightly larger than estimated. Even 2 in is a fair increase in size, as bulk would also increase markedly. Shoeing short has adverse veterinary implications, as does the reverse. With the shoe nailed to the very back of the hoof, constrictive pressure would have affected blood supply to the hoof. Eventually, this would have resulted in contracted heels and a boxy shaped hoof, again erroneously indicating a smaller horse.

In the thirteenth century the wavy rim became less prominent, disappearing by the fourteenth century. Web width increased and shoes grew heavier, weighing from 4 oz to 7 oz, and the number of holes, now square and fixed with square-headed nails, increased to seven, then eight. During the late fourteenth and early fifteenth centuries shoes again increased in weight and web-width, with six to eight nail holes, fixed with T-shaped nails. Calkins were not always present.[10]

Not all horses needed shoeing, but the gradual size and weight increase indicates horse-size progression and greater carrying capacity in those shod: the long-haul hackney hireling, sumpters, draughthorses, palfreys, coursers and destriers. Indicative to a certain degree of this size/date progression are measurements taken of two sets of my own horses' shoes compared against shoes from the Museum of London. My 15.1 hh, 950 lb Arab mare's shoes were almost identical with a set of Norman shoes. Hot-blood horses tend to have smaller, tougher hooves than warm-blood horses. The other set belonged to my 16.1 hh, 1,200 lb horse Granicus, an Arab/Standardbred. His shoes were a close match for a set of late medieval shoes. Both sets from the Museum of London are the largest from their respective eras.

VETERINARY CARE AND ADVICE ON HORSE MANAGEMENT

The combination of the farrier's and veterinarian's crafts continued beyond the eighteenth century. The creation of veterinary schools in France in 1762 and 1766, and in England in 1792, marked the start of specialization.[11] Many veterinary treatises were written during the Greek and Roman eras, the most notable those of Chiron, Apsyrtus, Pelagonius and Publius Vegetius Renatus. They were devoted mostly to equine medicine. Practice and medicaments now seem a very strange mix, derived from observations and treatments that worked, plus a huge range of other medicaments, some of which were efficacious, some definitely harmful, others merely traditional and while doing no harm did little good.

Herbal remedies, caustic ingredients and metallic substances were commonly used; there was a residue of ancient Assyrian dung pharmacopoeia. The active ingredients, some of which are still used, can be extrapolated from the remedies. Where medicine failed, sympathetic magic was used, although the Greek *Hippiatrik* Chiron called a practitioner using it, 'minus intelligentes . . . idotae et minus scientes'.[12]

During the early medieval period veterinary advances in the occident were halted for several centuries. The old treatises continued as the 'authorities' together with peasant magic practices.[13] The Byzantine Emperor Constantine Porphyrogenitus (905–59) had a compilation of Greek and Roman works produced under the title *Hippiatrika*. Until the high medieval period no further works were published in the west. In the orient greater advances were made in human and veterinary medicine. These influenced the resumption of veterinary care on a more scientific basis, although some 'charms' were present in Arabic works. One of the most comprehensive Arabic works was compiled by Abou Bekr ibn Bedr, stud manager and veterinarian to El Nacer (see p. 21). Another was that of Aly ben Abderrahman ben Hodeil el Andalusy, written by order of Sultan Mohammed VI (1392–1408) of Granada.[14] Both drew on earlier Arabic works.

Sicily, southern Italy and Spain had long had an Islamic equestrian and military presence which influenced equine veterinary practice in the west. The catalyst was the Hohenstauffen Emperor Frederick II (1215–50). In 1198 he inherited Naples and Sicily through his Norman mother and spent much of his life in Sicily. He wrote a book on the art of falconry, and directed his Catalan knight-farrier Jordanus Rufus to translate Arabic veterinary treatises.[15] Shortly after Frederick's death Jordanus produced the first 'modern' book of European equine veterinary care, and although he wrote largely from his own observations it was clear oriental science influenced medieval European work. Later European writings drew on that of Jordanus. Vegetius also continued to influence the equine practitioner.[16] His work was copied for rich patrons during the medieval period, and one copy came up for auction at Sotheby's in 1994; the *Independent* of 15 June described it as, 'a 15th century lavish ms on horse medicine produced for the King of Naples'. Although the text was that of Vegetius, illustrations were from the fifteenth century.

Most veterinary works included advice on choosing a horse, especially a warhorse, and its early training. Although England was slow to get on the 'veterinary book wagon' some works were being produced.

THE BOKE OF MARCHALSI

There are seven extant manuscripts of the fifteenth-century *Boke of Marchalsi* by an unknown author. In Oxford the Bodleian has three and Balliol College one; the British Museum two; and Trinity College, Cambridge, one. The British Museum's Harleian 6398 folios 1a–58a and Trinity College's R.14.51 folios 48a–77b, are almost complete. For the version edited by Bengt Odenstedt of Uppsala's Stockholm University, the British Museum's manuscript was used.[17]

The sections on selection, care and early training are basic and reasonably sound. The veterinary section has many weaknesses. Obvious external ailments such as lameness are reasonably described as being due to poor conformation and/or strain,[18] but some are way off the mark, or very patchy. Sometimes good advice is given but partially for the wrong reason; for example, 'because the flesh of the horse is cold and to prevent disease he should not be allowed to get too fat.' Many diseases common to the medieval era are absent such as anthrax, pneumonia, tuberculosis and stomach ruptures. The reasons given for certain conditions are ludicrous: 'cataract is caused by excess of blood and heat arising when the horse chews hard food, such as beans, barley or chaff'.[19] As these were staple foods one wonders about medieval horses' vision!

Commenting on the sources the editor concludes there were French and native English elements, probably from a work written in England during the Norman era.[20]

The text is in a question and answer form of student to master (the author). An impressive passage, much of it sound, advises:

a horse of good conformation shall have a little head, great round eyes, short ears, large front (forehead), large nostrils and large jowls, and narrow space between the jowls, long neck and well rising, a little arched, even back, large chest with muscles ?loose, great muscles beneath the shoulders without (outside of), large sides, broad legs and large, and great sinews (tendons), short pastern and large, ever the larger the better it is, easied (?) coronet, large croup, large wither, the sheath of the penis well protruding, the testicles well ?loose, the smaller they be, the better it is, the hips compactly framed, with large muscles, short hair and not rough, the shorter that it is, the better it is . . .

The editor used the word 'loose' with a query for *hangende* (chest muscles) and *wel-hangende* (for the testicles). A horseman's terminology would be *prominent* chest muscles and *well-descended* testicles.

Warhorses of the above conformation from 'the Mount of Olives, Venice, Nubia, or the Damascus mountains, or Aleppo were all good'. Warhorses of Hungary and Lombardy were 'not so good'. Also recommended were chargers of the Tarsus mountains, even though they were small, and Rabites (Arabians) of Alexandria and Carthage. Mountain breeds were the best, and horses foaled in high, stony land were esteemed because they were certain to be surefooted, have good wind, agility and excellent loins, shoulders and better sight. They were stronger, lighter and better than horses foaled in low marshy ground which had broad, thin feet, a big belly, rough (coarse) hair, and 'they shall have heavy breath' (i.e., thick-winded); when they worked in hard, stony country they tired easily and bruised (i.e., hoof soles were stone-bruised, rendering them lame). The low-country horse, 'warhorse is he not'.

Later the author says there are good horses in Hungary, and good warhorses in Calabria and Aragon and good mules in Lombardy. From the Low Countries, Frisia and Germany came good rouncies for pack work (to *bere*). However, all had bad feet and eyes due to being foaled in low marshy land, and once out of their homeland they did not acclimatize well but needed constant veterinary care. England, Ireland and Scotland produced good horses for saddle and harness (draught and/or pack) but were not suitable for war as they 'be fat and that is their downfall'. When the student asked, 'Why be these Lombardies little to prize?', the author answered that they were too soft, large and heavy, and on that account were weak and could not flourish in a 'hard country', but Spanish horses were the best because foaled in a 'high and hard country'.[21]

These passages are notable on several counts. Some were controversial in contemporary terms and the references to the Levant, Egypt and North Africa were most unusual in a European, let alone an English work. Warhorses from the Low Countries, Germany, Frisia, Hungary and Lombardy were highly rated. Oriental breeds were barely known in Europe. Where did the author get his information? Had a now lost Anglo-Norman treatise written around the Crusading era recommended horses based on information supplied by a returning Crusader who had learned to appreciate their qualities, perhaps when his own Low Country, heavy fleshed, splay-hooved European destrier was lost and he had used an eastern breed? Had our author travelled to the Levant? Read Arabic treatises? and/or gained wide experience of the types of horses raised there? This section alone makes the *Boke* very unusual and the observations very sound, unlike much of the veterinary section. Apart from Raymond of Aguiliers, a cleric on Crusade who esteemed the Arabian, this is probably the first documented European reference to the Arabian, although it is possible that the horses from Carthage were Berbers.[22]

The spare-framed, hard-footed oriental horse generally has better wind and endurance capabilities and is sounder in hooves and legs in tough hard going than European cold- and warm-blood horses; in spite of a relatively smaller size it is up to considerable weight. Marsh-bred horses and heavy breeds often have 'dinner-plate' hooves with softer horn and low soles prone to stone bruising. They are often gross with water-laden tissues that make them sweat more in adverse conditions, and such characteristics can lead to all manner of ailments: founder (laminitis), dehydration and azoturia, which although he may not have correctly assessed them, the author meant they needed frequent veterinary care.

Much advice on caring for a young warhorse is designed to prevent disorders, some real and other imaginary, that come from bad horsemastership. Because of youth and delicacy foals were to be stabled in cold weather. Food was to be fed off the floor on the assumption that because a foal has to spread its legs to reach it its chest muscles would be strengthened. Strong foals were to be kept apart from mares and feeble foals who were to receive supplementary oats, dampened to prevent 'the veins of the head from getting too large and thus causing eye disease'! Damping feed lays dust and causes mould spores to swell, preventing their passage past the alveoli in the nasal tract, thus inhibiting broken wind. Keeping a floor and/or bedding dry was necessary for wet feet 'grow broad and long and curved'. Fouled, wet bedding softens hoof horn and induces thrush, a cankerlike, foul-smelling substance in the frog of the hoof.

At two-and-a-half years old, colts were tied up (a little late to teach them this restraint); confusingly, later, when haltered, they were not to be tied but allowed to drag the halter rope so that when stepped on the colt(s) would jerk to a halt and therefore be easier to tie up. When sent to pasture colts were to be strongly tied to prevent halter breakage; should they do so it both frightened them and taught bad manners – timely advice. Such horses are a nuisance, now as then. This suggests that horses were tethered at grass.

Blanketing and girthing came next. A warhorse had to cope with cloth housings and body armour, so needed a gradual introduction to anything that flapped or clanked. A first girthing sometimes produces a volatile eruption – disastrous if a young warhorse scattered armour in all directions. Tapping their hooves with a hammer was advised to ready the warhorses for their first shoeing. On early bridling: 'Do him to have a bridle with huge iron and that it be loose and easy for always he should fear a hard bridle when it is necessary. For often he grows bad mannered with faulty keeping.' This can only be a snaffle bridle, which was the most common 'easy' bit; the 'hard bridle' meant a curb bit which can be made more severe by tightening the curb chain. The last comment could apply to faulty keeping in general, and/or that overbitting caused undesirable traits. When an overbitted horse reacts adversely, a bad horseman resorts to increased severity and risks turning the horse into a rogue. At three-and-a-half years old the colt was backed, and ridden slowly 'and soft. But not run for his joints be tender and soft'. No horse was to be ridden (hard) till it was full-mouthed at four-years-and-a-quarter, or at the latest by five, 'for the tenderness of his joints and of his marrow. And on that account many horses is maimed, and one knows not how but for default of good keeping'. Regular exercise taught the horse its paces and kept it gentle and well mannered. It should become accustomed to spurs being used each time it changed gait. If a warhorse, it was to be ridden at a trot, then sprinted for two or three furlongs, and got used to all manner of things so it was unafraid of anything. It should be taught to stand still when dismounted from in the field and then mounted again – important for a warhorse so its unhorsed rider could remount (it is a fallacy that weight of armour prevented this; a winded/injured man could not remount, but a thrown rider could). Final advice, particularly for a warhorse, is that after the age of five it should never be allowed to stand up in the stable for more than three or four days, and it should never be allowed to get fat. The groom was to be a good rider and was not to change his bit as it would make the horse 'lose his paces and grow bad mannered'.[23]

There is much reiteration in the pages on many aspects of care and training. The sensible parts are still relevant, but the veterinary reasons are strange in some cases, while in others they are partly correct, partly muddled. Many conditions are not described, presumably on the assumption that the marshal knew what they were; the author thought it sufficient to detail treatment, and occasionally reasons for horses suffering from them. Where descriptions do occur it is sometimes impossible to recognize the disease. For the most common external disorders the descriptions are fairly accurate.

WORMS: 'The worm' was considered the cause of many disorders. Our author names three conditions he considered directly caused by it (not to be confused with the parasitic worms we regularly dose horses for today). These were Farcy, the Trenchelouns (colic) and the Lowe (warbles). Farcy, or glanders, is not caused by worms but is a highly contagious condition caused by the *Pfeifferella mallei*. Rare now, in past times it often flared in wartime when horses were both debilitated and held close together. It manifested itself in ulcerative conditions via the lymphatic systems, accompanied by other symptoms. Veterinarians advised that affected animals be destroyed.

Our medieval vet notes four types of farcy and described one called 'tourte' that 'gaderynge withinne þe skyn in þe manere of a cake . . . of humours þat be bitwext þe hyde and þe holde', (an abscess forming under the skin). In a rare case of recognizing infection he states it could be caught by smelling where an infected horse had been, or from such a horse's breath when it was stabled alongside. He then ruins this by saying that the smelling of a sow in heat, or a boar, also passed the malady.

Among cures was a lengthy charm or prayer to Jesus Christ to be said while holding a layered cross of dock root, red dead nettle, lead and leather; the skin was then to be slit, the cross inserted and the wound stitched. As true farcy needs stringent disinfection of all objects in contact with an infected horse, outbreaks in medieval stables were likely to have been frequent and losses high, even though most horses have a degree of immunity to the disease.[24]

Our author states that domesticated horses suffered from disorders more frequently than wild horses because of the worms caused by eating 'unkende metis' (strange food), such as bread, bran and oats. When a wild horse felt worms growing in its body it knew how to 'kell' them with 'vertus of herbis þat grown in wildernes'. A wild horse kept itself in 'good poynte' (condition), travelled every day and for that reason would never be fat and stayed fit so as to be able to withstand being preyed upon by wild beasts.[25] He was wrong about 'unkende metis' causing worms, but right to recognize that wild horses, moving to fresh pasture, were less burdened with parasites than their stabled kin who, when tethered at grass, could not avoid fouling the land with parasite-laden faeces, and then ingesting the same grass. Wild horses do know which herbs to eat to worm themselves.

COLIC: This was said to be caused by worms, and in a young horse especially it was caused by feeding 'bred . . . and also bren and otys'[26] – horse bread, a mix of grains and pulses, and bran and oats. Colic can be caused by a heavy worm infestation, and young horses are more affected if not regularly wormed, but unless fed on fouled ground the feed would not carry a parasite burden. Colic remedies were strange: hen's dung and well water, presumably given as a drench; or, more likely to harm than cure, herbs – sage, broom or savin – mixed with vinegar and *vitriol*, given in strong doses of 'platefuls'.[27] The dung of various animals was used as plasters, or to plug wounds. My late neighbour, who called himself 'a heavy hossman', said that rather than call the vet out to his workhorses he would smear a wound with cow dung, with no ill effects. Recently, the veterinary advisor to the Endurance Horse and Pony Society of GB, Jim Kerr, MRCVS, recommended the addition of dried droppings from a healthy donor horse to the feed of a yearling who had a bacterial imbalance of the gut. Also recommended to correct the same problem was the administration of fresh droppings from a donor horse via the rectum or a naso-gastric avenue.

THE LOWE: Warble is not a worm but could be mistaken for one. It is the larvae of the warble fly that burrows under the skin, usually of the back, and when mature it erupts through the skin.

BROKEN WIND:[28]   The core of the author's reasoning on broken wind is good, but not wholly accurate. Nevertheless he was aware that an overweight horse worked excessively hard after overeating would suffer broken wind, but not for the reason given 'that the overloaded midriff destroys the lungs'. He says a broken-winded horse can be cured by reducing his bulk, feeding all hay and oats dampened, and by regular exercise. He warns not 'to take in hand' a horse whose respiration is 'as though it were small bellows for he may not be helped with no medicine'. Also recommended were two eggs seethed in vinegar and half a gallon of cow's milk on ten successive days. This was a nutritious dietary supplement but not medicinal. Our vet calls the thick-winded, overexerted horse 'broken winded' when he was only overstrained. But he recognized the true broken-winded animal with the double-lift as having an irreversible condition; the palliative regimen of dampened feed and grazing is a course still followed today.

CANKER OF THE TONGUE:[29]   This was attributed to many causes, some were cogently reasoned, while others had superstitious overtones that could have some common-sense explanation. 'It comes sometimes from his own bridle' – so far so good. Many mouth lesions are caused by rough handling, and would have been more severe with some of the harsh medieval bits, but our author reasoned differently, blaming toad dung and/or a spider on the bit. Presumably the first being insanitary could infect an already open sore, and the latter may have been mildly venemous. Although no known venemous spider now resides in England such may not always have been so. Chewing food and letting it fall out, one of his diagnostic signs, suggests buccal pain. Another was the cluster of blisters under the tongue which *may* suggest a form of poisoning. In some parts of the United States hay can become infested with toxic blister beetles that can kill if eaten in sufficient quantity. Our author states: 'in July (medu month) when great plenty of spiders fall among the hay and men go and make it all up together, the horse that eats of it may get canker upon the tongue. And of that malady he may be dead before anyone take any notice, for then he shall refuse his food.' Could this have been a similar case and not wholly superstitious? Unfortunately, treatment was the useless medieval remedy of bleeding, a course resorted to for all manner of ailments not understood.

LEG AILMENTS: The owner was advised to look first for obvious causes in the foot, such as a nail prick in the hoof, embedded thorns, or damage to the bulb of the heel or pastern; 'for he may ben greued on many maners, or with euel steppyng of þe fet, or wyth an nayll in þe midward of þe fot, and berrore do a fferowre to sekyn þe fot . . .' Many horses overreach, cutting a front heel, or even the pastern in high overreach. Such needed the 'Fferowre's' attention. Remedial shoeing can often lessen or prevent occurrences.
    Leg ailments, mostly those induced by being worked hard too young, among which were ringbone, synovial enlargements, spavins curbs, windgalls and splints, were first to be treated with a lotion of vinegar, gall nuts, mullein leaves and vitriol,[31] a crude astringent mix rather like a modern blistering agent that reduces soft swellings; in the case of bony enlargements such as splints it eventually reduces them. Our author is correct in attributing many leg ailments to working an immature animal: if the conditions did not respond to external applications, cauterizing was recommended.[32] Firing and/or pinfiring was in use until relatively recently but, fortunately, it is now obsolete. For a lameness arising from poor conformation the sensible advice was not to take 'a crippled animal in hand for it will never do well'.[33] This advice was attached to many of the hopeless cases.

The Boke of Marchalsi was aimed at the prevention of equine maladies by good stable management and sensible use of the horse. The author comes across as very humane, only resorting to the crude methods after all other remedies had been tried. In the rearing and training departments he was far ahead of his time in his kindly methods with a young horse!

MANUFACTURING SKILLS AND PRODUCTS

The saddle horse's equipment consisted of functional saddle, bridle and saddlecloth; decorative cloth housings and leather embellished with embroidery, silver, gold and gilt, and in the case of a warhorse armour.

SADDLERY: Craftsmen making saddles, bridles, bits and spurs were governed by their respective town guilds, the medieval equivalent of Trade Unions. In 1422, out of 111 guild trades in London eleven were connected with saddlery. Leather was first tanned and curried. England imported so much Córdoban leather, tanned using a Moorish process, that leatherworkers became known as cordwainers whose craft is referred to as early as 1087. The Saddlers' Guild claimed to be London's oldest organized guild. Documents from 1154 and *c.*1164–74 attest to its existence. In 1272 it received its royal charter.[34] The Loriner's Guild did not receive its royal charter until 1711, but a document from 1269 shows that London's mayor and barons had approved their ordinances.[35] Loriners also made stirrups and metal saddle fittings.

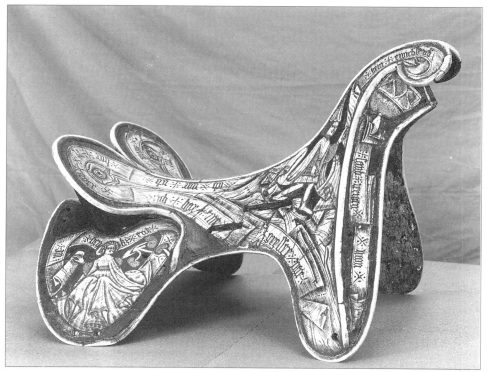

A highly ornamental riding saddle, definitely for the wealthy.

SPURS: The prick spur dates from ancient days. Today, the business end is blunted; in medieval times its form varied – as a single goad, sometimes lozenge-shaped, or with multiple prickers similar to a fork. The neck was usually short. The rowel spur did not appear until the thirteenth century,[36] and came with moderate and very long necks; the rotating rowel could be a simple six-point type or have multiple and finer points. One type was slightly offset to enable a rider to spur a horse without altering the angle of the foot in the stirrup. I consider the very long shanked spur was designed to allow contact with the horse's sides by reaching underneath trappers or armour. It enabled the knight who rode extremely long to engage the business end with minimal leg movement, and to reach further back. *The Articles of the Spurriers* of 1345 required London spurriers to keep to a strict code of work, maintain quality of raw materials, implement safety precautions with their forges and exhibit seemly conduct.[37]

Allied crafts were also bound by quality control in England and Europe. Although just outside the medieval period, a sixteenth-century Assize of Tanners stated that anyone breaking the guild's rules and offering inadequately tanned leather was to be fined 6*s* 8*d* at the first two offences and forfeit 'all that is forfeitable . . . the third time to be judged according unto the statute'. The first leatherworkers' guild in France was established in 1397. Prospective members purchased the right of entry from the king, and took an oath to observe the customs and moral precepts of the trade. An English law of 1283 decreed that for saddle decoration only 'good colours tempered with oil' were to be used on gold or silver and 'no silver rough or partly old on saddles. No one shall use tinfoil or plaster on saddle bows nor any other thing except to be applied with a brush . . . any false work is to be burnt, and he who made it shall suffer the penalty of the court'.[38]

The 1403 statutes of the Saddlers' Company of Limoges stipulated that the tree's joints were to be well glued and reinforced by rivets, that it be 'well sinewed above and below and that the underneath should be well covered so that the horse's sweat shall not damage the sinews'.[39]

The Wallace Collection in London has several medieval saddles ranging from beautifully carved state saddles, weighing only 7 lb, to tournament and war saddles weighing 21–33 lb. With contoured trees and sufficient under-tree padding they would sit comfortably on a horse's back, the load evenly distributed.

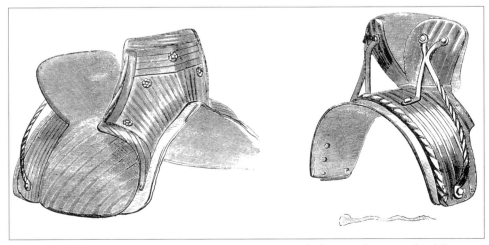

A war saddle with cantle bracers that absorbed the impact of a lance and prevented saddle breakage.

Not all medieval saddles protected the horse's back from pressure galls; Henry V's war saddle is an example. Although the tree is somewhat shaped to the horse's back, the seat has the load-bearing sectors at four points; the two in the shoulder region could hamper action, and cause pressure areas which could have become hard and painful, the skin thickening and sloughing with new hair coming in white from damaged follicles.

Although a warhorse was ridden only in, not to, battle, the immense activity of a weapon-wielding rider imposed heavy strains on a horse's back and saddle. The Breton knight de Tournemine knew this; he instructed his saddler:

> first shall my said horse . . . be saddled with a saddle whose pommel and cantle are of wood, garnished with bound horn, and garnished in iron and steel, or in one of these two, and ribbed and glued, the pommel and cantle high in front and back and open at the sides as they should be, garnished and covered in leather, linen, or light silk, studded and garnished with iron, steel or other metal, gilt or tinned.[40]

Henry V's saddle has the seat well stuffed with straw – easier on his backside than on his horse's back; we must assume efficient padding went under the saddles or back lesions would have rendered most horses unusable. Various accounts stipulate stuffing, but it is not clear if it was for the rider's or the horse's benefit. A requirement for a Windsor Tournament of 6 Edward I was 'a sadell wele stuffid'.[41] Guided by Henry V's saddle, it was probably for the jouster's benefit.

True saddles, as distinct from pad saddles, trace back to well before the Christian era, as shown by the Pazyryk burial saddles from the last centuries of the first millennium BC. Later, the Romans developed a four-horned rigid treed saddle which was definitely the forerunner of early medieval saddles.[42] These saddles had raised continuous front and rear

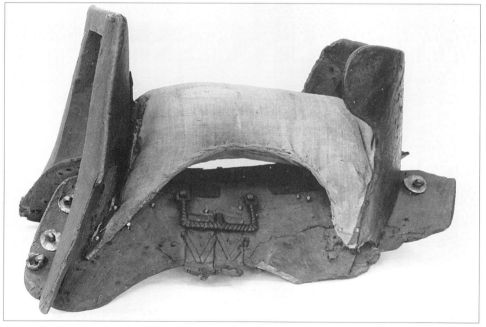

Henry V's war saddle. Note the seat raised off the bars, the retaining cantle, and the protection to the lower abdomen afforded by the high pommel.

bars, as shown on the Bayeux tapestry. In the high medieval era war saddles became more
elaborate with greater integral safety factors. The front arch got much higher and wider,
giving some protection to the rider's midriff and thigh. With the addition of saddle steels
the rider's legs to the knees were protected, enabling him to dispense with plate armour in
that region. The cantle became higher and wider, the lateral sectors curving around the
rider's hips. Being butted out of the saddle was now only possible if one's opponent was
immensely strong and able to hoist the knight upwards on his lance. The great
disadvantage was that if the horse fell the trapped rider could be crushed.

Ordinary riding and ceremonial saddles were far simpler and lighter in construction,
from the simple cheap saddle for everyman and his wife to the elaborate carved and/or
tooled and gilded saddles of the wealthy. These still retained some integral safety factors,
with a high but not overly wide pommel and a moderately high but non-encasing cantle.
Ann of Bohemia, Richard II's queen, popularized sidesaddles in England. In place of the
modern double-horn a footrest was all that kept the very insecure rider from hitting the
deck. For other than slow paced ceremonial parades medieval women sensibly rode astride.

STIRRUPS: The shape of some medieval stirrups is preserved in those used on western
saddles, which also retain a semblance of a war saddle with a raised front arch and a higher
cantle. The rounded stirrup, with a wide flat tread attributed to Avar design, gave way in

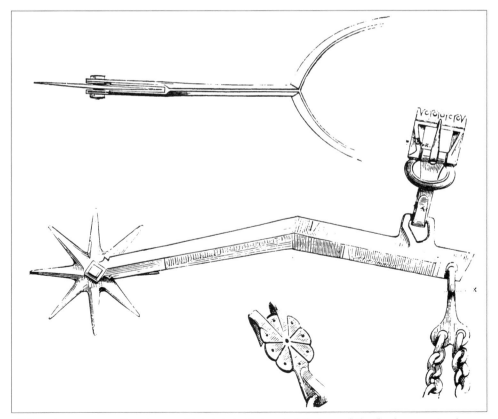

*Fifteenth-century medieval spur with points inclining slightly toward the flanks, meaning less
leg movement was needed to apply the spur.*

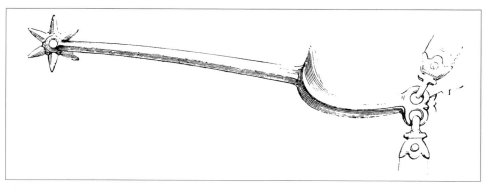

An example of winklepicker sabaton and shaped footplate.

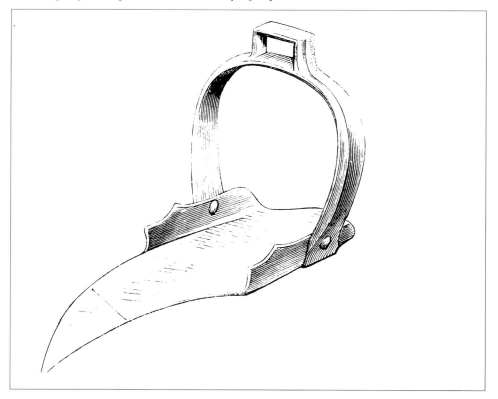

Saxon times to what is termed the Viking-style stirrup, which was triangular and much larger. Later medieval stirrups included a daintier, triangular shape; others had the modern outline, and another a heavy, box-like shape with metal sides and wide treads which were sometimes constructed of several bars of twisted metal. The wide sides protected the foot, the twisted treads gave stability and stopped the foot slipping out of the stirrup. When sabatons developed into the metal equivalent of 'winkle pickers', far longer than any foot, some stirrups enabled the whole foot with 'toe extensions' to rest on a similar shaped footplate.

ORIENTAL TACK: Saddles used by steppe peoples from the Middle East, in Persia and India, were never as exaggerated in style as those in Europe. Modern steppe peoples now use tack little changed over the centuries and with no 'safety' features. Mamlūk, Arab, Levantine, Turkish and Persian equipment utilized a moderately raised front and rear. Indian saddles, as shown by an ordinary trooper's outfit from Akbar's era (1556–1605) and exhibited in the Jaipur Armoury, had scarcely any retaining feature, being basically of felt construction. The equipment for India's wealthy followed the Persian style, with many Persian artisans working in India. Oriental horsemen had two tremendous advantages, however, over their occidental contemporaries – they usually rode superior horses and were themselves natural and excellent horsemen.

BITTING: Of two bit categories – snaffle and curb – snaffles are generally milder, but can injure a horse's mouth if used harshly. Basic varieties are two- or three-jointed, or single-bar mouthpiece. Less common are twisted snaffles, in which the mouthpiece resembles twisted rope; they are severe, with multiple edges, and would have been used on a hard-mouthed, overkeen horse. Snaffles act by a direct pull on the external bit ring. Pressures are applied to the lips, bars of the mouth and tongue. They have the undesirable effect of deadening a horse's mouth from the constant pressure normally applied. Medieval folk used the horse to ride on and as pack and draught animals; getting from A to B, not the niceties of horsemanship, was their prime consideration. The snaffle was easy and cheap to make.

Curbs, especially the more severe types, were likely to be used on horses ridden by the military, where immediate responses were vital for safety in battle and tournament. The

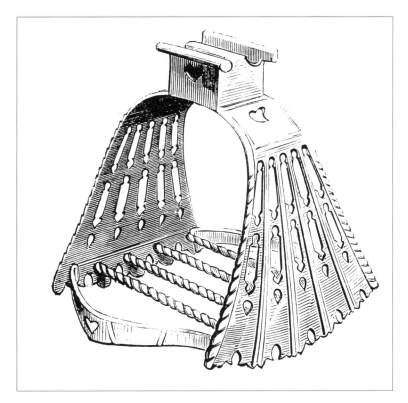

Stirrup with anti-slip treads. The wide sides protected the foot and the twisted treads prevented the foot slipping out of the stirrup.

medieval curb usually had single-rein control, even if two reins were buckled to the lower shank, the horse being turned by indirect, or neck, reining. Curbs exerted several points of pressure: to the chin groove via the curb strap or chain; from the port, often of extreme height, against the roof of the palate; to the poll, to the lips. The severity of these depended on the length of the lower shank, how tightly the curb chain was fixed, and the height of the cheek piece above the bit. An additional pressure point in some bits was the metal noseband attached, not to the headstall, but as an integral part of the mouthpiece so that pressure was exerted on the nose, as in a hackamore. Some medieval curb straps were of metal affixed to the mouthpiece so the jaw was in a vice and the mouth area greatly compressed. Such bits would stop the medieval tank of lumbering destrier working off his forehand. They were probably the last line of defence/control as the animal's mouth lost its sensitivity with repeated maulings. With excessively harsh bitting a horse sometimes reacts violently to the pain and becomes uncontrollable. From the inhumane varieties extant, clearly many medieval riders opted for increasing severity as their mounts got progressively more unruly – I have seen this with some modern riders; I will not call them horsemen. Not all medieval curbs were harsh. One from the ruins of Tannenberg Castle is very mild and exactly like a broken pelham used with four reins. It has short lower shanks and virtually no height above the bit, so poll pressure was minimal. Albrecht Dürer's *Knight, Death and the Devil* shows this type in use.

Some bits had rein chains, or metal covering the leather to avoid reins being slashed in combat. In 1285 when the king of Aragon fought the French, the king's reins were severed and his horse barged about uncontrollably until seized by four of his *almugavars* who tied

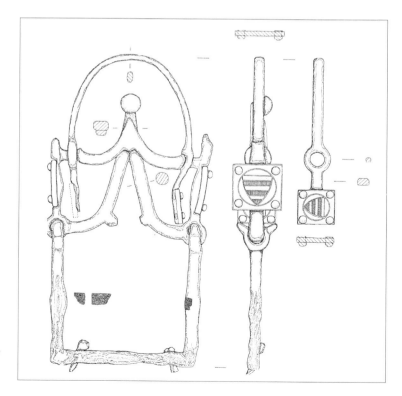

The bit found in Pergamon, dating between late 13th and early 14th century.

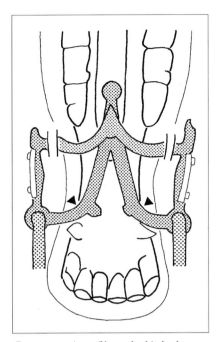

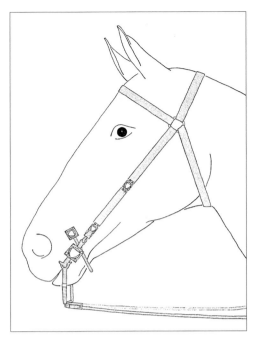

Reconstruction of how the bit looks inside a horse's mouth.

Reconstruction of the exterior appearance of the bit.

its reins together. Recommended too late were double-reins, with one of chain and the other of leather.[43] Another type of bit used in battle was a fifteenth-century example which had its lower shanks fenced with very long sharp spikes to prevent infantry grabbing the horse.

EMBELLISHMENTS: Medieval saddle and sumpter horses were often covered with a cloth trapper. For ceremonial and tournament purposes these were impressive, bearing the rider's armorial quarterings, and/or were expensively embroidered, and also embellished, with precious metals. Bridles, breastcollars and cruppers often had little bells or metal rosettes attached. A horse ostentatiously equipped advertised his rider's wealth and status.

Edward IV's funeral chariot horses were trapped in black. The late king's horse, covered in housings bearing the royal arms, was ridden by Sir William Parr accoutred in the king's armour. At the Quire door the customary offering of charger and equipment was made and accepted by the deacon. The late king's banner, Lord Howard, also rode a black trapped courser.[44]

In contrast to the sombreness of Edward's funeral, and following just three months later on 6 July 1483, the coronation of Richard III was a dazzling affair. The royal retinue was resplendent, as were the horses – coursers, palfreys, hackneys and chariot horses – all flamboyantly bedecked. The equestrian turnout was masterminded by Sir Thomas Tyrell, the new Master of the Horse. Prior to the coronation ceremony the king took possession of his court at Westminster. The three saddles and accompanying harness used by the king, his sword-bearer and attendant were to be covered with crimson cloth-of-gold wrought with nets of roses (the Yorkist emblem) using 13 yds of material – sufficient to make three elegant trappers. For the coronation the king's saddle of state and his horse were covered with nearly 4 yds of red cloth-of-gold, also covered with nets of roses. Crimson velvet covered the saddles of the seven coursers of the attendant *henxemen* who were attired in crimson satin and white cloth-of-gold. The king rode to his hallowing in a blue cloth-of-gold doublet covered with 'netts' and pineapples, his purple velvet riding gown trimmed with bogy shanks (budge; lambswool fur from the animals legs) and ermine, the whole powdered, or scattered, with spots, presumably following the golden theme, or maybe more ermine, as shown in some medieval illustrations.

The queen rode to Westminster in a two-horse litter, the horses were elegant coursers. Her seven ladies and five *henxemen* rode in saddles covered in crimson cloth-of-gold, while the male attendants were attired in crimson satin and blue velvet gowns. On coronation day the *henxemen* were in livery of green satin doublets and sarsenet-lined gowns of crimson velvet.

The unfortunately short-reigned Edward V attended with a small retinue, his horses' harness and saddles bedecked with blue velvet.[45]

The equestrian display continued as the Duke of Norfolk rode into Westminster Hall astride a charger trapped to the ground in cloth-of-gold. Once halted, he cleared the crowd so the banquet could begin. Later Sir Robert Dymmock, the king's champion, rode into the hall to deliver the customary challenge to anyone foolish enough to argue the king's right to the crown. Sir Robert wore pure white armour, his charger trappers of red and white silk.[46]

ARMOUR: Horses in the orient benefitted from fully protective head, neck and body armour centuries before their European cousins. Persian horses, for example, were fully armoured well before the medieval period. Their armour was varied and used in many combinations – layered fabric, felt, leather, mail, lamellar and scale.[47] The Arabs used Persian-style felt horse armours as early as Mohammed's times (seventh century). The

Early mêlée before horses were armoured and before the use of plate armour.

Khorassani's were armouring their horses in the eighth century. Khorassan and Ispahan were the main centres for armour manufacture in Persia, and Persian armourers found ready employment wherever they could be lured.[48] Many Indian armours are of Persian manufacture.[49] Timur is reputed to have transported Damascene armourers to Khorassan in 1401,[50] after his sack of Damascus, Aleppo and other Syrian cities. John of Plano Carpini described the Persian armour made for Mongol heavy cavalrymen:

> Whereas the majority wear leather armour, some have their harness completely wrought from iron which is made in the following manner. They beat out in large numbers thin iron plates, a finger broad and a full hand long. In each they bore eight small holes, through which they pull three straight leather thongs. Thereupon they arrange these plates one above the other, as it were, ascending by degrees, and tie the plates to the thongs as mentioned by means of other small and tender thongs drawn through the holes. And in the upper part they fasten a single, small thong, doubled on each side and sewn on to another, that the plates may be well and tightly knit together. . . . Suchlike armour is for their horses as well as for their men . . .[51]

How rare European use of horse armour was is shown by the surprised comment of Beha-ed-din Saladin's *qadi* (military judge) and biographer who described 'a man of high rank among the Franks who rode a great charger covered with a hammer cloth of chain

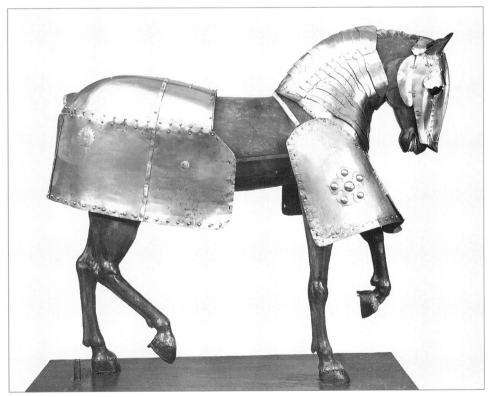

Horse almost fully protected, even to the sensitive poll area.

mail that reached down to its hoofs and he was apparelled in a *most extraordinary fashion*[52] [author's emphasis].

In the *Rule of the Templars* only one specific reference to barding occurs, so we are left wondering what the barding was: mail, fabric, leather? Only the very wealthy in Europe could afford such horse protection and art of the period only rarely shows full mail coverage. Occasionally a hint of mail shows beneath cloth trappers.[53]

By Edward I's time a covered horse was mandatory for the trooper drawing a shilling a day, but the armour was not necessarily total cover. By Edward III's day this was changing rapidly, again only for the wealthy as more and more plate armours came into existence.[54] As the weight of gear escalated, and the horse to carry it became bulkier, so the armourer's trade reached its apogee just before the use of full armour became more of an encumbrance to horse and bank account, and, with the coming of firearms and artillery, obsolete.

The main European centre for superior armours was Milan, but in the fifteenth and sixteenth centuries the output of armourers in Nuremberg, Augsburg and Innsbruck rivalled that of Milan.

Elaborate, although not very protective, armour.

From documents preserved in the Archivio Civico, Archivio Notarile and Archivio de Stato of Milan a list of armourers working between 1371 and 1565 shows a total of 241 names. Some workshops were those of single armourers, others family concerns with a long history of manufacture. In the latter half of the fifteenth century the house of Missaglia, with seventeen members noted between 1429 and 1507, had the highest profile; Antonio Missaglia, working from 1441 to 1488 had a tremendous international reputation. The house of Negroli is listed as having eighteen members working between 1492 and 1565. Some Milanese armourers manufactured weapons, bits and spurs. The aftermath of the Battle of Maclodio in 1427 shows Milan's output: when the Venetian general Carmagnola sent Milanese prisoners home stripped of their arms and armour, Duke Filippo Maria (Sforza) was able to outfit them in a few days; two Milanese armourers alone were able to supply the duke with armour for 4,000 cavalry and 2,000 infantry.[55]

CHAPTER 6

The Black Prince's *Register*

Edward, the Black Prince, was best known for his military exploits. He first saw action aged sixteen at Crécy in 1346, fighting in the thick of the battle. In 1355 he led a brilliant campaign prior to his victory at Poitiers in 1356, followed by his 1357 triumph at Najera. Less well known is *The Register of the Black Prince* covering his estate management throughout England and Wales from 1346 to 1365. Entries include the simplest, such as felling and sale of trees; the attachment of equine heriots; 'weifs and strays'; guarding royal privileges in hunting domains; the feverish activity prior to a military campaign, especially that of 1355; and landgrants, gifts, purchases, etc. Hundreds of entries, directly and indirectly, concern cart-, saddle-, pack- and warhorses. The *Register* affords a rounded picture of the horse in medieval England, its use, breeding, movements, and its economic and prestige value. Aspects of the Black Prince's character emerge, some of which contradict historians who highlight the negative elements, such as his ferocious sacking of Limoges in 1370[1]; his harshness to tenants in Cheshire; and the exploitation of miners in his Cornish stannaries.[2] The *Register* shows him as innovative, businesslike, tough in demanding good service, but fair and a good boss. Certain names stand out for seniority, tenure of office, periodic advancement, or family involvement. Many come from his equestrian establishment, others from his military and household retinue. He was generous to his household, from kitchen staff to the most senior knights, especially John Chaundos. Although served by an army of officials it is clear he regularly consulted his 'despatch box'.

Forty-four of the Black Prince's knights bachelor are named in the volume concerning English estates.[3] Others appear in volumes covering Cornwall and Cheshire. Notable are John Chaundos, the prince's biographer who was a steadying influence at critical times and fought alongside him at Crécy and Poitiers; Sir Bartholomew de Burghersh, Senior, his 'dear Master' who also fought at Crécy (his son was castellan of the Wallingford estate); and Sir Baldwin de Botetourt, Surveyor and Master of the Prince's Great Horses.

THE STUDS, STABLES AND ACQUISITIONS

The many establishments associated with the Black Prince illustrate his keen interest in equine matters and how vital horses were to the efficient running of his household and estates in peace and war. There were at least nine studs. Some venues were used for lodgement, but were not specifically named as studs. When the Black Prince was in residence at any park, chase, forest or moor, his personal horses would also have been lodged, in addition to the permanent nucleus of horses for parkers, huntsmen and some foresters classed as 'riding foresters'.[4]

The Black Prince acquired horses from many sources. At least three big horse markets are named: Smithfield in London, Stamford in Lincolnshire and Chester in Cheshire.[5] He purchased from his knights and his stable staff. Palfreyman Rocelyn (also called Rothelyn, Rottelin) sold him two horses for £9 6s 8d at the Battle of Poitiers,[6] not being paid until two years later in 1358. Palfreyman Roger Ragaz also traded with him, selling him two falcons for £19 8s 8d in 1353 and one for £3 6s 8d in 1355.[7] By 1361 Ragaz had been promoted to lieutenant under the new Surveyor and Master of the Prince's Great Horses, Sir Robert Nevyll who succeeded de Botetourt.[8] In many cases sellers' names were not recorded.

Only two entries note specific imports, both from Germany. In 1358 the prince gave Sir Tuderik van Dale, one of his indentured foreign knights, £39 4s to cover 'his costs in going to Almain to buy horses'. Such a large sum was surely because Sir Tuderik was the prince's agent.[9] Many of the prince's gifts were actually payments, e.g. for expenses incurred on his business, or for horses spoilt in his service; but some of course, were real gifts. In 1359 the Lord of Brunegg was paid £129 9s for eight coursers and trotting horses bought by him for the prince in 'parts of Alemaigne'.[10] Other imports can be deduced from the unimaginative names of horses, being noted by type, colour, seller/donor's name or place of origin: for example, 'Bayard de Brucell', given to Sir Thomas de Ferrariis; and courser 'morel de Cippenham' (a stud location) to Roland Daneys in Normandy; destrier 'Morel Burghersh' to a minstrel at a tournament – a very expensive gift; and 'Liard Scarre' for a blemished silvergrey. An exception, which suggests a plump little horse, was the small hackney called Welyfed given to Richard de Bekensfeld the elder, keeper of the prince's stud at 'Risbergh' (Prince's Risborough).[11] This naming system indicates the prince had horses, mostly destriers and coursers, from France, Cologne, Brussels, and either Lombardy or from a Lombard horsedealer. Others had foreign origins, being bred from animals imported from Spain, France, Lombardy, Sicily, Germany, etc. (see ch.2 on Royal Studs).

The studs noted in the *Register* were: Princes Risborough, his principal stud; Woking, Byfleet and Wisshele (Wisley) in Surrey; Cippenham in Buckinghamshire; Somersham in either Cambridgeshire or Suffolk; Cotyngham (Cottingham) in Yorkshire; Macclesfield in Cheshire; and Denbigh in Wales,[12] plus another not noted in the *Register* at Beckley in Oxfordshire.[13] Other major holding venues were the manors of Donington, Leicestershire; Kennington, Surrey; and Berkhamstead, Buckinghamshire. Possibly destriers were also held at Huntingdon, as there is an intriguing 1347 entry of an order to Oliver Danys, the prince's yeoman and Keeper of his Great Horses, to look into the complaint by the Bishop of Ely whose carters were beaten and his poulterer robbed of 500 eggs in the town of Huntingdon by royal grooms, who were to be sacked if guilty.[14]

STAFFING

An army of staff serviced the equestrian establishments. Senior posts were by royal appointment. Heading the list was the Surveyor and Master of the Prince's Great Horses, a post sometimes honorary with the actual work delegated to others. Sir Baldwin de Botetourt appears to have held it by royal favour, and because he knew his horses. He was involved in selecting courser and destrier stallions for the covering season,[15] and choosing and purchasing mounts for the Prince – e.g., a sorrel courser for £6 13s 4d.[16] He received coursers and stallions into his care when sent from studs for war or tournament use,[17] together with their tack, which was usually made by the German saddler Lambkyn based in London.[18] Sir Baldwin also sold the prince quality horses and received expensive equine gifts, such as the destrier *Morel de Coloign*. The prince spent heavily, his treasurer William de Northwell noted horses given by the Prince up to '31st January, 23 Edward III':[19]

Destriers	14	Sumpters	9
Coursers	19	Horses	13
Palfreys	26	Trotter	1
Hobbies	2	Carthorses	33
Hackneys	2	TOTAL	119

STUD KEEPERS

Stud keepers were answerable to de Botetourt, and for stud financing to the prince's chief officials such as John de Kendale, Receiver of Issues; John de Dabernoun, Keeper of the Prince's Fees in Cornwall; John de Brunham, Receiver of Dynebegh (Denbigh); and Sir Peter Lacy, a prominent clerk in the London secretariat.

Princes Risborough's keepers between 1347 and 1364 were: (1347) John de Geytford[20]; (1351–58, and maybe longer) Richard de Bekensfeld the elder; (1363) John Bassett, who was joined a few months later by William Spirk. Bassett was soon appointed as keeper of the prince's foals at Woking. Spirk remained keeper at Princes Risborough until at least 1364.[21]

In January 1356 Alexander atte Crosse of Prestwich was keeper and surveyor of all the prince's stock throughout Cheshire, and keeper of the manor and park of Macclesfield. The care of mares and the Macclesfield stud came under his remit. His annual pay was initially 40s and a robe or 13s 4d and the right to keep a mare and two cows in the park. He had to provide food other than pasture. Later, Alexander asked for a rise saying his wage was insufficient. He succeeded, being better off by 16s 8d a year.[22]

Hugh Fairchild ran the Denbigh stud[23] with a host of grooms, each paid a penny a day plus expenses whenever they accompanied horses to the prince's manors, London, or overseas on a military campaign.

BRANDING

This is hinted at by the 1358 order to the Princes Risborough keeper to ensure skins shown to the auditors of de Bekensfeld's stud account were those of dead mares and foals he was claiming for.[24] Branding was done in European, Asiatic and oriental spheres, especially for warhorses. Hungarian brandings are noted in the Kallay family records for 1336. At Henry VIII's Caersws Stud in the Severn Valley stock was branded, as were Moghul cavalry horses.[25] When claiming for a dead cavalry or stud horse, the evidence was a branded piece of hide. A check on stock levels and staff honesty was necessary, particularly as establishments were so widely spread with horses regularly in transit from stud to stud, to war, hunting lodges, tournaments, and of course to pageants in London. At Caersws employees' nefarious dealings are recorded.[26]

EQUIPMENT

The Black Prince, reputed to be an excellent horseman, designed his own bitting for the joust. The order to Lacy to see to their manufacture shows it was a joint effort between the prince and Roger, his smith.[27] Numerous entries concern saddles and equipment used in the studs such as tethers, shackles, halters, surcingles, housings, etc.,[28] but the bit order shows Edward had more than riding ability for the subject of correct bitting is very complex. He also had his favourite breeding stock. When generously giving to Sir John de Beauchamp a mare of his choice from select Princes Risborough broodmares he stipulated 'except the Prince's grey mare there'.[29]

Experienced staff, such as John Pryme and Henry Neuman, usually made his 'bulk' purchases, or these were commissioned by senior officials such as John Dabernoun in Chester, and John de Brunham and John de Kendale in Cornwall who, in 1347, 1353, 1357 and 1363, made huge purchases of riding, sumpter and carthorses.[30] A 1359 entry records £50 for a destrier 'bought by the prince himself' from Little Watte of Smithfield.[31]

BREEDING POLICIES

At key points in the Black Prince's life destriers and coursers are prominent in stud entries, but palfreys, sumpters and carthorses also feature. As a prince Edward had his own household from childhood, but at Princes Risborough and Macclesfield parallel studs were owned by his father. Under Edward III the military equestrian establishment expanded to its greatest extent with numerous purchases (see ch.2) during the decades covered by the *Register*. The king also received gifts from the Counts of Juliers and Guelders and the Italian bankers, the Benefacie of the Peruchie Society. Spanish and Sicilian hot-bloods and the heavier cold-bloods from the Low Countries would have produced the coursers and destriers. Irish horses ranging from £24 to 12 marks would have been a mix – lightweight Irish hobbies, possibly some at the higher price with Spanish blood, as Ireland had long had Spanish connections, and some of Norman extraction, as Ireland's involvement with the Plantagenets went back to Henry II.[32] It is to be expected that much of the prince's stock came from his father's nuclei of prime breeding animals.

As early as 1347 the Black Prince operated studs at Byfleet, Wisley and Princes Risborough. In March 1347 William Bynorth, bailiff of Byfleet, was ordered to send all mares 'fit for foaling this season' to John Geytford with enough grooms to drive them to Princes Risborough Park. Five young mares were to be sent to Byfleet and Wisley. In November that year Bynorth was allowed 13s 4d to pay the Parson of Wisley his 'tithes of the Prince's meadows in the close of Whissele' where mares and foals grazed. Other expenses were for feed and incidentals for the prince's stallions, mares and foals, and keepers' wages.[33]

Tithes to the parish parson were customary, in this case his share of the value of pasture. In 1358 Richard Bekensfeld noted the foals 'he had reasonably delivered to the Parson of Risbergh as tithe'. Many foals must have been dropped for the parson to receive several, but this was balanced by mare and foal losses that year, already noted.[34]

The removal of in-foal mares in Princes Risborough illustrates the practice of stock rotation to allow covering by different stallions, thus widening the gene pool. Stallions were frequently relocated and fresh blood introduced via imported horses and by loans received and made by the Black Prince. Several movements are recorded. Sir Richard Destafford was loaned one of the prince's great horses, called *Grisel de Suffolk*, in November 1351 for the 1352 covering season, and Botetourt loaned two destriers for covering at Risbergh and Cippenham in 1359.[35] In May 1351 Botetourt was ordered to select from the horses in his care those most suitable for the current season's stallions at Risbergh, except Grisel King, Grisel Tankarvill and Morel de Salesbirs.[36] This shows covering started late in the spring by modern standards. Grisel Tankarvill and three others were to be sold that November 'as quickly as possible'.[37] Had he failed to meet standards as a stockgetter? The Princes Risborough population appears to have fluctuated wildly: in 1363 only one stallion and eight mares were resident,[38] but the next year the Black Prince sent a grey courser stallion there and purchased a black stallion from Nicholas Westerdale to cover mares at Princes Risborough and Byfleet; a final Princes Risborough entry has stallions in the plural.[39] The other studs show the extent of the prince's breeding policy.

On occasion Byfleet received great horses for an indefinite stay, such as seven from Princes Risborough in 1355.[40] Somersham had destrier Grisel de Lancastre and three young horses lodged in 1359 awaiting the prince's return to England.[41]

In December 1358 Bekensfeld delivered three destriers and five coursers to Botetourt;[42] and in 1359 one four-year-old and seven three-year-olds were withdrawn from Macclesfield accompanied by John Haket who was to deliver them to Roger Ragaz, currently Keeper of the Prince's Great Horses. Horses belonging to Sir John Wengefeld, one seven-year-old, two four-year-olds, and one three-year-old were to be kept with the prince's other horses.[43]

In 1360 John Haket and assistants were sent to Macclesfield to break and train the young horses of the prince and Sir John, and then bring them to London.[44] Clearly Haket was, in cavalry terms, a 'rough-rider' – rather a misnomer as the rider often got the initial rough treatment on first backing a young colt. Breaking colts must have been his forte – only two batches are recorded but training was required annually. In 1362 nine horses were withdrawn from the Denbigh stud and transferred to London,[45] and the Yorkshire stud at Cotyngham (Cottingham) was being run down with the removal to London of a destrier stallion; a year later the mares and foals were sold, the remaining stallion being given to the Priory of Hautemprise.[46]

PURVEYANCE AND FURTHER ACQUISITION

For the equestrian establishments provender was requisitioned at royal not market price. Oats, beans and peas could be bought more profitably by the heaped measure, giving a small surplus on each, or 'with advantage', getting twenty-one bushels for the price of twenty. Hay, grass and litter (bedding) were also bought, although purveyance was frequent. One comprehensive 1352 order was for comestibles, wood and underwood for cooking and heating, and various items for the chamber(s): John de Palyngton, Purveyor of the Avenary (horse-feed department); John Cotelyn and John Otewell for the 'menee'; and Eustace Wisman for the great horses were to purvey hay, litter and oats, etc., and to commandeer carriage for the same.[47]

Although purveyance was much disliked it was not always heavily imposed; indeed, some instances show the prince in a kindly light. In 1351 many carthorses and grass and hay were purveyed for war. While awaiting departure for Gascony, Edward permitted carters John Spede and Richard Adam to 'take their profit of their carts and horses in the meantime'.[48] Sometimes the prince's hand was altogether removed; in 1347 the Abbot of Hayles was let off purveyance from the abbey's estates,[49] and many other ecclesiastics were also treated lightly. In 1359 thirteen tenants of Wynewyk (Winwick) benefitted when the prince ordered Sir Thomas Rasen, the prince's clerk and avener of the household 'to allow the tenants to keep their horses in peace, as the Prince . . . wishes to do them a special favour'.[50]

Breeding, of course, filled only a portion of the prince's needs, especially for wars. Acquisition was also by gifts, individual purchases, large-scale buying at horse fairs, at market prices, and countrywide purveyance. For the 1355/56 expedition Cornwall produced '30 of the best and strongest baggage horses' plus many other horses, hay and oats. In 1357 Devonshire granted 2,000 quarters of oats and £200 to pay for them as horse provender in Gascony was scarce.[51]

Prior to the Aquitaine campaign huge purchases were made in February 1363. John Pryme was commissioned to buy horses of all types at Staunford (Stamford) Fair, payment coming from 'issues' of Rehale, Eston, Upton, Caldecote, Wissenden and Torpel. Others were sought in Leicestershire and all kept at the prince's manor at Castle Donington in the county. In November purchases continued and were still resident at Donington in February 1364.[52] Cornwall was scoured for riding horses, sumpters and carthorses.[53] From Wirral Forest 100 harts and 100 bucks were hunted, salted and transported to Bordeaux.[54] Cornwall and Dartmoor sent large consignments of venison and oats.[55] Good prices were paid for some purchases:

1358 – £70, for two horses from Sir Baldwin.
1359 – £50, for a destrier from Little Watte of Smithfield.
1360 – 80 marks, for a horse from Sir John Hide.
1362 – £50, for a horse from John Paladyn.[56]

Little or 'Petitwatte' often sold the prince quality horses, appearing as vendor in the 1352 list supplying three palfreys which Edward gave to the Earl of Northampton, the queen and Sir Hugh Despenser.[57]

Cheaper horses ranged from approximately £10 down to £1:

1347   –   an order to buy forty carthorses each worth between one and two marks; and later fifty more, not paying more than £2 each.[58]

1353   –   £6 for a horse given to Sir Biscaud (Boucicaut) Knight of France.[59]

1358   –   £3 6s 8d for a bay palfrey from John Mabbessone.
            £5 6s 8d for a ferrand horse from Roger Ragaz.
            £6 13s 4d for a sorrel courser from Sir Baldwin.[60]

HERIOTS AND DEODANDS

Heriots provided a few good horses when the Black Prince exercised his right to the best beast. Bishops' and nobility's holdings from the prince provided the best, the Bishop of Llandaff rendering one in 1362.[61] A courser belonging to the deceased Earl of Garren was owed and claimed in 1347,[62] but a horse and foal arrested for the Manor of Careswelle was questioned. The prince ordered an enquiry and their return to the rightful owner if a heriot was not due.[63]

Another courser which belonged to William Boydel was owed as a deodand.[64] This is an intriguing entry as a deodand was a forfeit, in this case to the prince, to be used for 'pious purposes' if the object had caused a tenant's death. Had the courser done so? There are instances of dangers involved with horses. In one, surely a deodand, a horse which caused death by drowning to two friars in Macclesfield was given by the prince to the Friars Preachers of Newcastle,[65] a rather tactless gift in the circumstances! Another was the surrender to the prince by the Bishop of Lincoln of an iron-tyred cart and four horses which had killed their carter, John.[66]

EQUINE USAGE

There was a constant drain on resources. Royal households moved constantly and it was easier to move the household, which included furniture and departmental objects such as cooking utensils, etc., to the manor or hunting lodge and consume estate produce, relying on purveyance to top up their needs for an extended stay, than to remain at a main base with comestibles and other needs being hauled in by carthorses and strings of baggage horses. There was also the frequent need to, to coin a Tudor phrase, 'sweeten' residences – a thorough cleansing, with new rushes, an airing, etc., and an emptying of odiferous cesspits. There were times when extended stays at the capital or at a muster venue prior to transit to France put a strain on equine transport systems – and on the need for drovers, as the prince regularly instructed his county officials to procure cattle and have them driven where needed, such as the 1360 order to have '100 great beasts from the County of Cestre [Chester] and 100 from North Wales', making sure they were large and vigorous since small beasts would be unable to withstand travel in winter weather without losing flesh.[67] Parkers and foresters provided venison, which was transported by cart.

INDENTURES AND *RESTAURO*

The demands of war depleted equine stocks. Among war indentures are some in which the prince undertook to provide his own knight with his warhorse(s), although their mounted retinues were at the bachelor's expense, or subcontracted with his own retinue.

Indentures had a basic outline but sometimes had special clauses inserted, as shown by a 1347 clutch:

Name	Length of Indenture	No. (incl. leader)	Knights	Esquires	Fee per annum	Mounted Archers	Warhorses
Sir John Hide	1 year	3	1	2	£20	Not stated but sixpence per day each	Valued
Sir Wm. de Ros	1 year	7	2	5	80 marks	Not stated	Valued
Sir John Fitzwauter	6 months	20	5	15	100 marks for 6 months	12 at sixpence per day	
Sir Thomas Furnival	1 year	10	2	8	100 marks	6	14 horses

The differences in the first three indentures were only over method of payment, as follows:

Name	Fee	Pay
Hide	25 per cent in advance, rest quarterly	1 month in advance, rest quarterly
Ros	50 per cent in advance, rest quarterly	2 months in advance, rest quarterly
Fitzwauter	50 per cent in advance, rest quarterly	6 weeks in advance, rest monthly
Furnival	50 per cent in advance, rest quarterly	1 month in advance, then monthly or quarterly at prince's choice (Pay was 2s per day for knights, 1s per day for esquires)

Furnival's indenture shows a more complex contract. He, another knight and two esquires ate in hall when at court. When victuals were taken in lieu, as on manoeuvres, a carriage allowance was granted. Fourteen horses for himself, his companion knight and two esquires were to have livery whenever the prince's other bachelors obtained the same, i.e., hay, oats, litter and shoeing for four horses at a penny per day, and fourteen grooms at wages. Two chamberlains at wages were allowed. Transit to and from the war zone was provided. The other esquires were at Furnival's cost.[68]

In 1353 Sir John Sully was retained for life, in peace and war, with one esquire. He, his esquire and his chamberlain ate in hall. Five horses were allowed at livery and four grooms at wages. In wartime he was to have court rations or be at livery and wages with nine horses and eight grooms. The Black Prince provided his horse. When summoned Sully was to receive travel costs.[69]

Occasionally, complaints were made. In 1347 Sir William Belesby complained that although he had been with the prince in the recent French war he had received only half his £20 fee, and he had incurred great losses because his horses could not be accommodated in the prince's livery around Tichfield (Tichfeld), where the prince's retinue was, but were lodged fifteen miles distant, so he could not get them valued when other knights' horses were appraised. The Black Prince agreed he should have £10 for the remainder of his fee and his other losses.[70] This appears to have been sharp practice as only the balance of the fee was paid, and the whole incident leaves a question mark about why Belesby was apart from the others. Had he fallen into disfavour on some account?

Restauro payments were sometimes considerable, but at other times moderate. Sir Bernard van Zedeles, his companion knights and retinue received £359 6s 8d for horses lost in war; the sum was paid in 1358 but related to the Poitiers and Spanish campaigns. Expenses of £246 for returning to Germany were also paid. Deossent, leader of the

Spaniards, received £96 to replace ten horses lost fighting in the Black Prince's company. Henry de Berkhamstead, the prince's yeoman and pantler, received only £6 to replace horses lost in Gascony, a low reparation, in this case probably for sumpters or carthorses lost in the back-up system.[71]

Restoration was also made for non-war losses. The prince pushed horses hard, requiring his servants to do the same: courier John Wetherherde lost a courser riding to Romney, receiving £1 in recompense. William Merkeshale received £2 when the prince commandeered his horse and 'spoilt', i.e. foundered it by hard riding from the coast to London in 1360 after landing from the continent.[72]

HORSES IN ESTATE MANAGEMENT

In running the Black Prince's huge estates the hidden horse was active; that is, animals used daily by household servants, estate workers and tenants whose horses could be pressed into use to boost the prince's coffers in diverse ways. These find occasional mention in sources and give a sketch of equines in estate and household management.

Hunting, falconry and the tournament were major sporting activities claiming much royal and noble leisure time. The Black Prince's involvement called on his equine and/or financial resources, for even if the riding foresters' horses were not owned by the prince their costs were reflected in wages. Falconers were often posted to manors around the country. In April 1352 William Whitton escorted two falcons and two tercelets with their bearer to Wallingford. His daily wage of one shilling indicates his senior position, and that he was mounted.[73] Wallingford features prominently in the *Register*, especially in regard to falconry.

Game took precedence on grazing land, but agistments (taking in livestock to feed) realized a moderate sum. In Cornwall and Devonshire parks, forests and chases, agistments for horses and cattle were banned from 1354, except on Dartmoor where they were to be increased when pasture permitted. Foresters were ordered to go easy on folk who grazed horses and cattle there to encourage their use of pasture, thus increasing the prince's profit.[74] Agistments were ordered in 1355 for the wastes within the Manor of Kirketon, Nottinghamshire. Periodically the wastes were to be driven for 'weifs and strais which the Prince ought rightfully have' and for animals grazing illegally. If anyone else claimed the waifs and strays, a day was to be fixed to ascertain rights in these animals before the prince's council.[75] The law was tough, normally resulting in a fine or loss of the animal to the landowner. Waifs (unclaimed stock) also became the landowner's property.

When hunting game, foresters often had the right to commandeer tenant's horses. This is illustrated by the claim, among others duly agreed, made by William Stanlegh, Forester of Wirral, to use horses belonging to the town in which the deer was found to pack the meat to Chester Castle.[76]

In addition, other agricultural spin-offs appear. Sir Hugh de Hop was ordered to negotiate for the 1347 wool clip from the monastic lands in Cheshire on terms advantageous to the prince.[77] Once purchased, strings of pack ponies, which most farming monasteries owned, would have transported the clip. The prince also claimed customs dues on Welsh wool, a charge accounted for in 1357 by a Lombard merchant being taxed on both sacks and woolfells in a huge consignment.[78]

Horses carrying corn to the mill aided the economy, but although the peasant was obliged to use the lord's mill, he at least got free grazing for it while there in the 'stanks'. Mills, and other agricultural lands, were let out at farm. Ikelyngham Mill was sub-let to Edmund Pernhill by Sir John Berners of Ikelyngham Manor, who held of the prince.[79] The Cheshire towns of Northwiz and Menewiz (Northwick and Middlewich) levied tolls of fourpence for a cartload and twopence for a horseload,[80] this being the countrywide fee.

Cumulatively these small amounts added considerably to the prince's exchequer. On the other hand his officials also dealt with complaints. One poor Cheshire parson, of Gropenhale Church, complained of persecution by Sir John Danyers who illegally proclaimed a tournament at Werynton; entered the rectory; stole torches and burnt them at his revels; stole timber; allowed his men to take the parson's horses and ride them at will; his men threatened grievous bodily harm to the parson's servants, chasing them from the house; stole his crops so he lost half his harvest; and when the Bishop of Chester ordered the parson to make legal execution, Danyers stole the parson's personal horse in retribution.[81] Unfortunately the *Register* does not relate if Danyers had his just come-uppance for such banditry.

Anketin, also an ecclesiastic, fell foul of Thomas Pountfreit of Stamford who accused him, with others, of stealing five marks and a horse worth £2. Anketin was surrendered to the ecclesiastical court and managed to clear himself, upon which the prince ordered his distrained goods returned.[82]

Throughout the *Register* it is clear that the prince, or his council and 'legal eagles', oversaw every aspect, no matter how small, concerning his estates. The register gives a comprehensive overview of estate management, not only the equestrian side of it. But a large portion of the documentation centred around the horse, illustrating how, in its many guises, it was essential to the smooth running of every department, whether as transport, carriage, war tool, sporting partner, baggage beast or drover's pony; even a child's pony is recorded – Lyard Hobyn, a grey hobby/pony given to Edward, the prince's godson.[83]

Introduction to Chapters 7 and 8

In the High Middle Ages occidental literacy diversified. It was no longer restricted to monastic chroniclers writing histories of Church and kings, or to the occasional compilation of military advice, or to the cleric employed in a secular household as a scribe cum accountant. Literature grew as more of the secular classes, albeit those of higher social and economic standing, were educated. Guide books appeared – on farming, veterinary matters (too early to be called a science), and even on household management. Young men doing their 'Grand Tour' left travelogues. Poems on secular and romantic themes were popular. The novel made an occasional appearance. These had much to offer on equestrianism, especially the romanticized legends such as *Sir Gawain and the Green Knight*, *Willehalm* and *Parsival*. The war, tournament and hunting scenes in these were works of fiction, or at best had shreds of fact, but where the equestrian scenes occur they can be relied on – there was no political axe to grind, hero to eulogize, or villain to damn. The foxhunt in *Sir Gawain and the Green Knight* almost parallels a modern hunt, the main difference being the use of leashed hounds. Today's 'leash' is the control exerted by huntsmen and whippers-in. The warhorses are a good guide to the international horse mart. The *Roland* describes occidental and oriental equine differences. *Tirant Lo Blanc*, a fifteenth-century Catalan novel, draws heavily on the real-life Spanish wars over the possession of Sicily, with Sicilian chargers making frequent appearances.

To medieval literature we owe much accurate information on the place, provenance and use of the horse. From the Oriental sphere, where literacy came earlier to the social elite, we have a wealth of information, mostly from military treatises, or from military men writing of equestrian matters and veterinary practitioners writing not only of medical matters but of the selection and use of the horse in war and peace. Oriental hunting retained practices little changed over the centuries. In India this was perhaps the most marked and long-lived, as recounted in *The Centaur* by S.A.H.A.A. Imam, historian, raconteur and Indian 'Big Game' hunter.

CHAPTER 7
Hunting

Hunting was sport, training for war, and provider of meat. In the first two categories it was bound by rules and class distinctions. For a member of the lower social classes riding horses out hunting was a right that had to be earned, achieved as the young man went up the scale of hunting appointments. He would first have taken part on foot as a page, or as a *varlet des chiens* (dog/hound handler). When promoted, at around the age of twenty years, to *aide de la venerie* (assistant huntsman) he would have acquired several horses, and his own varlet who handled his leashed lymers until they had scented the hart; the *aide de la venerie* controlled hounds from horseback once they had been unleashed. That young huntsmen of non-noble descent could aspire to enter the ranks of the nobility via their hunting duties is borne out by a passage in John of Portugal's *Livro da Montaria* where he

St Hubert's vision.

stressed that foot huntsmen should consider how they may become squires. As squires and potential knights they automatically had the right to ride to hounds.[1]

The part the horse played in European and English hunting has to be extrapolated from accounts, poems, and from contemporary illustrations of hunting and hawking. In hunting treatises information on the hunting horse is scant. No doubt in nobles' stables certain horses were valued for their performance in the field, but unlike today, where a hunter is a certain stamp of horse which does not exclude other suitable horses, medieval hunting horses were not specially designated. The usual mount was the courser, swift and not too heavy, and the palfrey, elegant and comfortable.

In the mid-fifteenth-century translation of the French *Le Livre de l'Ordre de Chevalerie* by Gilbert Hay, hunting is recommended as an activity for training kings and knights, who were advised to be 'good riders both on war horses and on coursers and that they hawk and hunt for hart, hind, doe, roe, boar, bear, wolf and lion and practice all such honourable pleasures.'[2] Where lion were encountered in Europe is a mystery.

Potential warriors and their horses benefitted from riding to hounds. Hunting sharpened their perception, gave them aptitude for crossing country safely at speed, taught split-second timing, especially in an encounter with boar, and tested their courage. Any natural aggression the horse possessed, which is often shown when a horse, particularly a stallion, is pitted against another animal, would be sharpened and could be channelled at the rider's dictat. It would be too late if their first test came on the battlefield.

The role and the costs of hounds loom large. Information on hounds and handlers is voluminous, and on that point space allows only a brief summary of types (see below), while the horse's role is searched for. I have always thought it odd that twenty couple of hounds are needed to catch one fox, and usually do not. Maybe the collective brain is necessary to do so! But I admit I hunted for the equestrian element, as do most. Medieval hunting would have charmed the purist huntsmen today who are enthralled when they see hounds work.

THE ORIENT

In oriental hunting the horse was far more important. Dangers were more frequent, as many of the animals hunted were themselves large predators. Here the Asiatic lion was encountered. Today its last stronghold is in the Gir National Forest in Gujarat, India, where it is now a protected animal.

Oriental hunting followed a centuries-old tradition; for example, 'Big Game' hunting in India was inherited from the Moghul era and even earlier. Much Levantine hunting was with very intelligent, trained raptors; hounds took only a minor role. The horse was an essential part of the hunt, rather than a mere conveyance. Fortunately, much contemporary literature concerns hunting methods and equestrian participation, starting with possibly the earliest medieval account of a hunting preserve. Of course, texts from classical Greece and Rome, especially those of Xenophon, Oppian, and, the best, that of Arrian, give excellent accounts of hunting.

The life of the Roman soldier and historian Ammianus Marcellinus spanned the end of the old Roman era and the beginning of the earliest medieval years, allocated by some historians to AD 378 when the Goths thrashed the Roman army at Adrianople. Ammianus is an excellent source for equestrian detail and describes a Persian paled hunting preserve near Seleucia – very much like the later European parks where game was harboured until needed for the hunt.

Ammianus lists the game reserved for the sport of Persian kings. Similar game was hunted throughout most oriental hunting tracts for the next 1,000 and more years, though game was not necessarily emparked.

there were lions with long manes, bristly wild boars, bears of the extraordinarily savage type peculiar to Persia, and other choice beasts of enormous size . . .

In AD 363 rampaging Romans broke in and dispatched all the game.[3]

THE BYZANTINE HUNT

The Byzantine military manual *The Strategicon of the Emperor Maurice* has a chapter on hunting. Aside from acquiring meat and hides, hunting was used:

> to make them (men and horses) more alert and provide exercise for their horses . . . give them good experience in military tactics.

Scouts went out the day before to locate and report back on game numbers. On the appointed day what is now termed 'the field' in British hunting was ranged on military lines with a centre and wings spread over a large enough stretch of country so that game was not alerted. Width, allowing 800–1,000 men per mile, was preferable to depth as the intent was to drive the catchment area. When within about four miles of the game the wings gradually moved into the horns of a crescent before contracting into a huge circle, the horn-tips overlapping and gradually spiralling down as the circle tightened until the circumference was only one to two miles in total, leaving a centre large enough for marksmen to shoot while encircling troopers remained safe. The space between horses shrank and to prevent small game slipping between the horses' legs, infantry or dismounted troopers from the rear ranks were to be stationed in front of the horsemen with shields locked to form a wall. Throughout the round-up discipline and quiet was maintained. A trooper was not to spur his horse or to shoot until permitted, unless before encirclement was complete some game escaped; then only the trooper nearest the animal was to shoot at it, but without leaving the ranks. If, prior to closing the circle, game was alerted the horses were to quicken their pace to entrap it. The final phases of the hunt were when officers gave the order to designated marksmen, armed according to expertise with either bow or spear, to dispatch the quarry. If night was closing in the circle was further tightened so game could be dispatched by hand.[4] Hounds had no part in the hunt.

THE MONGOL HUNT

Mongol hunting procedures were similar to those of the Byzantines except the Mongol army indulged in a month-long annual affair organized as a campaign and led by the khan. Game was driven to a designated area, sentinels posted at strategic points and signal fires lit to advise on progress. Once the game was encircled the khan opened the slaughter before allowing his princes and nobles their turn at the game. At the end of the hunt the 'campaign' was discussed and approbation and/or criticisms of the procedures rendered.[5]

Ser Marco Polo has left us an excellent description of Great Khan Kubilai on his annual *nerge* (hunt); although run as a military operation, great variety was apparent in the different aspects of hunting, which took place from the beginning of March until Eastertide.[6] Kubilai's hunting establishment was enormous, involving many species of raptor, hounds by the thousand, and several types of big cat trained to hunt (for man). Game included roebuck, deer, wild ox, wild ass, bear and wolves. Ser Marco rounds all his estimates off in multiples of hundreds and thousands, as was the medieval custom when aiming to impress. Certainly the khan's hunt was a grand affair – travelling city, royal household and army combined. The trappings of 'après hunt' were magnificent, with luxuriously appointed tented quarters for the khan and his nobles.

The hound department was controlled by two *kyukchi*, brothers Bayan and Mingan, each with a staff of 10,000; when hunting, 2,000 men from each unit were accompanied by from one to three led-mastiffs per man. From October to March the *kyukchi* hunted for meat, being expected to send daily to the court at least 1,000 head, not counting quail and fish that were also required. When hunting with the khan one *kyukchi* rode on the khan's left, the other on his right; each led his full complement with as many as 5,000 hounds to each sector. The range to be driven extended in width to a day's march. Considering a Mongol day's march could be anything from the fifteen miles per day covered by the Il Khan Gazan's forces in the 1299 campaign against Syria[7] to the sixty miles per day plus covered in the 1241 invasion of Europe under Batu Khan,[8] Mongol hunting was of epic proportions. The Kubilai hunt witnessed by Ser Marco was in the army formation of centre under Kubilai, with two wings which gradually contracted to encircle the game. Dispatch of game was by various means: mastiffs and men bringing it down; lynxes taught to chase and catch; trained hunting leopards (cheetahs) which rode pillion behind horsemen until unleashed on their quarry. The most fearsome hunters were the so-called 'lions' with striped pelts of orange, black, and white (in other words, tigers) which were carted to the hunt in cages, then loosed on larger game. (Unfortunately, no mention is made about how the tigers were persuaded back into their cages.) Large, powerful eagles brought down wolves, roebuck and deer, and gerfalcons, peregrine and saker falcons and goshawks did the same to smaller game and birds. The best gerfalcons were set onto cranes.

From May to October, the breeding season, hunting ceased under threat of severe penalties. Ser Marco does not outline these, but as the death penalty was commonplace for even minor infractions the close season guaranteed the animals peace for at least a few months.

Non-sporting hunting was incumbent on subjects in order to supply the royal table. Those living within a thirty-day distance from the court sent suitably prepared game; those further away sent the cured skins to be used for making army equipment.[9]

The horses would have learned to watch the quarry and anticipate its movements, as animals usually indicate their next move to those skilled enough to recognize it – a cutting horse instinctively knows which way the calf is going to move and reacts to block it. By the end of a successful hunt horses would have become 'bomb proof'; if they did not they would probably have joined the game in the stew pot as the Mongols were very partial to horsemeat!

THE MAMLŪKS

As the Mongols swept into Persia and Asia Minor and advanced into Mamlūk territory in Syria, so their hunting methods influenced the Mamlūks who were the medieval oriental riders *par excellence*, each trooper having been honed to military perfection by assiduous training in *Furusiyya* exercises which were obligatory for all Mamlūks. Of twelve branches of *Furusiyya*, ten involved horsemanship.[10] Hunting, polo and horseracing were three exercises that, though not directly linked to warfare, gave good training to man and mount; the last named exercise implied the horse's military expertise as, according to contemporary historian Maqrizi, only horses used in war were entitled to race.[11]

The sultan and his Mamlūks based in Egypt hunted in the Libyan and Egyptian deserts. In Syria the Mamlūks hunted in their respective territories, which included the major viceroyalties of Damascus and Aleppo, and the smaller ones such as Gaza, Hims, Hamah, Safad and Tarabulus (Tripoli).[12]

THE TURKS

Not all oriental hunting was on the *nerge* format. Jahiz of Basra gives us a cameo of the Turk hunting and fighting in the ninth century. Superlative horsemen, Turks virtually lived astride their horses; both men and mounts were indefatigable. The distinctive horses, mostly of Turcoman stock, were used in almost every aspect of Turkish life:

> The Turk rides a stallion or a mare, and goes forth on a peaceful or a warlike expedition, far in pursuit of game or for any other reason, with his mare and her colt following. If he cannot hunt human beings he hunts wild beasts . . . All their interest is in raids and incursions and hunting and riding and the flights of warriors and seeking plunder and subduing countries . . .[13]

In other words Turks were expert and formidable in every equestrian exploit.

PERSIA

For hunting out of necessity we turn to the *Qabus Nama* (*A Mirror for Princes*), a Persian tract written in 1082 by Kai Ka'us ibn Iskander ibn Qabus ibn Washmgir, Prince of Gurgan of the Ziyanid dynasty, for the enlightenment of his son, Gilanshah. Horsemanship and selection of mounts loom large; hunting is recommended as a princely activity, but in moderation, and for personal aggrandisement with a strong element of self-preservation. Hunting was to be indulged in circumspectly on no more than two days a week; to enhance his appearance the prince was to ride a large, mettlesome horse at a conservative pace. A comfortable ambler was unsuitable as it induced sloppy riding. Chasing after 'ferocious beasts' was to be eschewed as several close family members had been killed so doing. Only when needing to impress 'great princes' was Gilanshah to forge ahead and risk his person. Hunting was to be used to stock the larder, and in order to lessen the odds and increase personal safety trained hawks, falcons, leopards (cheetahs) and hounds were to be used. Kai Ka'us then contradicts his advice on utility saying the prince should hunt for sport not meat; that it was unfitting to handle hounds himself or allow the cheetah to ride pillion behind him – this was undignified for a prince and imprudent to keep a wild beast at his back 'particularly if one is a king'.[14] In that era of Seljuk overlordship and constant bickering and infighting between princely houses, I should think an assassin's knife was more likely to be encountered than a cheetah's claws! Gilanshah himself only reigned for seven years before being overthrown in 1090/91 by Hasan-i-Sabbah, the Old Man of the Mountain,[15] the leader of the Battiniya, or Assassins. One wonders with so much intrigue around him whether Gilanshah took the preservation hints to heart, or, as would most youngsters, enjoyed the thrills and dangers of the wilder side of hunting?

SYRIA

Dangers certainly were present when Usamāh ibn Munqidh and his father, Amir of Shaizar in Syria, hunted in the middle of the twelfth century. Usamāh's memoirs have a superb chapter on hunting in Syria, Mesopotamia and Egypt, which ends saying he had hunted 'for seventy years of my life'.[16]

As well as hawking and hunting with hounds, encirclement was used to entrap deer, wolf and hyena for summary dispatch, but when tried with a hare, even though a lynx carried pillion on horseback was set on it, it escaped through the horses' legs. Usamāh was experienced in all branches of equestrianism; he recounts clashes with Frankish knights, describes their horses, and his and those mounts of other Arabs, speaking of them with knowledge, pride and affection, his family breeding Arabian horses of high renown. When praising or describing horses of 'the best breed' Usamāh always meant Arabians. Other horses got scant reference other than to note their use, or any individual's peculiarity.

A Persian hunt with bow and sword and beasts of the chase – graceful deer 'and ferocious lion'.

The horse features regularly in Usamāh's almost daily hunting exploits, which were part of the weft of Arab life. Most hunting was with raptors; hounds, although used, were not the major part of the hunt as they were in Europe. Invariably Usamāh, his father, friends and hunting establishment retainers, hunted on horseback, with falconers sometimes proceeding on foot.

Arabs have always excelled with birds of prey and Usamāh and his contemporaries were no different, hawking with falcons, sakers and river shahins, whose prey included cranes, herons, partridge, sand grouse, quail and geese – anything that flew – as well as game. A fast horse was necessary to retrieve a stricken bird from the falcon. Usamāh described an alternative method of retrieval favoured by the Franks. A Genoese had brought with him a large falcon for hunting cranes and a bitch to pin down a stricken crane until the huntsman could retrieve it . . .

In a foxhunt the tables could be turned on the pursuing hound, as Usamāh related when galloping after a fox outside Aleppo. As the bitch overtook the fox she seized its tail, but was bitten on the nose by the fox; the bitch yelped, let go, and the fox escaped into its nearby hole to the merriment of the hunters.

Usamāh's father constantly sought rare falcons for his sport, sending even as far as Constantinople for birds. In Shaizar the amir's chief falconer was Ghanā'im, a great expert on hunting with and training falcons, treating injured birds or imping their broken feathers. As he was always seeking new birds the amir's mews were stocked to bursting.

On one Munqidh expedition the amir's hunting establishment provided ten or more falcons, accompanied by the saker men; two cheetah keepers; two masters of hounds – one for the salukis, one for the braches; attendants, extra horses and weapons for the hunters for security against the Franks whose territory was adjacent to Shaizar. The field of forty mounted men included the amir, his four sons, comrades, and the amir's own mamlūks, all experienced hunters. Hunting often took place in the marshes outside the town and along riverbanks; wider territories were ridden when hunting stretched over a longer period. Strict discipline and silence was maintained, members being assigned a specific task. Game included francolins and hares for the falcons. Should a hare escape, a cheetah was loosed. Cheetahs also hunted gazelles; if they lost it a saker would be flown at it. Wild boar were quarry for the mounted men and great skill and bravery was needed from man and horse when closing with it.[17]

In old age Usamāh recalled memorable hunts. An occasion where the horse turned hunter was when a gazelle was startled in the marshy canebrakes; Usamāh, galloping his horse 'which was a horse of one of the best breeds', tried to turn the gazelle towards the cheetah, but the horse hit the gazelle, bringing it down for the cheetah (a privileged cat that lived in the Munqidh house cared for by its own personal maid).[18]

Arabians were definitely the preferred mounts for Syrian hunting. Usamāh compared an Arabian mare with a Berdhun, inaccurately translated as a hackney, as a Berdhun was a horse with no Arabian blood – one of common breeding. The amir was hunting roe on a black Arab mare called The Khurji; she put a front leg into a pit dug for wild boar, fell and somersaulted over the amir who broke his collarbone. Startled, the mare galloped a short way off, then returned to stand guard over her master, neighing till help came, 'such is the way Arab horses behave'! But a Berdhun ridden by the amir's huntsman Lu'lu threw its rider by spooking at the shadow of the rider's quiver, hightailing it into the distance. It took all morning and until late in the afternoon for Usamāh and an attendant to recapture it, eventually lassoing it when it took refuge in a flock of animals.[19] (The translation says 'trapped with a rope'. Lassoing was probably the method used, as the lasso was a part of Mongol and Turkic riding/hunting/war equipment.)

Boar hunting, as ever, caused casualties. Usamāh's brother had a mare killed underneath him; while spearing the boar, his lance broke, the boar charged and gored the

Lassoing a horse – a method of capture used by Asiatics, Persians, Syrians and Turks, and modern-day American ranch hands.

mare who fell, dislocating its thigh and dying from its wounds. Usamāh took up the chase but lost the boar in a thicket where his horse was suddenly charged by an enraged bull, struck in the chest and brought down. Remounting the horse the chase continued; the bull took a direct lance hit and, endeavouring to escape across a river, was brought to bay in the water and dispatched by a hunter's knife. Usamāh's comments on boar hunting were to the point:

> If the boar had claws and teeth like the lion, it would be even more deadly than the lion.[20]

INDIA

Both boar and lion were hunted in India for centuries; in the lion's case only the weaponry changed, from bows to guns as firepower took over from archery. Lion hunting continued in India until the mid-nineteenth century when for default of lion, having been shot out, it ceased.[21] Boar hunting with spears changed little for the Indian custom was to retain the weapon as it offered the closest and most dangerous of encounters, and required, vitally, a very agile, brave horse. Throughout the medieval period, which in India runs until the eighteenth century, only blood horses were used. My friend, Tootoo Imam, a retired professional 'Big Game' hunter with much experience of boar hunting says the Indian boar is 'the only beast which will attack from a distance unprovoked'.[22]

Although Indian game hunting predates the medieval period, it is only with the memoirs of Bābur, the first Mughal Emperor (1526–30), that it began to be recorded in other than epic Indian poetry. The *Bābur Nāma* outlines Bābur's early years when he was fighting to retain his inheritance of Andijan, Ferghana's capital. Once secure he set his sights on Samarkand. In between annual campaigns he went into winter quarters, spending the months hunting for game to feed his troops.[23] Years later, when he was making regular forays across the Sind into Hindustan, he combined raiding with hunting.[24] The *Bābur Nāma* indicates that the three focal points of Bābur's life were war, hunting and food; the first two were constantly indulged in, the third was always on his mind because so often in his early years he and his army were pinched for lack of it, and hunting and raiding flocks was vital to keep his army operational. In happier times it afforded him much sport.

THE OCCIDENT

By the seventh century there is evidence of hunting reserves in Europe. The first we know that was recorded as such was the Forest of Ardennes, noted in a charter of Sigbert, King of the Franks (634–56).[25] References to hunting occur in the *Royal Frankish Annals* but their content is minimal; pieced together, however, the details extrapolated give an overview of the system.

As well as spontaneous hunting it was customary to spend late summer and autumn, until early October, hunting in either the Vosges Mountains or the Ardennes before returning to the court at Aachen. Louis the Pious (814–40) devoted himself annually to the chase.[26] His father, Charlemagne, according to Einhard, spent much of his time on horseback and out hunting.[27] Notker, in his *Life of Charlemagne*, describes him hunting bison and wild oxen at Easter, accompanied by the Persian envoys who had brought gifts from Harun al Raschid. The envoys who were scared of 'these immense animals . . . turned and ran'. Charlemagne 'sitting astride his spirited horse' rode up to a huge beast, tried to cut its head off with his sword, but failed. Wounded, it gored him in the foot and fled to wooded shelter; Warin, a retainer, rode after it and dispatched it with a spear hurled into its heart. Charlemagne's reciprocal gifts to Harun included Spanish horses, mules and dogs chosen for ferocity and nimbleness. Only the hounds impressed the Persian who had asked for them to use against lions and tigers.[28]

The *De Villis Capitulary*, a document on royal estate management, gives a little more information. Woods and forests were to be well protected; game well cared for; and hawks and falcons kept ready for the king's use. Tithes for pannage were to be collected from men fattening pigs in the forest. Cordage was to be strictly controlled.[29] Falconers and those making nets for hunting or fishing are among craftsmen stewards were to keep on each royal estate.[30] Stewards were to take good care of walled parks.[31] Hunters and falconers who were permanently assigned to court were always to be assisted in their work 'when we send them out on an errand or when the seneschal or butler gives them some task to do in our name',[32] i.e. hunting and hawking for the royal table as opposed to sport hunting. The system of raising hounds was a precursor of today's 'puppy walking' for the local hunt. The royal puppies were to be either farmed out to estate stewards to care for at their expense, or if kept on the royal estate(s) stewards were to send a man to care for them together with dog food for their sustenance.[33] For poaching in royal forests fines were levied which went into the royal coffers, along with tithes and payments exacted on every commodity produced on royal estates where freemen or servants made their living.[34] Wolves, which were considered a plague, were to be poisoned, trapped and hunted with hounds.[35]

As well as the information on Frankish horsebreeding contained in the *De Villis* (see p. 12), the *Brevium Exempla*, dating to the last fourteen years of Charlemagne's reign, or to the early part of Louis the Pious' reign, shows other studs existed. Some idea of the scale of these can be gained from the livestock numbers kept on four royal estates in northern France. Aspanius (Annappes, Departement du Nord) had ninety-one head of mature stock and youngsters, two others, unnamed, had livestock of ninety and 150 respectively, and for the fourth there was a blank in the manuscript for numbers of older horses and three-year-old colts and fillies, but other young stock and the stallions came to thirty-eight head.[36] Many of these horses would have been used in the utility and sporting aspects of hunting to which all European kings and their households were addicted.

Later hunting establishments had much in common with those of the Frankish annals. By 1066 ducal and baronial hunting preserves were well established in Normandy, and from there translated to England and Scotland.[37]

Under Canute (1016–35) laws governing hunting in England were reasonable and sensible:

> It is my will that every man shall be entitled to hunt in the woods and fields on his own property, but everyone, under threat of incurring the full penalty, shall avoid hunting on my preserves, wherever they may be.

This probably meant a fine of 120*s* for insubordination to the king.[38]

The Norman kings were avid hunters, especially William Rufus (1087–1100). Increasingly lands were taken into royal forests and henceforth governed by severe 'forest law', which operated solely at the king's dictat and was separate from judicial procedure. Although one of Bastard William's laws forbade the death penalty he substituted it with blinding and castration,[39] and mutilation was common for forest offences. The *Anglo-Saxon Chronicle* for the year 1087 states that he forbade the killing of harts, hinds, boars and stags – animals that came to be known as 'royal game'; poachers who were caught were blinded.[40] Henry of Huntingdon enlarges on the Bastard's hunting saying:

> Beasts of chace he cherished as if they were his children; so that to form the hunting ground of the New Forest he caused the churches and villages to be destroyed, and driving out the people, made it an habitation for deer.[41]

In the twelfth century forest amounted to about one-third of England's landmass, including not only forests as we know them, but marsh, heath, woods and scrubland, as well as areas of cultivation, villages and townships – i.e. any land within the boundaries designated as royal forests. Within these boundaries only kings could take red, fallow and roe deer and wild boar. Any other lord or landowner whose land was within forest boundaries was limited to hunting small game such as hares, fox, wolves, badgers, etc. The king could and did issue warrants to favoured subjects to hunt royal game,[42] but usually stipulated the number allowed to be taken. The Black Prince did the same in 1351 for his parks in Cornwall, making grants to the local nobility and to several non-noble folk, some of them his servants, to take does from his parks providing they did it at their own cost and did as little damage as possible on the days appointed for their hunting, which, although not stipulated in this case, would have been done in sight of the keeper(s), as happened in 1362 in his park in the Forest of Dertemore (Dartmoor).[43]

Within the forest, areas were emparked by being fenced, hedged about, or surrounded with a ditch for preservation of game, or in some cases if game was destroying tenants' crops a park would be empaled. The forest was managed by huntsmen, foresters and parkers whose job, in addition to caring for game and vert (habitat), and providing meat for the table, was to exploit timber, pannage, pasture, etc. produced by the forest and to arrest any person found poaching.[44]

In England the 'forest law' continued exacting savage punishment, even if mutilation was not always carried out. Poaching incurred a fine and a year's imprisonment, or even banishment. Under Richard I (1189–99) this was again punished by blinding and castration. Damage against the vert incurred fines and forfeiture of livestock. In Scotland the law was less harsh; a £10 fine was levied for both offences. Persons travelling within the forest boundaries paid levies in both countries. In England even landowners going to their own woods within a forest paid twopence per half year. In Scotland trespassing incurred a 30-shilling fine. Lawing of dogs (removing claws) and a total ban on carrying bow and arrows was in force in England; whereas in Scotland dogs were not mutilated and the carrying of bow and arrows was not so rigidly banned.[45] In the Forest of Delamere and Murdrem in the Palatinate of Chester lawing was not customary. Elsewhere a three yearly check was made by foresters to ensure dogs had been lawed.[46] In Scotland although the king could hunt game over all forests this was also permitted to the owners of forest lands.[47]

In the emparked areas in both Scotland and England there were several royal studs. In 1330 the Scottish royal stud in the mountainous area of Mar was moved to Ettrick Forest, remaining there till 1501.[48] One example, among many, in England was the Black Prince's stud in Macclesfield Park under the care of keeper Alexander Atte Crosse of Prestwich and his groom, who also cared for the venison and vert of the park within the forest.[49]

The hunting preserve management system endured throughout the medieval period. Documents for Henry VII (1485–1509) included many grants from the king to subjects he wished to reward for service 'for repressing of our rebelles' (i.e. helped him when he usurped the throne). These grants took the form, usually for life, of the posts of parker, forester, bailiff, master of game, etc.: William Grene became parker of Wyldgolet, Essex; John Cheverell became parker of Ramesham, Dorset; and Christopher Savage became Master of Game and parker of Fekneham (Fekenham) Forest, Worcestershire. Savage's brother James became keeper of the Park of Beskewode (Bestwood), Nottinghamshire, and another brother John, a knight, among other grants, became parker of Hanley, Blakemore, Ridmarley and Bussheley, and Master of Game at Malvern, Gloucestershire.[50] Scattered throughout Henry's lands, dozens of other grants were made for similar positions.

WORKING THE FOREST HUNTING GROUNDS

The privileged enjoyed three types of hunting: casual hunting as the opportunity arose; formal hunting conducted on horseback following a pack of hounds; and the 'stable' hunt, shooting driven deer from butts and conducted on foot.[51]

The stable hunting, however, was not always on foot, as shown in *The Hound and the Hawk*: ideally it was (with) three archers and three horsemen dressed in green to merge with the vert. When deer were located the role of the horse was crucial as the horsemen rode downwind from deer with a brachet hound carried on the horse's crupper. The archers walked alongside, concealed by the horses and stopped one by one to position themselves, while the riders moved by fits and starts as the horses grazed, working in a circle called in French *metre le bestes autour*. Once they were upwind the horsemen edged ever closer. This was considered the most productive form of hunting for meat.[52] The shooting from the butts variety would have been done more for sport, if it can be called so with this method! Edward I's wardrobe accounts for 1285/6 hint at this type of hunting with horses. Two horses were purchased, one called Rudde, probably a chestnut, for Walter Sturton at 43s 5d, the other a black at 46s 8d for Peter Cornhall. Both men were employed as beaters on the royal hunt.[53]

The casual hunt could be on foot but was more often conducted on horseback. In the extremely peripatetic lifestyle of most royals and aristocrats there were plenty of occasions for hunting; hounds and hawks were always part of a medieval progress, whether it was a peaceful perambulation or a military progress. Apart from the social and royal hunts the greatest need was to provide meat for the huge royal and baronial households, and, in

Medieval 'hunt servants'.

Falconry, showing three stages: the hooded bird; the bird's hood just removed; and the falcom being cast.

times of war, venison to be salted and sent overseas as part of stores accompanying the baggage train, as shown above by the Black Prince's *Register* (see p. 75).

Hounds hunted by scent or by sight. Scent hounds were the lymers (leashed hounds), bercelets, brachets, raches and harriers. Sight hounds were the greyhounds, wolfhounds and alaunts, the latter big powerful hounds used in boar hunting. In charge of scent hounds was the berner, of the greyhounds the fewterer (vewtrer), and of the bercelets the berselleter. On hunting duty with the scent hounds was the cacheken (*the chasse chien*).[54] According to Gaston Phoebus, in his *Master of Game*, an alaunt was a dimwitted hound so savage its handlers and the hunting horses were as much at risk as its quarry.[55] Foxhounds were also used and Edward I had a pack of thirty hunted by William Foxhunter.[56]

Some idea of the part hunting and horses played in medieval life can be gathered from the royal accounts and the Black Prince's *Register*. In May 1285 Edward I and his huge household crossed to Wissant from Dover. It was the beginning of several years' absence from England during which he travelled in leisurely fashion to Paris, hunting as he went. Once there he did homage for his French possessions and entered into negotiations over Gascony. Subsequently he spent three years in Gascony, not returning to England until August 1289.

The wardrobe accounts for these years 1285/6 and 1286–89 have separate rolls for falconry and hunting expenses.[57] The horse appears in these accounts mainly as an aid for falconers and huntsmen to ride when performing their duties. Other uses for horses were to carry foxhounds at 3*d* per day per horse. Two mounted huntsmen each with two horses received 1*s* per day per man when sent into Essex, presumably to hunt for the royal pot. Expenses of a mounted man, of Sir Jollano Bavant's retinue, hunting herons with the king's gyrfalcon, were 9*d* a day. Sir Jollano received 2*s* per day for travel with the king's gyrfalcon; his son Robert, for the same duty, received 1*s* and Robert's brother with a royal falcon received 9*d*. Sir Jollano also had three lanner falcons, a brachet and several greyhounds belonging to the king in his care.[58] The payments set out the standing of men employed, being tied to the rates of pay for knights and men-at-arms at the 2*s* and 1*s* rates, and as a plain mounted man received the same fee for hunting with a raptor as Sir Jollano's son, who was at least a member of minor nobility, it would seem that the standing of raptors is also represented in the payments, the gyrfalcon being the more prestigious bird.

Many other costs relating to equines that were not warhorses appear in the accounts which show that in 1286 1,000 were shipped out of Dover and the same number brought back in 1289.[59] As many horse purchases and other costs for shipping low numbers of horses are also scattered throughout the accounts, and costs for hiring horses in France are also shown, one wonders whether the exact 1,000 out and back was a 'job lot' contract at 4*s* 8*d* each, and not the actual number shipped at what may have been more per head. There was also a considerable number of items showing *restor* (replacing dead horses). The main equine categories were cart and sumpter horses, but palfreys and coursers show more often than destriers, indicating much travel and recreational horse usage.

Other equine expenses directly bearing on hunting were the purchase and/or hire of horses for other hunt servants. Richard the ferreter was supplied with a packhorse to carry the rabbits his little animals caught.[60] There are other references to ferrets and presumably a packhorse was only needed occasionally. For falconers and austringers they were used on a regular basis, and the accounts suggest that these horses were sometimes hard-pressed. The costs of these horses was generally low at £2; sometimes, as above, a few shillings more. One was purchased for an austringer and two others for falconers whose previous mounts had died in service. An exception to the cheap horse was the £3 paid for a rouncy to equip a riding forester.[61] These hirings and purchases were in addition to those bought for the beaters and to the costs shown in the falconry and hunting account rolls.

Records for the Palatinate of Chester between 1351 and 1365 have many items dealing with aspects of hunting; although the horse is rarely mentioned, its use is suggested as the activities could not have proceeded without it. These records show that it was not only the landowner who was rapacious; his staff, among others, turned the tables. Robert de Leghe, riding forester appointed to the Forest of Macclesfield, was fined because his mother acquired the Manor of Macclesfield without licence.[62] This suggests that such a licence could have been granted if applied for (or not), and highlights the seniority of a riding forester.

Other abuses stemmed from a much higher social strand. In 1351 the Black Prince granted the abbot and monks of Vaureal the privilege of hunting fox and hare in his Forest of Delamere providing they did not disturb his other game. Later the same year we find the abbot had allowed others to hunt there and the prince had forbidden him 'to allow no living man henceforth to hunt there privily, on pain of forfeiture of all that he can forfeit'. In April of the same year the prince relented towards Vaureal – just one among other abbeys, including St Werburge, Oestre, Cumbremere and Dieulencresce – because they '. . . are so excessively burdened by the frequent visits of people of the country with grooms, horses, and greyhounds . . .' He decreed 'no such visits or charges fall on them henceforth'.[63] Clearly here was a situation where the prince and the county aristocracy had abused the hospitality of these abbeys, and the initial grant of hunting privileges to the monks was a 'you scratch my back' scenario, until Vaureal's abbot went too far.

Even the minor nobility, or rather their teenage sons, flouted custom and authority. In 1361 the Earl of Richemont complained to the Black Prince that the son of Sir Hugh Venables and others had poached five tame harts in the earl's wood of Northwode. The earl petitioned that if found guilty they not be allowed to go free without special order from the prince.[64] This was a case of the Earl of Richemont owning woods within the boundaries of the prince's forest. As the larger game was not the earl's (unless permitted to hunt by licence) maybe the complaint was made to register that the loss of game was not his fault, or maybe he was infuriated at what today would be likened to hooliganism.

The most illuminating section in the Palatinate of Chester records on forest administration concerns William de Stanlegh (riding) forester in Wyrhall (Wirral) Forest who claimed for himself and his heirs a great many rights:

(1) to hunt hares and foxes year round.
(2) to have six walking sergeants under him who shall be given food everywhere in Wirral, except at the four manors of the abbot of Cestre at Estham, Bromburgh, Hyrb, and Sutton.
(3) to have in fawning season escape moneys for all cattle taken in a wood.
(4) the shoulder of every beast taken in his bailiwick . . . and hide and offal of any wounded beast.
(5) all pelf [pilfered goods/spoil] in any house searched where poaching of venison was suspected, if such be found.
(6) provision of a horse by the town nearest to where a wounded animal was found so that the venison could be taken to Chester Castle.

Fifty villages/towns were named with amounts varying from 2 to 4s – a considerable sum from a tiny village in those days. These sums were to pay for the walking sergeants' food. All other townships in the Wirral area were also to contribute.

The local court and twelve jurors decided that de Stanlegh should not be allowed to keep greyhounds or running dogs in the forest, and hunting of hares and foxes was forbidden to him. All other terms were agreed, except the keeping of stolen goods (pelf) which pertained to the earl (the Black Prince), and the provision of puture (food) to the sergeants; cash was to be levied instead. When the findings were submitted to the prince he ordered all but the fines and the pelfs were to be allowed to de Stanlegh. These he kept for himself.[65]

This document illustrates the burden the preservation of game and other forest rights put upon the local people. Before the reign of Edward III (1327–77) the exaction of forest rights by the king had been a great cause of anger and unrest among the populace, but its place as a major source of revenue declined, to be superseded by parliamentary taxation.[66] The lessening of the burden must have been very gradual. Throughout the Black Prince's

Register it is clear that the prince stuck to the letter of the law, made generous gifts from the forests, and was assiduous in granting the customary perquisites of the forest to his forest servants, such as housebote and haybote – the right to take wood for house repair and hay for animals.[67]

William de Stanlegh no doubt felt his very taxing office merited his requests, as in 1365 he is reported to have taken, at the prince's orders, during the 1363 'season of grease' (Midsummer to Holyrood): eighteen harts, forty-nine bucks, one soar, three sorrels and one pricket, and during the last season of fermeson (the close season) five prickets, four hinds, thirteen does, two stags, three calves, and eleven fawns – all from Wirral Forest.[68] This shows that although hunting for sport ceased in the close season, hunting for the pot did not.

CHAPTER 8

Tournaments

Tournaments reflect two strands of human endeavour. One, easily recognized, was training for war; the other was exhibitionism in an equestrian event which drew extensive coverage from medieval 'sports reporters'. Reporters drew their inspiration from brave deeds (or idiocy) at countless tournaments, although some tales were peopled by ancient heroes, or even by mythical gallants; the equestrian facts, however, come direct from the sand of the arena. Much of value has been written on the tournament, especially by Juliet Barker. However, significantly, modern literature lacks information about the tourneyer's equine partner in their joint risky endeavours – although its appurtenances are dealt with, sometimes profusely. When it does appear briefly, although acknowledged as important, it is minus flesh, nerves, and above all temperament and mental capacity, yet these two in particular are what made success or failure possible, for without a suitable, well-trained mount, especially in the mêlée, mere adroitness with weapons was insufficient for victory.

Nowhere in medieval literature – in the occident at least, the orient being far more appreciative of equine abilities – is the horse celebrated so descriptively as in the romances and poems of the era. The equestrian detail is striking, and when noting performance and psyche of the horse there are many links with the modern era – our ways of acting and thinking may have changed, but the basic thought processes of the horse have not.

GROWTH OF THE TOURNAMENT

The earliest reference to a tournament is in 842, made in Nithard's *Histories*. At Mainz, Charlemagne's grandsons, Charles the Bald and Louis, were awaiting the arrival of Carloman, Louis' son, and his Bavarian and Alamanni soldiers prior to continuing war against their brother Lothair. Frequent 'games' were played which resembled the mêlée. Teams of equal numbers charged each other as if to attack, whereupon one team turned back as if fleeing, turned and recharged 'swinging their lances', riders taking turn and turn about to attack and flee. Discipline ensured a good, injury-free show, unlike other events when 'as often happens' injuries occurred 'even when the opponents are few and familiar to each other'.[1] Unusually for the period, Nithard was a secular writer and a warrior in Charles the Bald's retinue. He described what clearly was not an isolated incident.

The first set of tournament rules came in 934, drawn up by Emperor Henry I of Germany. Entry was restricted to the upper classes and infringement of the rules meant a tourneyer forfeited his horse.[2] The author and date have been challenged: some German writers place it 100 years later under another Henry; the French quote the *Chronicle of Tours* which states that Geoffrey, Lord of Preville in Anjou, invented the tournament. As far as England goes it came over about sixty years after the Norman Conquest, although it had been popular in Normandy and France well before Bastard William's usurpation of the English throne.[3]

The House of Anjou, in common with other noble houses, had a long history of involvement with the tournament. In 960 Count Geoffrey of Anjou fought on horseback against the Danish champion Ethelwulf whom he killed, beheaded, and took his horse.[4] His descendant Geoffrey Plantagenet, father of Henry II of England, was knighted in 1128 at the young age of fifteen, the event marked with a tournament. Geoffrey's armour and weapons were first rate, double-thickness mail, jewelled helmet, ash spear tipped with Poitevin iron and a sword reputedly forged by the mythical Weyland; his Spanish horse was 'wonderfully fleet and poised, and graceful in his speed'. The jam-packed mêlée was between Bretons, Geoffrey's side, and Normans with 'foot bruised by foot, and shoulder pushed back by shoulder'; horsemen were thrown, their mounts running around whinnying. Geoffrey's Bretons won. Subsequently, a huge Saxon, hearing of the tournament, came over and offered single combat in which Geoffrey killed him and took his horse, then set off for Flanders to seek competition.[5] Further down the line, in the 1450s, Rene of Anjou, titular King of Sicily, wrote one of the many books on the tournament.[6]

The popularity of the tournament increased so rapidly that in 1130 the Council of Clermont issued the first Papal ban, reiterating it on many occasions in the next 200 years. The last formal ban came in 1312 and spelled out the reasons: endangering souls, imperilling men's lives, wasting money, and destroying horses which were much needed for the crusades.[7] (In the crusades the horses were legitimately hazarded and faced starvation and sickness on top of injuries!) Penalties of excommunication and withholding burial in consecrated ground were applied not only to the tourneyer, but to his servants, grooms, etc., as well as to spectators. If a combatant was at the point of death excommunication could be reversed,[8] but with some fatal injuries death could arrive quicker than the priest. In spite of Papal fulminations tourneying and its later spin-off, jousting, flourished. In England the kings sought to control it. Henry I banned it; Stephen relaxed the ban; Henry II reimposed it; those who could not resist the challenge, risks, and excitement went abroad to tourney. In 1194 Richard I put it on a legal and financial footing that gave him some measure of control, and a lot of boodle for the treasury. He decreed tournaments could be held in only five locales, between these places: Salisbury and Wilton, Wiltshire; Warwick and Kenilworth, Warwickshire; Stamford, Lincolnshire, Warmington, Brackley and Mixbury, Northamptonshire; and Blyth and Tickhill, Nottinghamshire.

London's venue at Smithfield held tournaments on Saturdays. Participants paid entry fees – an earl 20 marks, a baron 10, a landed knight four and a landless knight two. Foreigners were excluded. Richard also decreed that the peace should not be broken, justice be unhindered, and no damage was to be done to royal forests.[9] An extra expense was a one-off payment on tourneying for the first time which covered first-time entry at the joust, but not vice versa as tourneying was considered the superior sport.[10] The law was frequently flouted by subjects holding their own events, or participating in those held by others. Sir Robert Mortimer did both. In 1195 he lost his lands and had to seek to recover them after holding an illicit event, and a year later had to seek the king's peace for participating in an event without a licence. Several times in the thirteenth century knights temporarily lost their lands for participation in tourneys: in 1302 Giles d'Argentine, an habitual offender, and six other knights, committed an even worse offence by going 'over the hill' – leaving the army in Scotland to attend a tourney in Surrey. In 1306 sixteen more knights were arrested for a similar offence.[11] This was the same d'Argentine who later led Edward II to safety from the field of Bannockburn in 1314, before returning to the fray only to be cut down. Numerous similar examples show that tourneying and jousting were as compulsive for medieval equestrians as are many equestrian events today, where the bank balance is often stretched to and beyond breaking point; royal and noble household accounts attest to a similar state of medieval financial affairs.

THE POLITICAL ASPECT

Before the joust superseded the mêlée, the political aspect could be an integral part of a tournament. In times of national unrest it gave a cover under which potential rebels could bring large armed retinues, ostensibly to boost the magnificence of a wealthy nobleman's turnout. In a flash this could threaten authority, especially at major tournaments where many powerful magnates would be present, each with a sizeable following. As a recruiting ground a major tournament also offered opportunities to a lord wishing to enlarge his armed retinue, and to tourneyers seeking prestigious employment. In the reign of Henry III (1216–72) it is significant that his most powerful rebel, Simon de Montfort, Earl of Leicester, was forbidden to attend tournaments.[12]

Victory tournaments hammered home the winning side's superiority, notably in the reign of Edward III when tournaments celebrated the successful English campaigns in Scotland during 1333/4 and 1342, and the Crécy celebrations in 1348 in which French prisoners tourneyed.[13] Joyful events were also celebrated. The Black Prince's *Register* shows tips to various yeomen who brought destriers for the Woodstock tournament held to celebrate the churching of the queen who had given birth to Thomas, later Duke of Gloucester, in 1355. Among the tourneyers were the Duke of Lancaster, the Earl of Arundel, Sir Ralph de Nevill and Lord de Percy; the Bishop of Durham also sent a yeoman with a destrier,[14] so presumably a knight of his household competed, or the horse was a gift to the prince.

TYPES OF EVENT

The original tournament consisted of a mêlée where groups of equal numbers fought each other using weapons of war. As war training it was ideal, but the aim was not to kill but to capture or batter one's adversary into submission. Nevertheless, many fatalities occurred. Starting as a massed charge with lances, it taught the value of cohesion, discipline and manoeuvrability on horseback and group tactics. When lances shattered, and/or were useless in close-order fighting, swords, axes and maces were used in one-to-one combat. As numbers diminished one man could find himself beset by several of the opposing team. A mêlée could range over a considerable stretch of countryside and include terrain suitable for ambush – houses, barns, woods and defiles; the law against taking royal game remained in force, but the farmer and peasant had no such protection against ruined crops. By the thirteenth century fenced lists or palisades were the norm; and often a town square was the venue. Once a knight had acknowledged defeat, he retired and arranged terms with his captor as to the ransom for himself, his horse, armour and weapons.[15]

By Edward I's day the mêlée had reached its high point and the joust, a combat between two individuals using only the lance, began to be the more popular event. It was also considerably less expensive to stage and outfit, and resulted in fewer fatalities. In both mêlée and jousting there were two main forms – *à plaisance*, fighting with blunted weapons, and *à outrance* where, technically speaking, knights put their lives at risk. In the former no booty or ransoms were allowed, in the latter they were, but could be ransomed back, including the sum decided for the knight's life. Eventually there were many variations on both themes. A 'Feat of Arms' developed from the joust and was fought *à outrance* using lance, sword, dagger and axe; it could be on horseback or foot, or a combination of both. When challenges to a Feat of Arms were issued the number of courses, weapons and manner of fighting were spelled out. These were popular in unsettled border areas, particularly between Scots and English, and English and French, and were always *à outrance*. Though defeat and surrender were the stated objects, fatalities were common, especially in bitter fights fuelled by national hostilities. The behourd was the informal practice joust in which armour was not always worn, and seems

A town square mêlée. Note the many horses devoid of any protection. One, on the centre left, wears a stechsack. A few are caparisoned.

A mêlée crush in a town square. Note the downed horses and knocked-back rider in the foreground. Also all combat horses are armoured.

to have been for esquires, who would later be dubbed knights. They were most frequent at festivities, as part of the pageants and general rejoicings, and were not included in the Church's ban on jousting.[16]

A clear note of Papal tolerance for the behourd is found in the *Rule of the Knights Templar*. Rule No. 128 specifically bans jousting, but rule No. 315 has several clauses concerned with galloping horses, some of which are directly aimed at the way in which brothers were permitted to behourd. If two brothers wished to do so, equipped with lances, they had to seek permission to run at half-speed and were not to throw lances because of the danger involved. If brothers wished to carry arms and run at full speed chausses had to be worn,[17] which implies that for a behourd they went unarmoured. That the Church permitted its premier fighting order to behourd indicates the sport lacked the antagonistic intent of the real joust. For the Knights Templar it was a means of keeping horses running true without flinching, in the knowledge that they would not be hurt. It enabled the knights to keep their eyes in with regard to weapons' handling and aim without undue risk to either man or mount, although of course accidents could and did happen at behourds.

TRIAL BY COMBAT

Definitely not a sport, but with the trappings of the joust, the chivalric duel was trial by combat *à outrance* when a case could not be settled at law. Fought on horseback, in armour with sword and spear, it was held only before the king, constable, marshal, and very rarely before a deputy. Such a duel could be stopped and arbitrary judgement given by the king. In 1398 a duel was held between the dukes of Hereford and Norfolk. Hereford accused Norfolk of treason for speaking against the king's honour; however, Richard II, who hated and feared Hereford because of his ambition, stopped the duel and banished both. Norfolk never returned, but Hereford did the following year when Richard II was usurped by Bolingbroke.

In such a duel the appellant (accuser) came on first, then the defender. The convicted man (the loser) was taken out of the lists and executed. The constable took the man's equipment and the marshal his horse, its tack, armour and trappings.[18] In 1395 a treason trial was scheduled to take place at Berwick between Thomas Beverlee, a Scottish esquire, and Walter Stratherne, esquire. The king funded both men, Beverlee receiving £45 to equip himself with horses, armour and other necessaries; while Stratherne received £20. Unfortunately, the records do not state the outcome, but the disparity in grants suggests where the king's sympathies lay.[19]

Hastiludes is a word which came to cover the spectrum of occidental medieval competitive equestrianism, apart from a limited amount of informal racing. One type, of which there were many similar, is an indenture and shows how a knight was engaged to serve for war, tournaments, and any of the lord's 'affairs'. On 8 November 1303 Robert le Fuiz Paen indentured with Sir Aymer de Valence, who was one of Edward I's principal commanders in the Scottish Wars. Robert agreed to stay with Aymer for the forthcoming Christmas tournament and until the following Easter, then extend his indenture for a further year. In return Sir Aymer agreed to provide 'fitting and honourable equipment for the tournament' for Robert and his two bachelors (knights) and replacement of the bachelors' two horses; robes and saddles for all three, and for Robert's son if he should be knighted within the term of the indenture. 'Diet at table' was to be provided for Robert, three valets, four bachelors, and each horse of the two esquires in the town where the tournament was to be held; en route to the tournament, food for himself, two knights and two esquires was to be provided. Sir Aymer also agreed to pay Robert £100 sterling in instalments of £20. If Sir Aymer went to other 'turnays' within the term of the indenture

Robert and his retinue were to accompany him. He also agreed to be sent on Sir Aymer's business to parliaments or 'elsewhere on his affairs', expenses paid for himself, one knight, three esquires and two sumpters, plus hay and oats for (space blank for number of horses, but more than the minimum of seven that the foregoing implies; wages for eight grooms were also to be paid while Robert remained 'on duty' as it were). Sir Aymer also agreed to legal distraint if he reneged on any part of the contract.[20]

THE HORSE'S ROLE: HIS TYPE AND SKILL

Literary works describing the equestrian element of the tournament span several centuries, from Wolfram von Eschenbach's *Parsival*, written between 1190 and 1210, and *Willehalm*, written mostly after 1221, to the fifteenth and early sixteenth centuries with its outpourings of lay writings, many of which were travellers' diaries with excellent sports coverage. Additional information on national customs, often strange to foreign travellers, adds to the broad overview as writers came from Germany, Castile, Catalonia, Bohemia, France and Brandenburg.

Maybe Gutierre Diaz de Games, standard-bearer to Don Pero Niño, Count of Buelna, in his eulogy of his master (written between 1431 and 1449, but about deeds at least as early as 1409), captures the interlocking roles of man and mount, knight and destrier or courser, both being used at tournament events:

> . . . there is no other beast which so befits a knight as a good horse. Thus have horses been found who are strong and full of energy that in the thick of battle have shown themselves so loyal to their masters as if they had been men. There are horses who are strong, fierce, swift, and faithfull, that a brave man mounted on a good horse may do more in an hour of fighting than ten or maybe a hundred could have done afoot . . .[21]

When mentioning the horses, most contemporary writers praise their size, courage, speed, etc., but few tell us what they were really like; even fewer state their breeding, and those who do assure us they were not the heavy carthorses thick in wind and mind that are the popular picture of a tournament horse.

Maybe they did become gross when armour escalated, so that the all-up weight could reach 425 lb with man, his armour, tack and horse armour – 250 lb of equipment for man and horse, *c*.175 lb for the man. These are weights taken from equipment in the Museum of Electoral Hesse.[22] But when the mêlée was the premier sport armour was lighter and the horse was not always fully armoured, or even armoured at all. And excessively heavy horses had not yet been bred. By the time the joust began to be popular, larger horses were more often bred. When the joust was at its height of compulsive participation, horsebreeding and armourers could cater for the heavyweight duo – note the bulk of Henry VIII and his efforts to import better (in his estimation, better meant bigger) breeding stock.[23] Even then animals brought in were not what we consider heavy horses, many being of Spanish and Italian breeds, though doubtless some German knights rode draught types. A horse can carry considerably more than the modern sports rider gives him credit for. My farrier was Harold Parr when I lived in the New Forest. In his youth he had been in the 14/20th King's Hussar Regiment in the early 1930s. Stationed in Egypt, War Office orders came for an endurance march. Each troop took three days to do a ninety-mile trek across shifting desert sands from Cairo to Wadi le Trunie, taking a twenty-four-hour break before doing the return trip in twelve hours, starting at 4 a.m. Each horse, of middleweight hunter stamp, carried over 300 lb; due to good management there was no attrition.

From measurements I took at the Royal Armouries, from horse armour of the late fifteenth and early sixteenth centuries,[24] it is clear horses were neither overly tall nor excessively bulky, more the stamp of a heavy hunter, but not as tall, or a heavyweight cob of 15–15.2 hh, and capable of carrying well in excess of the 300 lb noted above. The measurements I took were then compared against two of my own horses: a 14.3 hh stocky little horse, and a 16.1 hh, elegant but substantial, with no coarseness, Arab-cross Standardbred. The 14.3 hh horse was a little too small, but not by much, although the Royal Armouries armour would not have fitted the 16.1 horse, weighing *c.*1300 lb. Some of the critical measurements were: distance from cantle to dock; point of hip to point of hip across the loin; point of shoulder to wither; and across the widest point of chest. It has to be remembered, too, that under the armour went thick padding to prevent metal scalding or rubbing the skin, and to absorb some of the impact of weaponry misdirected at the horse, and certain areas of armour had to allow for considerable limb extension, so the overall outward appearance of a set of horse armour can be somewhat misleading.

A tournament horse only bore his burden for a very short time in which he used explosive energy. A palfrey or rouncy carried the peripatetic tourneyer on his annual competition circuit, the tournament horse being led at the squire's right side, hence it is considered destrier. In his book *A Knight and His Horse*, Ewart Oakshott writes that destrier could mean the horse leads with his right leg and is thus placed to veer away from the point of impact if necessary.[25] This is tenable, but I consider it doubtful such a refinement was taught to horse and rider in the crude western horsemanship of the early jousts. Some horses are naturally well balanced, even carrying weight, and can execute a flying change of leads in a sudden directional change. My reasoning on the state of early occidental horsemanship is derived from several considerations:

(1) In a mêlée such directional change would not have been called for and the mêlée was current with the use of the word destrier.
(2) Abou Bekr ibn Bedr, veterinarian and training adviser to the Mamlūk Sultan El Melik el Nacer Mohammed ibn Kalouan (1290–1340) at a time of the joust's increasing popularity, commented on the lack of equestrian skill among the 'barbarians', i.e. the Franks. He recognized the Franks' bravery, but deplored their bad seat on a horse. They needed a great space in which to manoeuvre their clumsy horses which were therefore only suitable for a head-on charge. However, he considered the Frankish lack of equestrian skill could be corrected. By schooling and a change of bit the Franks and their horses could be taught Arab skills. This was at a time when the Arabian horse and Arab trainers were *the* skilled equestrian exponents.[26]
(3) Aly ben Abderrahman ben Hodeil el Andalusy wrote an equestrian treatise by order of Sultan Mohammed VI (1392–1408) of Granada. Ibn Hodeil notes rapid directional and lead changes, saying it was a vital manoeuvre for a lancer.[27] Ibn Hodeil was writing only a few decades prior to Duarte, King of Portugal, who produced a book on horsemanship around 1434. Portuguese and Spanish horses and horsemanship are from the same mould. The Andalusian and the Lusitano have the same genetic background, and the equestrian skills of the Iberian Peninsula owe much to the long Moorish occupation, even though much was adapted to suit European needs.

PROVENANCE

Several sources indicate Spain and her connections in Sicily and southern Italy provided class tournament horses. Both the *Willehalm* and the *Parsival* refer to breeds of horses. Wolfram von Eschenbach came from northern Bavaria and entered the service of the Landgrave Herman I of Thuringia in *c.* 1200. The *Willehalm* covered the second battle of Aliscans in 803 when William of Toulouse led a flying column against the relief contingent of Moors coming from Córdoba to Barcelona, which had fallen to

Charlemagne in 801.[28] The *Parsival* is about the Legend of the Holy Grail. Both works contain much on war, tournaments and the joust, from a writer who had quite clearly experienced all three. His comments show he was knowledgeable about, understood and had empathy with horses, and his equestrian facts can be accepted as accurate.

The *Willehalm*'s equestrian content illustrates the impact of oriental equestrianism on Spain and contains several references to Castilian horses.[29] William's horse Puzzat is described as brown with white spots, i.e. an Appaloosa[30] (or what came to be termed an Appaloosa in our day). Volatin, captured from the Muslim Arofel, is variously termed Arabian, Persian, Syrian and Aragonese. This at first seems contradictory, whereas all the other equestrian facts are spot on. But when the Arabs exited Arabia in the seventh century, riding mainly on camels, they rapidly put Byzantium and Persia under their yoke, then carried the Islamic conquest into Spain. Their military commanders came from Damascus, the early Arab post-conquest capital, and Syria had long been renowned for horsebreeding. By Wolfram's era Syria had absorbed the equine element of various Turcoman tribes to add to the mix of home-bred Syrian horses, Persian infiltrates, and the horses of the Arab tribes that made Syria their tribal home, especially the Anazeh. Volatin may well represent a type of horse evolved in Spain from horses captured from the Moors; indeed, the Moors were also quick to take advantage of Spain's natural heritage of indigenous horses. The combination could have produced a distinct type.[31] Brahane is another Muslim-owned horse; the poem's translator equates it with the horse in the earlier French poem 'Aliscans' – L'Aufage Brahaigne, *aufage* being the Arabic *al faras*, meaning gelding.[32] But according to Abou Bekr, *faras* means a purebred Arabian.[33] The *Parsival*'s Arabian came from Spain; noted as a tall horse,[34] this indicates what was considered large. It is only in recent years that most purebred Arabians have increased to the 15 hh mark; the old desert-bred stock were much smaller. However, a crossbred (with a Spanish horse) could have been much larger, as hybrid vigour frequently enhances size while still retaining the dominant parent's looks. The Castilian appears repeatedly,[35] and as one of Parsival's mounts there is also a good description – a horse with long slim legs, a tough enduring physique, inured to heat and cold, so fit it never sweated (foamy sweat indicates an unfit horse, thin clear sweat a fit one). With constant work the girth never needed tightening,[36] indicating a good shoulder for holding a saddle in place, and a fit horse of the dry type. The heavy-fleshed northern types – cobs and draught horses – usually sweat profusely and lose much weight under severe work conditions. Danish and Hungarian horses are noted, but the only other tournament horse was Gringuljete, which appears with slight spelling variations in other medieval romances and is of legendary character.[37]

Gutierre Diaz de Games singles out Castilian horses as superior mounts. King Enrique of Castile:

> . . . knew all about horses; he sought for them; tended them; made much of them. In his time had no man in Castile so many good mounts; he rode them and trained them to his liking, some for war, some for parade and others for jousting.[38]

The inference drawn is that they were Castilian. Although de Games never describes Pero Niño's adversaries' mounts he implies some jousting horses were large, bulky and clumsy. The Spaniard on his lighter-framed Castilian was pitted against the French champion Jean de One who rode '. . . a strong jousting horse of great size', but due to adroit horsemanship and perfect timing, although connecting full tilt with the Frenchman's horse, it was the latter who crashed to the ground. Most telling of all is the analogy between speedy, light craft which evaded heavy shipping as 'the swift courser manoeuvres between great and heavy horses'.[39]

Tirant Lo Blanc, although a Catalan novel, incorporates much reliable background information. Favoured horses were 'mighty Sicilian chargers'.[40] The hero Tirant rode a 'much lighter horse' than his adversary.[41] A Sicilian charger suitable as a royal gift was 'tall, strong, light and a 4 y.o.'.[42] Other horses were from Tuscany and Lombardy.[43] In that era the Spanish presence and the frequent dispatch of Spanish horses into Sicily meant a strong Andalusian element in Sicily's horses – a trend that was marked in the Neapolitan breed. Lombard and Tuscan horses are well illustrated in works by Leonardo da Vinci and show the Spanish influence in a class horse, with good body mass, but retaining quality.

From engravings by Albrecht Dürer and Lucas Cranach we can see the type of animal favoured by Germanic jousters – heavier by far, with the draught blood evident in feather at the heels and the broad, flatter hooves, but they are not of the huge drayhorse stamp.

There was a lively trade in horses, with dealers scouring many lands for them. Studs produced some of the tourneyer's needs, and they bought in when necessary.

THE HORSE'S PARTNER

The tourneyer took his string with him and this could be diminished by frequent horse fatalities and severe injuries, which are mentioned all too often; the string could also expand or contract according to the knight's proficiency.

THE HORSE'S PARTNER: SOME FAMOUS KNIGHTS

The legendary Parsival had a winning lance, gathering a remuda of over fifteen horses at one tournament, all of which he gave away to his attendant squires. The fact that all were unwounded implied his fair play and accurate weapon delivery.[44] Striking a horse brought disqualification according to the 1466 rules, drawn up by John Tiptoft, Earl of Worcester, based on earlier customs.[45]

An outstanding tourneyer was William Marshall who, riding a borrowed horse, started a glamorous and lucrative career in 1167 by winning nine horses, shared equally between himself and his esquires. Teaming up later with another proficient knight, they captured 103 knights, their horses, equipment and baggage in the ten-month period between Pentecost and Lent.[46]

Marshal Jean de Boucicaut the younger won fame in battle and tourney. In May 1390 he, Regnault de Roye and Jean de Sempy, held a month-long tourney at St Inglevert. Froissart catalogues feats run in the four days during which the English took up the challenge, relating that the three Frenchmen fought more than forty Englishmen for a total of 136 lances.[47] Actual details were that about forty other foreign knights also attended. Only thirty-nine *venants* eventually fought the French. No serious injuries were recorded and after the four days no further knights took up the challenge.[48]

DANGERS TO JOUSTERS

Hard knocks did not necessarily result in immediate damage to knights constantly being battered around the head. Because the helm was a prime target many knights were unhelmed, the faces of many knights being bruised, cut, and generally bludgeoned; of those who were helmed, some were killed with lance points entering the eye slits. During one of the St Inglevert courses Boucicaut was hit so hard on the helm by Sherborne that he was unhelmed and got a violent nosebleed.[49] In 1559 Henri II of France was killed as a result of a splinter from a shattered lance going through his visor and entering his temple.[50] Other deaths too numerous to mention occurred from a great variety of injuries.

On a lighter note was the joust between two notable knights in the early sixteenth century: Frederick, Palsgrave of the Rhine, and Charles de Lannoy, Seigneur de

Maingoval. A quarrel arose over a stupid matter – whether music was a manly pursuit. Frederick said it was, others disagreed, so a three-a-side joust was determined to settle the point. Frederick's opponent was de Lannoy. Both were armoured to the knees and used only blunt lances and blunt but heavy swords. Frederick landed a terrific blow on de Lannoy's arm which brought an outcry as it was against the rules of the tourney, since combatants could only strike at the head. Frederick countered by saying 'why then do you not keep your head still where I can hit it instead of bobbing it backwards at every stroke?' for this also was against the rules. Frederick then dealt him a blow on the temple which sent de Lannoy back in his saddle and Frederick would have leaped the barrier and continued had not Emperor Charles V intervened. When de Lannoy and his comrades removed their helms their lips and cheeks were 'swollen with rage'.[51] For 'rage' read, most likely, heavy bruising. Many knights must have had injuries similar to those suffered by boxers – i.e. were punch drunk.

Jousters needed to be supreme athletes. One of those for whom we have physical evidence of excess activity was Bartholomew de Burghersh, prominent in Edward III's diplomacy. On one occasion at Reims he was challenged by a French knight to a fight *à outrance*. In the fight one Frenchman was killed and two others wounded by the lance. Recent investigations on de Burghersh's tomb at Walsingham, Norfolk, revealed he was 5 ft 10 in tall, of an erect and powerful build with broad shoulders and a narrow waist. His right side and arm were markedly more developed than his left. Evident was a fracture of two ribs, a twisted ankle, and some wear on the right elbow joint. For a man in his fifties he was in remarkably good fettle, showing little evidence of the common medieval incidence of arthritis, and he had almost a full set of very worn teeth.[52]

Boucicaut was a supreme athlete and exhibitionist. Several feats are chronicled. Two strong arm exploits indicate the height of some horses used in tournament and war:

> item: he leapt onto a courser without placing his foot in the stirrup, fully armed . . .
> item: placing one hand on the saddle pommel of a great courser and the other near the horse's ears, seizing the mane, he leapt from the ground through his arms and over the horse . . .[53]

These moves are similar to some trick-riding done today with a western saddle equipped with a high horn, which would have matched the height of a tournament/war saddle. To be able to reach up and grip such a high pommel and mount, or vault over the horse's back as in the second feat, a man would need great strength in his arms, tremendous spring in his legs, split-second timing and a horse of a height that enabled the man to bear down with his arms to achieve extra elevation over the animal's back. Doing a pre-Fosbury Flop high jump, 6 ft would have been an award-winning achievement for an athlete.[54] An excessively tall horse with the added height of the saddle pommel to take into account would have meant the man could not press down for added leverage. Boucicaut's horse cannot have been much above 15 hh.

COSTS OF TOURNEYING

Many accounts remain in which tournament costs are registered. Edward I, before becoming king, was an avid tourneyer, being blooded at Blyth in 1256 and going on the French circuit in 1260, but not too successfully according to the Dunstable annalist who recorded that he was wounded and lost most of his and his retinue's armour and horses. The *restauro* payments were not completed until 1285/6. As king he held many celebratory tournaments, such as those at Nefyn in 1284 at the conclusion of the Welsh War and in 1302 at Falkirk.[55]

The account roll for the 1278 Windsor behourd, or *Justus of Pees*, survives. Requirements for the event are set out, including the knights' armour and weapons; plus an armourer with hammer, pincers, nails and anvil whose job must have been on-the-spot repairs; judging by his tools he was equally well equipped to reshoe a horse, which was to be a 'good courser, newly shodde and waring a softe bitte'. There was to be 'a grete halter for the reyne of the bridell', a well-stuffed saddle fitted with a pair of 'jambus' (these must have been an early type of integral armour for the rider's legs and later this developed into the saddle for the German *Hohenzeuggestech* which incorporated a stomach-to-foot shield), three double-girths with double-buckles and a double-'singull' (surcingle) with double-buckles, 'a rayne of lethir hungry tied from the horse hede unto the girthis beneth between the ferthir bouse of the horse for renasshyng, a rynnyng patrel, a croper of lethir hungrye'. When a horse is exerting maximum energy with his respiratory tract working overtime his barrel expands by several inches, thus putting enormous pressure on leatherwork, especially when the horse was set on its haunches at point of lance impact, exerting a snatch effect on girth fastenings. Hence the need for several stout girths and the additional protection of a surcingle to go over the saddle. The strap from head to girth is a standing martingale to stop the horse throwing his head in excitement, or fighting against bit restraint. Doing so could impair the knight's aim, or even strike his helm. The 'patrel' and 'croper' protected chest, flank and haunch. Over all went a trapper. Two mounted- and six foot servants were to attend each knight.

The king provided all entrants with armour of gilded leather, consisting of a tunic, surcoat, ailettes, crest, shield and leather helmet. The thirty-eight swords bought were of whalebone; twelve helmets for senior knights were gilded, the rest silvered. Pommels and hilts of swords were gilded. Milo the currier fashioned thirty-eight pieces of leather to resemble horse's heads – presumably leather chamfrons. There were other gewgaws – little bells to jingle on horses' harness; fancy leather for crests; and cruppers; silk cords for tying on the ailettes. Total cost for these came to £80 11*s* 8*d*. Among other purchases from

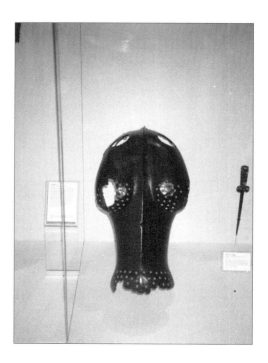

The Warwick chamfron.

Paris was a clutch of richly embroidered saddles made by Felis the saddler: eight with the royal arms, four for coursers. Five saddles were bought for Robert Tibetot, John de Neele, Imberti Guidonis, John de Grely, and the Count of Cornwall. John de Grely's saddle cost the huge (for the time) sum of 38 pounds parisis (£9 10s). All five were embroidered with the arms of respective knights. A variety of more moderate saddles were bought for sumpters and mules. Paris costs were £447 12s 5d.[56]

Longshanks' grandson Edward III was extravagant in his participation in and funding of tournaments. In 1343 his household accounts register costs of £15 per day, but for jousting at Dunstable they rocketed to £317.[57] At that event 135 named knights took part.[58]

EDWARD I'S SONS-IN-LAW: JOHN OF BRABANT AND JOHN OF BRITTANY

The accounts for 1285/6 and 1286–89, the period of Edward's sojourn in France and Gascony, have many entries for the two youngsters. Possibly John of Brabant, who joined the household in 1285, was too young to tourney immediately, but he lived with the royal children at King's Langley and enjoyed hunting, hawking and, eventually, jousting.[59]

John of Brittany appeared in both sets of accounts and must have been a tourney addict as most of his expenses relate directly to his tournament costs. £7 0s 7d covered (some) saddlery and armour purchased and hackneys hired to transport it from London to tournaments at Warwick, Wynton and Reading. Other hackneys were hired to go from London to the event at Kingston, and others bought ready for John's arrival from Bedford and Warwick.[59] Other equipment for the Reading tournament cost £13 6s 8d, plus £2 as John's 'pocket money'. Expenses at Reading and Bedford ran up another £48 8s 5d. Wight, the king's palfreyman, was paid for looking after two of the king's destriers from Ringwood, Hampshire, to be loaned to John for tournaments at Bedford and Kingston. Other expenses were incurred taking John's equipment to the Croydon tournament; and he and his knight companion purchased more equipment for Croydon costing £11 6s 8d. Other frequent expenses were for minor tack items. A sumpter costing £6 13s 4d was purchased for him,[60] quite pricey for a pack animal considering some saddlehorses cost under £10. A white horse cost £5 but the king lashed out on two great horses for John to compete on at the Tours tournament, the pair setting him back £52 10s. John's expenses for this event and another at Libourne were £20.[61] All in all, John of Brittany was a pretty busy lad on the circuit. There are no instances, in these accounts at any rate, of horses needing medical attention for sickness or injury so maybe he was successful, as all other ailing horses connected with the Edwardian household have the costs of medicine, care and place of recuperation noted in the accounts, and there were many such. It is pleasing to note their welfare was of concern to the royal household.

THE HORSE'S MENTAL AND PHYSICAL CAPACITIES

Horses selected for the mêlée and joust needed different physical and mental attributes. It is significant that as the joust developed, with increasingly larger lances and more protective and heavier plate armour for man and horse, so that the outfit for the joust and for war were no longer interchangeable, a horse was needed with a temperament and physique more suited to the stupid aim of bowling over horse and rider with the combined force of speeding horse and aggressive rider. In Tiptoft's system of scoring, unhorsing an opponent or bringing horse and rider down gained the highest score.[62]

In the mêlée horses were grouped together and operated under herd instincts, which elicited different responses. The use only of stallions ensured that shirking the issue was not such a problem, for once connection was made much of the horse's natural aggression would surface – there is only room for one mature entire in a group under normal herd conditions; unlike today when stallions are selected for amenable dispositions (among other attributes), an aggressive horse would be better suited to war and tournament. Training and severe bitting channelled aggression to the rider's advantage, with knight against knight, and to an extent stallion against stallion, yet with the overriding control of the knight. The excitement of speed, the constant flow of movement and the squeals of rage triggered by close contact increased the aggression. Stallion fights are usually prefaced by tentative nose sniffing, then squealing before the horses erupt.

The mêlée was unlikely to feature a balking horse; the only time they retired was in allotted sectors for knights to spell themselves and/or their mounts. Any injuries sustained by mêlée horses, unless totally incapacitating, would not immediately register as painful enough to back off – rather the reverse. Watch any two horses fighting; biting, powerful kicks with the hind feet and striking with the forefeet spur them on. Only later, when separated and tempers are calmed, do the injuries begin to stiffen and the pain register. However, though fatalities and injuries to horses were inevitable they would have been avoided where possible: horses of the right calibre were expensive, and no knight wanted a crippled horse as a prize!

Jousting one-to-one needed more precise training and a different type of courage; no herd instincts were available to the horse who faced its master's opponent solo. Incidents of shying off target were far more common and to be expected, particularly if the horse was not a novice; for after its first few encounters, it would anticipate impact poundage, concentrated in the back and mid-section of its anatomy, and the wrenching strain on its hocks in an abrupt, or even sliding halt. If and when overturned, the experienced horse would most probably have suffered wrenches in the back and loin muscles, resulting in prolonged lameness, as well as massive bruising from a fall at speed. When, as they occasionally did, heads connected, the injuries would have been in the head and neck; if the neck was severely twisted in the wither area the horse could have become very lame in the forehand. The most pernicious and difficult to diagnose lamenesses are not in the lower limbs, but in the shoulder, back and loin areas.

Froissart gives several examples when horses shied off course, their paths crossed, or they refused to charge. Added traumas were horses being stopped dead in their tracks by the force of blows where lances bent but did not break, and by blows so hard horses' forelegs were jerked off the ground.[63] The tournament at St Inglevert near Calais was held prior to the appearance of the tilt, which came into use via Spain and Portugal before becoming common in France around 1430. At first a flimsy cloth on a barrier, the tilt quickly developed into a padded wooden barrier.[64] This helped reduce accidents but horses still got overturned or severely jolted.

Another Holy Grail poem has the unknown writer cramming as many dangers in as possible. Destriers staggered under the weight of the armoured knight; knight and horse roll over 'all of a heap'; Lancelot pierces his opponent's shield, pins his arm to his side, and brings horse and rider down; two horses hurtle together so hard that both fall, and both riders perish from spear thrusts in the heart; horses stumble and almost fall. Injuries to the knights include a broken leg, broken collar bone and loss of blood. Knights are beaten back over the cantle, which must have resulted (in real life) in at least bad bruising, maybe kidney damage, and on occasion a broken back. In a mêlée unhorsings, tramplings, injuries and deaths were the casualty crop.[65]

THE HORSE'S BEHAVIOUR

Having felt these injuries no wonder horses became nervous and unreliable. Success depended as much on the mount as on the rider's expertise. And, it must be said, aggression of the rider could be transferred to some degree to the horse, provided it was of a courageous nature in the first place. A steady rider could hold a nervous and/or exciteable horse (not the same thing) together. Inevitably though, providing the horse's first engagement was not his last through injury or from totally funking it, temperament would quickly sort the destriers into courageous, honestly dependable or dodgy customers. The increasing use of cold-bloods to gain body mass also tended to produce a more placid animal, but also one not so readily manoeuvrable because of his bulk and lack of breed agility: hence De Games' comments above.

In his book on horsemanship Duarte of Portugal wrote a lengthy section on jousting: on lack of confidence he lists four reasons for failure. All affect the horse's performance:

(1) Wanting to avoid the encounter.
(2) Veering away, fearing the moment of encounter.
(3) Failure to keep body and lance steady because of the effort required.
(4) They are so anxious to gain an advantage over their adversary that they end up failing.

In respect of Nos. 1 and 2: A horse always senses a rider's hesitation; this tells the horse he can shirk, so he shies. With regard to No. 3: If the weight on a horse's back is unstable it will deflect him from his path. Finally, No. 4: The horse senses an overeager rider and anticipates by performing what he *assumes* the rider will instruct him to do, thus causing him to mistime or misplace his thrust because he has to divide his attention between keeping the horse in check and sighting down his lance onto target.

Similar equestrian elements can be seen today and illustrate the implications. A nervous rider approaching a high fence will not fool the horse who will react by refusing dead in front of the obstacle or by running around the wings. If the horse relishes jumping he may do so but will be hampered by an ineffective rider. Smart and keen horses are prone to anticipation. I have owned several horses used for western riding events that have manoeuvres performed in sequence. With one exceptionally talented horse I learned not to train in sequence but to do individual manoeuvres when he least expected it. When working cattle this horse thought for himself! Another, a competent but very dull mare, never anticipated, did the minimum required, but satisfactorily. I would suggest the latter temperament would have been suited to the joust; the former type worked in partnership, and would have been better suited to a mêlée. Some horses are so sensitive and highly schooled that according to how one indicates by weight displacement a lead or directional change can be achieved .

Other elements producing poor jousting were discomfort in the saddle and an insecure seat. Duarte recommends a saddle neither too wide nor too tight, which was to be cut deep where the legs went; it was to be well padded and designed so it neither threw the rider forwards nor backwards. An upright posture and long stirrups were advised. A saddle that throws the rider forwards puts excess weight on the horse's forehand; one that throws the rider back puts excess weight on the loin area, the weakest part of the horse's anatomy – and it also puts the rider behind the horse's motion. Some extant medieval war and tournament saddles are ill-designed for maintaining a clean back. The saddle for the *Hohenzeuggestech* resembles a perch with an encasing cage – it may be good for staying on board, but it is hell on horses' and riders' backs.

Other equine faults stemmed from bad collection and bad bit handling:

. . . a horse must be easy to control with the bit or the spurs; it should not be unruly, stop suddenly, or be so restless as to hinder the jousting rider. This can be remedied by being a little harder on the bit, but not so much that the horse shies or throws its head down; and you must not be heavy on the spurs, which should be short and blunt.

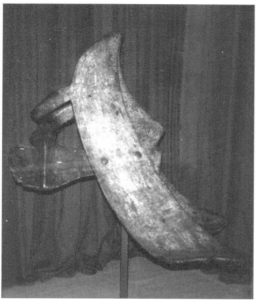

Totally encasing jousting saddle with integral stomach and thigh proection.

This advice shows that Duarte was either a talented horseman himself, or understood what was needed to be one; most of his advice would be acceptable today. It suggests he recommended moderation in severity and type of bit. Some excessively severe medieval bitting would incite a horse to rebel against pain in the mouth and induce head-throwing, rearing, and even bolting; or the mouth would eventually become so hard that the horse would bog his head, bore on the bit and ignore restraint. Some spurs were hardly short and blunt! Possibly Edward I understood moderation well when he ordered that coursers for the Windsor behourd were to wear a 'softe bitte'.

Horses for the joust were often difficult to procure. It was not unusual for one prince to loan destriers to another. In 1496 letters between Friedrich of Brandenburg and a Count Philip highlight several aspects of the joust. Friedrich replied to Philip's request for a loan of horses saying he only had two horses for himself; a chestnut that was so exhausted after travelling from Worms to Brandenburg that it was not fit enough to compete at a recent Nuremberg joust, but he was willing to let Philip borrow his stallion from Waldeck. He warned that it was inclined to bolt and hoped Philip could control it, adding that the horse was not to be lent to anyone else. This interchange illustrates the distances horse travelled between events. It is 300-plus miles, as the crow flies, from Worms to Brandenburg, a distance that would tire a heavy horse more than a lighter-framed animal more suited to an endurance march. The warning about the bolting horse reinforces the overbitting problem; the request that the horse not be lent to another suggests the animal was potentially good but a bit of a rogue, only too clever in taking advantage of an unwary rider, and that Friedrich realized the horse's vice would be that much harder to circumvent if it got the better of a succession of jousters.

Duarte condemned any jouster whose horse was brought to them in the lists and which needed another servant to prod it into action – surely the phlegmatic cold-blooded type. His ideal was a knight skilled in riding techniques who could place his horse where and when needed. He reasoned that if the knight was a passenger he could not control his lance even though the horse charged very fast. The mind boggles at the thought that some knights, a few bricks short of a load, even attempted to joust if they were such inept horsemen![66]

Ludwig von Eyb the younger, who was master of the household to the Palsgrave Frederick, afterwards the Elector Frederick II, composed an illustrated tournament book while at Frederick's court. In 1507 he wrote the biography of Wilwolt of Scaumberg who toured the German tournament circuit. Von Eyb's descriptions show many customs, some points disliked by Duarte, the atmosphere, complete with noisy equine rage, sweat and dust, and some unintentional humour.

A quarrel arose between Martin Zolner and Wilwolt which resulted in a fight:

> no sooner had the combatants been packed into their respective corners of the ground and the cords been cut, than Wilwolt's servant seized his master's horse by the reins and piloted him up to Martin Zolner, who being taken wholly by surprise, was without difficulty bound and bridled. This done up came all Wilwolt's friends and together they dragged the culprit off his tilting saddle; even up to his spurs, laid him on the back of his horse, beat him on the stomach till he fell to the ground, heaved him up again, and finally cut the girths and set him astride the lists on his saddle, even like a man who has earned the tournament penalty.

The impression is of foul play, two rather slow-witted knights and an even dumber horse standing while blows were rained on its rider. A horse's normal reaction, as it would not reason that it was not going to be struck, would be to retreat, but if the horse were a stallion it would be risky as some entires, rather than being cowed, turn aggressive.

A tournament at Stuttgart, again sparked by a quarrel, was between Margrave Frederick of Brandenburg and Lord Jorg of Rosenberg. Some 125 Brandenburgers and thirty-five of Lord Jorg's men, termed The Unicorns, set-to:

> no sooner were the ropes cut than the Brandenburgers were urged forward, but the Unicorns held to their corner, and defied all the efforts of the Margrave to break it. The throng became so dense the horses 'squealed like pigs', and the cloud of sweat so thick the ladies looking down from windows could hardly see the fight. Wilwolt was flanked on his right by Rosenberg and on his left by Diez Marshalk; and they were so hard pressed that soon all were unhorsed, prostrate, their tilting helms and themselves so severely trampled they came near to death.

Then came a break for the downed knights to be lifted back onto their horses:

> The Margrave then planned to attack in three groups, front, back and sides, and chose to be first to the fray to impress the ladies. He was trapped by the Unicorns closing behind his horse, and was then unhorsed. The Unicorns permitted the sergeants to come and pick the Margrave up, but he was so firmly attached to his saddle that they had to cut the girths to free him. He was set on the lists saddle and all, and his barebacked horse led away. When a Unicorn offered to give him a pick-up lift behind him Frederick refused because of the ignominy.[67]

These two escapades in which Wilwolt was engaged are definitely humorous, but one recounted about the Palatine Frederick is decidedly darker. As a result of the fight already noted Frederick's enemies sought to bring him down through a fight *à outrance* between the challenger Seigneur de Glayon and Frederick.

You shall choose out the best and strongest horses, whereon you shall lay high and deep saddles, and in these you shall sit up to the girdle clad in the heaviest arms and armour, so that it shall not be possible to be dislodged from the horse by the lance or pole . . . therewith the one runs at the other, and they strike one another as they can. If neither of them miss or swerve or loose the bridle – which is the most important matter of all – or fall backwards, then must the horse, of necessity and not without sore peril to the rider, tumble right back . . . Glayon to avoid the spear leaned a little to one side, though he afterwards declared it was his horse that was to blame. The blow caught him (Glayon) sideways on the shield so mightily that horse and rider fell together to the ground . . . and his horse (Frederick's) – whether terrified by the shock he had suffered, or feeling freed from the burden of the spear which the Palsgrave had cast from him – came down on its knees and fell right over squeezing the rider so sorely in his high saddle that a portion of his spine was damaged . . . Palsgrave Frederick so soon as he came again upon his horse, swung his arm aloft and gave her (Lady Eleonore, Charles V's sister) thereby to understand that naught was amiss with him. Though verily he did but counterfeit this, and must needs hide the pain in his back as best he might.

Afterwards de Glayon complained that all his body felt as if beaten; he felt the effects for the rest of his life. His physicians attributed his death (when it came) to this tilt. Frederick took to his bed for a lengthy period, and was never thereafter completely free of pain.[68]

Much more could be written about the horse's part in the tournament, but these passages reveal some hazards, though various rules helped minimize some dangers. Armour gave both horse and man some protection, the most remarkable pieces being the stomach-to-thigh shield, an integral part of the saddle, and the huge padded buffer from Germany call the *Stechsack*, which the horse wore like an enormous peytral around his neck and chest.

The reality of the joust: injured and mentally traumatized horses.

CHAPTER 9
Medieval Postal Services

Riding post in oriental and Asiatic spheres was better organized than in Europe where each monarch employed messengers, such as the English *nuncii regis*, who rode their own horses or hired animals at need.

THE FRANKISH KINGDOMS

Charlemagne's *missi dominici* had a multiple role, carrying information and inspecting conditions and hearing cases throughout his realm. The system contracted as counts appointed their own *missi*. Charlemagne's grandson, Charles the Bald, started a transalpine system of horse and foot couriers between France and Italy. *Caballarii*, serfs owing riding and cartage service to their lord, also supplied a courier service; *para veredarii* supplied similar services; *sindmanni* provided horsed courier and carriage (of light goods); *scaremanni* and *scararii* were armed retainers performing similar services on horseback, foot, or by boat.[1]

The Abbey of St Wandrille at Noyon was obliged, under the terms of an 854 land grant by Charles the Bald, to keep post horses,[2] and as religious houses were often endowed with land by the ruling house it was surely not the only establishment so obligated.

ANGLO-SAXON, NORMAN AND PLANTAGENET ENGLAND

Riding services were owed as in the Frankish kingdoms. When Bishop Oswald of Worcester granted leasehold of Church lands to certain thegns, one service demanded was delivery of the bishop's messages. Prior to the Norman Conquest superior peasants called *geneats* owed riding services.[3] This continued post-Conquest as shown in the Domesday Book where freemen had to provide escort and riding duty (see ch.1).

Under the Plantagenets, in addition to the *nuncii regis* system, horses could be commandeered. The 1392 *Calendar of Close Rolls* notes that Henry Draper was arrested at Northampton because, when the king's messengers came through the town, 'he withdrew himself and his horse, delaying the king's business in contempt of the king'. This shows that countrywide commandeering operated, and we can be sure avoidance was equally assiduous. However, a patent of 1396 regulating horse-hire payments on the Dover to London route (see below) clarifies that there was already a regular service, in this area at least. Pre-1396 the charge per stage was 1*s* 4*d*. This proved excessive, and there were other complaints. London hackneymen Thomas Athecok and Reginald Shrewsbury grumbled:

> Divers men passing through these parts take the horses against their will paying little or nothing . . . often lost or sold or taken quite away (the horses).

The king therefore ordains by this patent that there shall be taken for the hire of a *hakenei* from Southwark to Rochester 12d; from Rochester to Canterbury 12d; Canterbury to Dover 6d; and from town to town according to the rate of 12d. and the number of miles; that the petitioners be in no wise compelled to let their horses for hire unless paid promptly and that for the better security of the horses a branding iron be kept in each of those towns by an approved person for branding without payment, horses on hire.

A 1397 Act reiterated the abuses, and threatened imprisonment to:

people of evil condition which, of their own authority take and cause to be taken royally horses and other things . . . saying and devising that they be to ride on hasty messages and business, where of truth, they be in no wise privy to any business or messages.

A nationwide system with regular staging posts had to wait until the Tudor era.[4]

One super-efficient system, with every aspect of their organization harshly regulated, was the Teutonic Knights' communication network. Light, swift 'letter ponies' appear in records of various commanderies, and under the heading *Draught Horses and Letter Ponies* Elbing alone listed 121 head in 1414.[5]

NUNCII REGIS

The Kings Messengers 1199–1377 tabulates messengers, some merely as to when they operated, others with details of journeys – reasons, destinations, expenses, companions, etc. Messengers were not just medieval postmen but frequently performed other duties, such as escorting envoys to court, apprehending spies, arresting and conducting malefactors to penal lodgement, overseeing the loading of, and then accompanying wardrobe paraphernalia during court perambulations, and, very noteworthy, conducting large amounts of specie, often soldiers' wages, during wartime. Messengers had to be absolutely trustworthy.

Senior division messengers, the *nuncii regis*, were mounted; *cokini* (later called *cursores*) were foot messengers, some of whom, such as William Brehull in 1298–99,[6] were elevated to *nuncii regis*. Occasionally a *cursor* was provided with a horse, as happened, probably with a feeling of relief, to Robert of Chester for his 1315 journey to Gascony, accompanying *nuncii regis* Richard Swyn carrying writs to authorities at Agen, Bordeaux, Saintonge, Bayonne and other towns, as well as visiting local magnates.[7] *Nuncii regis* had to be freemen and reasonably affluent, as they rode their own horses, and although they daily drew threepence to a *cursor*'s twopence, their horse's bait and their own keep came out of that.[8]

To be ready for missions messengers ate in hall when not on the road. They carried a variety of legal documents, such as new statutes, writs, etc., and often performed 'secret business'. Documents concerning national government were usual, and county sheriffs were visited frequently. Circuits radiated from Westminster and riding and foot messengers covered between 30 and 35 miles per day. *Nuncii* rested their horses every 10 miles. One-day stints covered Surrey, Kent and Middlesex; two days took them as far as Hampshire, Northamptonshire and Oxford, while six days reached Yorkshire or the southwest to Cornwall, and eight days the English/Scots borders and Wales.[9] The return trip doubled the mileage. For this a good horse was vital, not what we now term a quality horse maybe, but a sturdy, although not coarse, animal with tough resilient hoof horn, good heart room, clean wind and legs, overall good conformation with a decent saddle back and a long stride, and a reasonable turn of foot. Today such a horse competes in long-distance riding where on successive days 40 miles-plus are covered, success being to finish fit and able to continue piling on the miles; a *nuncii*'s horse would have fitted the bill. With his periodic rests, a *nuncius* probably travelled at much the same average competition speed of 6–7 mph. The ability to accelerate, in case of ambush or to escape a running fight, was essential.

During 1284–86 Richard of Norwich made several journeys. In a twelve-day period he took a new statute and letters close to nine sheriffs: Norfolk, Suffolk, Essex, Hertfordshire, Middlesex, Canterbury, Buckinghamshire, Bedfordshire and Huntingdonshire.[10] Occasionally *nuncii* were ordered to ride with haste, as in 1300 when Geoffrey Simple rode from Carlisle to the treasurer at York and back.[11] Fast riding on urgent business usually meant riding post, *nuncii* having prior claim on animals for hire, with the cost being met by the wardrobe. In 1337/8 Nicholas Ufton was sent to magnates in the north and ordered to ride by night and day. He hired horses and between 1 July and 4 July rode a distance which normally took eight days. His return with answers from the magnates for the king at Stamford was equally expeditious and costly, horse-hire costing 20s.[12] Journeys to and from war zones were nearly always those ridden in utmost haste, Gascon and Scottish trackways in particular echoing to rapid hoofbeats from messengers' horses.

Though much was demanded of a *nuncius*' horse its value was set low. If lost as a result of enforced hard riding the king reimbursed his messenger, but the amounts shown indicate only a partial cost was paid in some cases, or in others only enough for a horse ranked alongside an ordinary man-at-arms' mount at £2. Several examples show that although wages had risen from threepence to sixpence per day towards the end of Edward III's reign, lower level horse values had not:

1299:   Brehull received 30s for one horse.
1305–7:   John Dunstall lost two horses, receiving 20s for one and a new horse for the other.
1351/2:   John Cardinal received 20s for one.
1357:   Richard Hert received only 6s 8d towards the replacement cost. Had he ridden carelessly?
1362:   Hert lost another, receiving 20s compensation.
1367:   Hert lost two more, receiving a total of 60s for both, even though promised 80s as he had been on urgent business to the north,[13] a trouble-spot throughout the reigns of Edward I to Edward III.

Senior *nuncii* and their horses often travelled overseas, the most common destinations being the Papal Court at Rome (later at Avignon 1309–77) and Gascony. The best documented career is that of Jack Faukes who operated from 1330 to 1360 as messenger to, first, the Bishop of Winchester, then to the Bishop of Durham, before transferring to the king's service in 1333. He was often employed on overseas missions for the king, even when in Winchester's employ, as shown by the wardrobe having paid £24 3s for wages, expenses and lost horses on a journey from York to Gascony. He went repeatedly to Avignon, Paris, Wissant, Calais, Gascony, and to Flanders and Germany. His domestic travels were equally numerous, many being from York to Carlisle and onwards to Scotland.

The most interesting is a trip to Avignon from 26 July to 23 August 1343, for which Faukes noted the itinerary and costs. He rode post, hiring horses. On his first day he covered about 80 miles to Dover. Landing at Wissant he had ridden about 150 miles to Paris by the end of the second day. On three subsequent days he averaged just over 100 miles per day and at Lyon took a boat to Avignon. He remained there until 10 August, then rode to Vienne, then to Chateauneuf sur Loire on business, before returning by a slightly longer route to Wissant. He reached London ten days after leaving Chateauneuf.

Out of the total time, he spent fourteen days in the saddle covering over 1,300 miles for which he received 74s 10d in wages and expenses, not being fully paid until 15 October 1345. Clearly messengers needed private means to tide them over.

Many *nuncii* served incredibly long terms in an age when longevity was not the norm. Maybe the outdoors, exercise, and frequent absences from congested conurbations kept them fitter and away from, or able to throw off, disease. Such careers meant frequent equine replacements which salaries would not have covered, but bonuses and extra cash for special messengers helped. Faukes received an additional £20, a huge sum then, from Edward III for 'his labours here and overseas'.[14] Others received lesser gifts, and these together with other perquisites boosted income.

Some exceptional long-term careers were: Donald of Athol 1309–44; Alan of Barley 1337–76; Arnald Bon 1281–1318; and John Somers 1283–1329.[15]

Many long-term *nuncii* received pensions and/or corrodies at abbeys receiving royal endowments. In his 1331 letter to the Prior of Kilmainan in Ireland the king named Donald of Athol a 'royal envoy', a higher status than mere messenger and an accolade for good service, for which his corrody had the added unusual benefit of maintenance of a groom and a horse for Donald to ride.[16] It is pleasant to think that maybe Donald's equine partner was also pensioned off after many years in the king's service.

ORIENTAL SYSTEMS

Oriental, Levantine, Asiatic and Indian postal systems utilized a supply of horses kept at each staging post. All were under their respective government's control, and far more sophisticated than anything in Europe. Successive cultures had maintained an efficient courier service which had depended on indigenous swift horses as far back as the Assyrians whose Amat Shurri (The King's Word) dated to the eighth century BC. Their Persian successors' system connected all local points, the best known being the 1,600-mile Susa to Sardis road with 111 divisions and fresh horses available every 15 miles. An *angaros* was expected to cover this distance in one week. Rome followed suit with the *cursus publicus* using the 53,000-mile road network. The system was maintained into the early medieval period under Justinian (527–65) when up to forty horses were held at post stations approximately eleven miles apart. Couriers daily covered between five and eight stages, but urgent business could see them riding 240 miles in a day.[17]

These systems operated where the best of the ancient world's horses were bred – Cappadocia, Phrygia, Armenia, Persia, Syria and Byzantium. Later empires had the tough Bactrian, Turkmene and Arabian horses. The Asiatics used steppe pony breeds and imported horses from the rich breeding grounds of the Upper Oxus (Amu Darya),[18] which went a long way to improving the speed of native ponies.

KOREA: The Korean royal postal system was begun in the fifth century AD by King So Chi for the use of royalty, nobility and government. In AD 935 the system was enlarged under the Silla dynasty. The Mongols disrupted it but it endured, being revitalized in the sixteenth century by King Song Jong with staffed staging posts every 50 miles holding a nucleus of five horses. Each post rider had an insignia – a *mae-pae* – designating rank and the number of horses allowed him. Should a post horse be incapable of completing a stage, one could be commandeered from a traveller or a village, payment being guaranteed by the government. Profiteering was punishable by death.[19]

MONGOLIA: The Mongol system was similar to the Korean, but far superior. It dated to Khan Ogodei's reign (1227–41), and ambassadors and couriers were entitled to use it. Stations were called *Tayan Yams*. The *Morin Yam* was a horse station; *Tergen Yam* a wagon station; *Marin Yam* a secret station for urgent military communication.[20] Marco Polo gives further details. There were 10,000 stations with more than 200,000 horses, kept in herds of up to 200 ready at each station, with an equal number at grass on a monthly rotation system. Stations were from 25 to 40 miles apart, and maintaining stock was a charge on the local community. In isolated stations the great Khan provided part of the stock, the locals the rest.[21]

TURKIC/MONGOLIAN: Timur used a similarly efficient system to keep in touch with his sons and military commanders. Ruy Gonzalez de Clavijo, Castile's ambassador to Samarkand in 1403–6, used the Tabriz to Samarkand road, noting stations at regular intervals with between 100 and 200 horses ready at each. He described the route as littered with horse carcasses, as Timur preferred a fast-riding courier who killed his horse(s) to one who conserved his mount. Even the king's son had to surrender his horse to a courier if so ordered.[22]

THE MAMLŪK SYSTEM: The *Al Barid* operated twenty-eight routes throughout Egypt, Syria and Arabia. The longest was Cairo to Mecca: 966 miles with fifty-seven stations. Cairo–Gaza–Damascus–Aleppo was 688 miles. The 475 miles from Cairo to Damascus normally took four days, but could be ridden in three. Mounts provided by enfeoffed Bedouin Arabs were changed monthly. Inaugurated by Sultan Baibars in 1261 the *Al Barid* lasted as a horse postal system till Damascus fell to Timur in January 1401. Thereafter camels were used.[23]

INDIA: Medieval historian Barani described the Indian system of the Delhi Sultanate under Alauddin Khalji (1296–1316). The *Barid i Mamalik* was in charge of the intelligence and postal departments. A chain of post houses was built, each horse station having a nucleus of horses ready, and officers and report writers in residence. In between horse stations were posts for foot couriers.[24] From Babur's memoirs come more details describing the Agra to Kabul road, and a model on which to view the Mughul system. Each 9 *kuroh* (18 miles) a tower was to be erected, open on all sides, and at each 36 miles six post horses were to be kept tied up in readiness. Arrangement was to be made for paying post masters and grooms, and for gathering and payment for horse corn. If the station was in a crown domain the inhabitants were to pay for its maintenance. In other areas the *beg* (lord) paid in whose domain the post house lay.[25]

CHAPTER 10

Travel

Today we think nothing of extensive travel, which is made easy by modern transport. If ever we reflect on the journeying of our medieval ancestors it can surprise us when we realize how far away many of their destinations were. And travel medieval man did: royal armies went to war, and whole households, royal and noble, went on progresses, considered necessary for taking the court to the produce, showing the king to his people, and enabling residences to be periodically sweetened or 'mucked out'. There was a host of travellers: messengers; servants on business; pilgrims; ecclesiastics touring their dioceses, serving as ambassadors, or travelling to the Papal court. Judges went on circuit, often with armed mounted escorts; national and county administrators rode about their business, as did purveyors; and following their often unwelcome visits, carters were employed to haul the provisions earmarked for royal households, especially when provisioning armies for war. Merchants were great travellers, from the international level down to the humble chapman, who gave his trade name to a type of Yorkshire packhorse (long since died out). There were adventurous pleasure jaunts too. The medieval 'Grand Tour' took in more than Europe, with many travellers visiting parts of the orient, Anatolia, Persia and India.

Travel was either by shanks' or a real pony (horse) inland, and initially by sea for Englishmen travelling abroad who often took their horses with them, needing licences to do so to prevent the illegal export of horses. Such prohibitions were frequently circumvented by the animals 'running away'!

Occidental and oriental journeyers criss-crossed land and sea routes and disseminated much of equestrian value to the bank of international lore. The sights, sounds and, in many instances, the horses of the 'mysterious east' crossed to and benefitted European stock. A reverse flow did not benefit the orient. European horses did not thrive in the orient; indeed most European chargers, palfreys and pack animals died in the biggest exodus of European stock – the Crusades.

INTO THE ASIAN STEPPES

The invasion of Europe had long been planned and in 1242 the Mongol war machine reached the outskirts of Vienna, but was suddenly recalled to Karakorum for the election of a new khan. Strangely, an unnamed Englishman worked in Karakorum; he appears briefly in Matthew Paris's *Chronicle* which relates that Robert Fitzwalter, one of the English barons who forced King John to sign *Magna Carta* in 1215, was among those whose excommunication was secured by John when he became reconciled with the Pope. Fitzwalter's household chaplain shared his excommunication and exile. When hounded from Europe this cleric rode east – 6,000 miles to Karakorum where he is *reputed* to have acted as adviser on Europe. A quarter of a century later he rode with Batu Khan and Subudei; when the Mongols evaporated before Vienna the cleric remained – a captive executed one month later in Wiener Neustadt.[1]

In 1245 Franciscan John of Plano Carpini and Dominicans Ascelin and Andrew of Longjumeau were sent east by Pope Innocent IV. Several years of travel were interspersed with lengthy stays at Mongol and oriental courts and military encampments. In 1253 William of Rubruck followed the trail east. The objectives were to gain political and military information of Mongol intentions and capabilities regarding Catholic Europe, to lay the ground for the conversion of non-Christians, and for unification under Papal authority of all Christian sects – Orthodox, Jacobite, Nestorian, etc. The envoys only partially succeeded. They reported on many aspects of Mongol life and military conduct, but proselytizing was unsuccessful. In an age of religious intolerance the Mongols accepted all religions. The Pope's desire, according to Carpini, 'that all Christians should be friends of the Tatars and at peace with them . . .' meant one thing to Innocent and another to Khan Kuyuk. He interpreted peace as submission and demanded personal appearance at the Mongol court from the Pope, Emperor Frederick II, Louis IX of France and Henry III of England.[2]

Carpini and Rubruck left fascinating accounts about geography, animals, and the warlike and domestic aspects of their Mongol hosts, who far from being undisciplined savages were highly organized. Much of their life centred around the indigenous Mongolian horse, which in the intervening centuries has changed little in type, methods of rearing, capture and capabilities. In the less harsh west many breeds have lost some ability to fend for themselves, while the Mongolian horse (pony) still thrives in its harsh environment.

The friars were advised to ride 'Tatar' horses as these could dig below the snow for food. Carpini travelled to the court of Kuyuk (1246–48), Rubruck to that of Mongke (1251–59). Both were corpulent and riding a 13–14 hh straight-shouldered, fast-trotting Mongolian pony, instead of easy paced ambling mules or palfreys, was uncomfortable.

Carpini changed to Tatar horses at Kiev. These may have been one of the indigenous Russian breeds whose modern descendants are the Kazakh, Altai, Trans-Baikal, Yakut

This Persian drawing shows an animal similar to the steppe-type mount common to the Asiatic and Oriental traveller.

and Kirghiz, which have great similarity to the Mongolian horses, and almost certainly interbred with Mongol warhorses.[3] The friars' route went via the Mongols' Russian conquests, crossing the rivers Dnieper, Don, Volga and Jaec. Packhorses were acquired at the first Mongol encampment. Some had been used as saddlehorses, showing there was no difference between pack- and saddlehorses in Mongolian herds. Thereafter fresh post horses were provided three or four times a day as they travelled first to the court of Batu Khan at Sarai on the Volga, then to Kuyuk at Karakorum. Carpini frequently notes the speed, always trotting, usually dawn till dusk, and sometimes at night too (which must have reduced his bulk after thousands of jolting miles). Once at Kuyuk's tented court he noted the discipline, the constant mounted activity of Mongol chieftains and their retinues near the court and in the adjacent countryside. Only *noyons* (chiefs) could freely go to the horse lines situated two bowshots from the royal tent. Mongolian horses might be less than beautiful to western eyes, but Carpini marked the lavish gold embellishments on bits, breastplates, saddles and cruppers, and later observed the brilliant lamellar armour of heavy cavalrymen and their horses. The less affluent heavy cavalryman had to make do with *cuir bouilli* armour for man and horse (and mule). Carpini also listed a full range of weaponry.[4] He was obeying Papal orders.

In Mongol life the horse was transport, food, drink (in the form of fermented mare's milk called *kumiss*), funeral sacrifice, feast and passport to the afterlife. Its skin provided leather for armour and harnesses. Special horses were consecrated to Chingis Khan and enjoyed a work-free life; others were selected, usually isabel (yellowish dun, possibly with black points) or iron grey, to be sacrificed for the well being of the herds. The chosen horse was called *Isik*, not to be ridden by its master until after snow had fallen, and reconsecrated annually. It would seem this was more of a dedication than a sacrifice, unless the ambiguous 'reconsecration' meant a new horse was offered each year. Burial customs did call for real sacrifices, according to Carpini, for the Mongols; and Rubruck describes an important Cuman burial with the flayed and stuffed remains of sixteen horses over the grave.[5]

Mongol women rode well astride, were fine archers and fought bravely in war. Wealthy women rode 'big stout palfreys' gorgeously harnessed;[6] these were clearly not the ordinary range-bred animals, but since 1220 Mongols had access to and tribute from the renowned herds of Transoxiania, Samarkand and Tabriz.[7]

Information was two-way. Mongke's secretary interrogated Rubruck who wrote:

> They began to question us greatly about the Kingdom of France, whether there were many sheep and cattle and horses there, and whether they had not better go there at once and take it all . . .'[8]

Mongol wealth resided mainly in the size of their livestock herds.

Sixteen years after Rubruck returned to the west Marco Polo embarked on his epic journey through Anatolia, Armenia, Persia and Afghanistan, and travelled the Silk Route into the Mongol empire, which then included part of China. The most comprehensive details noted by a European about oriental and Asiatic horse herds and marts appear in his travelogue. Early oriental travellers and writers such as Ibn Battuta, who travelled between 1325 and 1354, and writer and studmaster Abou Bekr ibn Bedr expanded the equine overview. Their information cross-referenced with much of Marco Polo's, and gives a clear picture of the variety and importance of equines in the oriental and Asiatic sphere.

Abou Bekr listed the purebred Arabian strains and breeds of the Middle East and neighbouring countries: *Faras* were purebred Arabians; *Hedjin* were partbreds; and *Berdhuns* were common horses. His list contains Berber (Maghrebin), Turkmene, Barqa, Egyptian and Khorassanian Chahri. Faras were superior, Egyptian stock weedy; Berber, especially those infused with Arabian blood, good; Chahri's excellent but savage warhorses; Barqas stocky, good but rather clumsy. He denigrated Mongol and Frankish horses, saying the former 'rarely has any noble characteristics', and the Frankish were ill-trained and extremely clumsy.

Marco admired the fine horses and sturdy mules of Anatolia, observed Armenian contrasts with lush summer grazing which drew the prolific herds of horses and other livestock of the Levantine Tatars, and the devastating winter cold which forced their retreat to warmer territory. At Baghdad he was told of the 100,000 cavalrymen and numberless foot that had been inadequate to withstand Hulegu, the first Ilkhan, in 1255.[10] Hulegu's uncle, Great Khan Ogodei had requested 'tall horses of western breed found at Baghdad and Bukhara'.[11] Some of Rashid's translators have 'Arabian horses', assuming all oriental horses were Arabian. At that period some Arab tribes' transhumance took them into 'Irak',[12] and Turcoman horses – 'the western breed' – were plentiful due to Turkic invasions. In Persia Marco was trebly impressed: with her magnificent horses which each cost the equivalent of £50 sterling, as much as the most expensive European destrier; with the finest donkeys which were fast, sturdy, and exceptionally economical to feed; and with cavalry equipment of high-grade steel – armour, swords, saddles, bits, spurs, stirrups, etc. Badakshan (Afghanistan) bred fine swift horses with hooves so hard shoeing was not needed, and so surefooted that mountainous terrain was no barrier. It was claimed they were descended from Alexander the Great's charger Bucephalus,[13] a legend still current. This area was ancient Bactria which produced estimable horses. Balkh, Kabul and Kandahar, among other places, were also noted for horses. Kabul was a major mart with up to 10,000 horses per annum, drawing horses from Kashgar, Turkestan, Samarkand, Bukhara, Balkh, Hisar and Badakshan, which raised horses valued in India and vied for by Hindustani traders. Kandahar was the main entrepôt for Khorassani trade, also supplying good warhorses, notably the Chahri.[14]

Marco Polo reiterates much of the friars' data on equestrian Mongolia. Horse stealing was a capital offence under Mongolian and Turkic law. To escape execution a Mongol horsethief had to repay the stolen horse with nine, or their value. A Turkic culprit had to return the stolen horse plus nine more. If he could not, his sons were taken; if he had no sons he was executed.[15]

Both Marco Polo and Ibn Battuta visited India and China, the latter staying some years in India. Their most impressive equestrian information was about the huge trade in Arabian, Persian and Turcoman horses to India – all breeds that European travellers, soldiers of fortune, and armies of the Crusades entering that sphere would have become familiar with.

DISTAFF TRAVEL

Women's travel was usually for shorter journeys close to home, but some women did travel long distances; the wealthy noblewoman travelling with her lord, or an emancipated widow travelling to please herself. Some women travelled to war zones, notably Eleanor of Aquitaine in the twelfth century. At the other end of the warhost were the camp followers, on foot, or mule back if lucky, the necessary laundresses/prostitutes. Nuns went on pilgrimage, either on foot or riding a mule or palfrey. A journeying noblewoman had an abundant household well supplied with horses. Pomp and extravagance marked her travels.

In 1332 Edward III's sister Eleanor travelled to Nijmegen to marry Reynald, Count of Guelders. Her journey began at Stratford le Bowe with the loan of dowager Queen Isabella's chariot and seven destriers, under the care of Isabella's farrier Adam. He accompanied the equipage to Dover, was paid a tip of one mark and returned the equipage to Stratford. At Dover a total of fifty-six horses belonging to Eleanor's household, plus many others belonging to lords Crombewell, Vallibus and Chaumpeyn, and the Abbot of Langdon, were embarked for Sluys on *The Percy*, *Simon Daniel*, *Nicholas* and *Hurtyn*. Eleanor's fifty-six comprised thirteen destriers, seven palfreys, nineteen sumpters and seventeen carthorses. The horses of the accompanying lords had a similar mix, with the addition of a few hackneys; the total number is not given as several account entries state 'horses and men' of various retinues, or named types and 'other horses'. Most of Eleanor's horses were intended as gifts; her husband Reynald received eleven destriers, two palfreys, six sumpters and six carthorses; St John of Jerusalem at Nijmegen and the Bishop of Winchester each received a destrier; Henry of Lancaster a dark grey Spanish palfrey and his companion knight a palfrey; other gifts of sumpters and carthorses brought the total of gifthorses to forty-one. The remaining sumpters and carthorses were sold off.[16] It is noticeable that the horses pulling Eleanor's chariot were referred to as destriers. Clearly a better class of carriage horse was needed on such a mission.

Great fluctuations in the numbers of stable occupants often indicate disruptive travel, illustrated by the 1265 household accounts for the Odiham estate of Eleanor, Countess of Leicester, sister of Henry III and wife of the rebellious Earl Simon de Montfort. In February she moved from her Wallingford residence and went via Reading to Odiham, where the normal stable complement ranged between thirty and thirty-eight horses. In March her marshall had to cope with feeding and stabling the huge influx of Earl Simon's horses when he arrived for a two-week stay. Forty-four horses were recorded for Sunday 15 March rising to 172 on 17 March, and 334 on 19 March. After Simon left for Hereford the accounts show repeated trips by messengers from Odiham to Hereford. The country boiled with the rebels still in the ascendant and holding the king captive. Prince Edward (future Edward I) escaped Earl Simon's captivity and raised his army. In June the countess and her son Amaury hastened to Dover Castle held by another son, Henry. Her entourage, including men-at-arms of her son Simon, used eighty-four horses, including carthorses, some of which were hired. They doubled the daily norm of 15 miles per day to 30 miles, which with baggage and carthorses was a considerable achievement.[17] On 4 August the rebels were defeated at Evesham and Earl Simon's mutilated corpse found among the battle carnage.

It paid to keep a well-stocked stable and stud and to cope with his peripatetic lifestyle Count Robert II of Artois founded a stud at Domfront, inherited by his grandson on Robert's death at the Battle of Courtrai in 1303. His daughter Mahaut, a very great noblewoman related to many of the French royal house, inherited her father's itchy feet, and no doubt used the stud's horses for her constant visits around Paris at Fontainebleau, Vincennes, Conflans, Pontoise and the Abbey of Maubuisson. Twice-yearly she visited the family home in Artois. Her retine of about forty persons used around sixty horses of riding, pack and carriage types.[18]

When travelling within their own domains great lords required an extraordinarily extravagant household. That of Philip the Bold was, at first, modest with only 100 persons and seventy-six horses needed for a visit to his brother, the Duke of Berry. In 1386 only three years after he had acquired Flanders through the death of his wife's father his expanded household of 353 people used 405 horses for a journey to Ypres.[19]

POMP AND CIRCUMSTANCE – LORDS AND AMBASSADORS

Ambassadors reflected the prestige of their kings by the pomp that surrounded their embassy. Chronicler William Fitzstephen described the 1158 embassy of Chancellor Thomas à Becket to France. No expense was spared. The retinue of 200 were all mounted, with the squires carrying shields and leading destriers belonging to the knights in the retinue. Thomas took with him falconers with their falcons and austringers with their hawks; hounds and greyhounds swelled the travelling zoo, which included monkeys trained to sit on the backs of each carthorse which were hitched, five to a team, to a convoy of eight baggage and provision wagons, each of which was guarded by a chained mastiff. Twenty-eight packhorses carried smaller items – books, specie, gold and silver plate, and chapel paraphernalia. The whole must have resembled a small township on the move. The pomp had the required effect with Frenchmen coming out to gawp as the cavalcade passed by, commenting, according to Fitzstephen, on 'what a magnificent man the King of England must be if his chancellor travels in such state'.[20]

Other ambassadors travelled with less pomp, much hardship and far from Europe. A surprising number of European courts sent ambassadors eastwards; there were some west/east links that seem strange until one recalls that in the closing years of the medieval era the west felt increasingly threatened by the aggressive Ottomans. Mercenaries travelled to hawk their military services, others out of curiosity to see what lay over the next hill, or country. All had need of horses.

Probably the most well-travelled man was the Maghrebin Ibn Battuta whose recorded journeys were interspersed with lengthy stays and various ambassadorial employments at courts and nomad encampments. His early record has little of equestrian interest, being mostly his itinerary around places of Muslim worship and the imams he met. An exception was his description of Mamlūk post stations between Egypt and Syria. Each had a hostelry, a khan (caravanserai) for travellers with a watering place for animals and a shop supplying the needs of travellers and their animals. The large border khan at Qatya (now Katteh or Katia) had fully staffed government offices. Customs dues – *zakat* – amounting daily to 1,000 gold dinars were collected; passports were required to pass from Egypt to Syria and vice versa, although the Mamlūks then controlled both Egypt and Syria.[21]

His travels in the entourage of Shaikh Muzaffar al Din took him to the Crimea where the people, collectively called Crimean Tatars by the west – were an ethnic mix of Mongol and Turk. His itinerary then took him to Khwarizm, Turkestan, Khorasan, Bukhara, India and China. Many Turkic and Mongolian equestrian customs were similar. Wagon transport used horse, ox, or camel according to the weight of the load. When horses, either a two- or four-horse hitch, were used, the driver rode one, guiding the team with a long stick and urging them with a whip. At night stock grazed loose, all fear of theft having been removed by strict laws. Animals were branded on the thigh and Ibn Battuta relates instances when missing horses were returned, once after a ten-day absence, and another after a twenty-two-day spell.[22]

Tatar gift-giving was lavish. At one Crimean encampment robes were given to all the important guests, and horses too – ten to the shaikh, six each to his brother and sons, and one to each important group member.[23] Later, when Ibn Battuta joined the entourage of Turkic Khan Uzbeg's wife, Khatun Bayalun, for her visit to her father, the Byzantine emperor, he was given 'a large number of horses', a robe and money by the khan, and other presents from Bayalun – furs, money, periodic gifts of horses for riding and from 'among the horses intended for the kitchen'. Being soft-hearted Ibn Battuta spared them, shortly collecting fifty head! Khatun Bayalun's retinue included Amir Badara with 5,000 troops, her 200 armed retainers, 200 slave girls and twenty pages. Four hundred wagons were needed and 2,000 horses for riding and draught, plus 200 oxen and 300 camels. On entering Greek (Byzantine) territory the rough going only allowed horse or mule travel. At Constantinople Bayalun's brother greeted her with 5,000 heavily armed cavalry. His immediate retinue and their horses were gorgeously apparelled; even the lances were covered with plaques of gold and silver. Khatun Bayalun's own horse wore a gold embroidered silk saddle cloth, its fetlocks flashing jewelled gold anklets.[24]

On entering Khwarizm the ruler, Amir Qutludumur (Qutlugh), gave Ibn Battuta 300 gold Moroccan dinars out of which he purchased a black horse for thirty-five silver dinars – a sizeable price. Although his band of horses 'reached a number which I dare not mention lest some sceptic accuse me of lying', he came to love this black horse, giving it preferential treatment and keeping it for three years. He said it brought him luck, and was with him when he left Khwarizm for Bukhara, an eighteen-day march across a sandy waste where it was so cold that even when travelling the spare horses were kept blanketed. On entering India the black horse died and with its passing so also went Ibn Battuta's good fortune,[25] but not for long.

In 1342 he was part of an Indian embassy to China which took 100 high-class horses among a huge array of diplomatic reciprocal gifts for the Chinese emperor. The embassy never reached China. Ibn Battuta did, but left no details of any Sino-equestrian exploits. This is the only record of any such embassy.[26]

In his note on India Ibn Battuta refers to Raja Jalansi,[27] ancestor of the present-day Jhalas of Jhalawar in Kathiawar. Shri Raghuraj Sinh Jhala, who gave me so much help on the Kathiawar horse for my book *Warhorse 1250–1600*, is a direct descendant of the Jhalas of Jhalawar – a lineage traceable for at least six and a half centuries.

CLAVIJO

Castilian Ruy Gonzalez de Clavijo started his three-year sojourn in 1403 travelling in company with Frankish ambassadors and the ambassador from the king of Babylon (Egypt). They travelled through Iraq on to Tabriz and being in Timur's territory were kept well equipped with mounts, travelling at night due to the tremendous heat and the swarms of bloodsucking insects that drove men and horses mad, and in some instances proved fatal. At Teheran he was introduced to a Turkic gastronomic feast of whole roast horse! Thereafter horse, roast and boiled, appeared at every meal.[28] At Tehran a tall ambling horse was given to de Clavijo, but he thought the saddle and bridle poor,[29] probably a snaffle bridle and a short-seated Mongol/Turkic saddle still common among steppe people, and unlike the *à la brida* style of saddle and bitting of the Spanish court. Rules governing the care of ambassadors and messengers going to Timur were harsh. They had the right to demand the horse of any traveller, including those of troops and royalty. Non-compliance cost the man his head. En route, robes, horses, food and fodder in abundance were to be made available. De Clavijo was amazed when negligent staff were beaten with whips and sticks and warned by Amir Mirabozar, sent by Timur to guide the Frankish ambassadors to his court, that a repeat drubbing would occur if the 'lord's orders' were again flouted.[30]

At Derbent – the Caucasian Iron Gates – ambassadors again received horses but of a local breed noted for its spirit.[31] In Timur's lands de Clavijo travelled in the breeding grounds of some of history's famous breeds known for endurance, courage and aptitude for war – Turcoman horses of the twenty-four Turkic tribes, Khorassanian Chahris and the fabled horses of Ferghana.

At Timur's court, feasting again on haunch of horse (which by now de Clavijo must have been sick of, as well as it being forbidden by Catholic Canon Law), the gift-giving commenced and included a batch of 300 horses. Then he saw Timur's summary justice. A great lord left in charge of 3,000 of Timur's horses failed to produce the whole complement, and in spite of promising to produce double the number if given time he was hanged.[32]

Timur's star was rising and de Clavijo must have been awed by the invader of India (1399) and the victor of Ankara (1402), where the Ottoman Bayazid I had suffered a catastrophic defeat. And maybe there is a hint of what was to be Timur's last campaign. At Samarkand de Clavijo met a man who had returned from China (Cathay) and reported that the emperor could field 400,000 cavalry.[33] Hyped medieval arithmetic? Disinformation? Whatever it was, Timur was not shaken, although the Chinese campaign was aborted because Timur sickened en route and died at Otrar in 1405, while de Clavijo was retracing his steps to Castile. Once Timur was dead the Ottomans surged again, and in the succeeding years wreaked havoc on Persia, Byzantium, the Mamlūk empire, and eventually rethreatened Europe whose armies had already suffered defeat at Nicopolis in 1396.

THE VENETIAN AMBASSADORS

In the early fifteenth century the great trading city of Venice either owned or controlled most of Dalmatia, Corfu, the Morean Coast, and islands in the Aegean and Crete. One of her citizens, Caterino Cornaro, became Queen of Cyprus on her marriage, thus giving Venice a stronghold in the Mediterranean.[34] As Venetian power burgeoned, so did the might of the Ottomans, but maritime Venice held her own against the Turkish fleet until a disastrous battle at sea and the loss of Negroponte (Euboea) to the Ottomans in 1470, leaving Venice's southern defences open.[35] At the same time Uzun Hassan, the Ak Koyunlu Turcoman ruler of Persia, faced the Ottomans on his border. So began a century-long exchange of Venetian and Persian ambassadors. Four Venetian ambassadors recorded much of equestrian and military value, as well as the hazards of international travel in their separate journeys by various routes to Persia.

The exchange began when the Persian ambassador arrived in Venice in 1471 briefed 'to comfort the Signoria to Folowe the warres against the said Ottomano'. If the Grand Turk could be weakened by the Persians he would have less punch to aim at Venetian territory. Venice answered with an arsenal of artillery intended for Uzun Hassan which was packed into the fleet gathered to attack the Ottomans, who held Corfu. When Corfu fell to Venice the Persian ambassador and the Venetian envoy, Josefa Barbaro, continued by sea to Adana and then struck inland, making for a Euphrates crossing to enter Uzun Hassan's territory. En route they ran into a Kurdish attack. The Persian (Turcoman) ambassador, Barbaro's secretary and two others were killed. The others, injured, fled on horseback. All their baggage and packhorses were lost. Eventually Barbaro arrived at Tabriz where he was impressed by the numbers and types of cavalry fielded by the Turcoman ruler, and by the horses from Baghdad presented to Uzun Hassan. He was less impressed with the cheap nags for sale in the ambulatory city which followed the army (see p. 24).[36]

Two years later a multinational embassy went east, Ambrogio Contarini representing Venice. He travelled the land route via Germany, Poland, Russia and the steppes to the Black Sea where he boarded ship. In Polish-governed Russia the German saddlehorse he presented to the governor so impressed him that Contarini was asked to exchange his stallions for Russian horses. At Caffa, where he disembarked his nine horses, he saw mounted slave catchers under a *subasi* (Turkish officer) on a round-up. Once in Ak Koyunlu territory he found the country in civil turmoil, which boded ill for Venice's hopes that Uzun Hassan would divert Ottoman attention away from Venetian holdings. His son Oghurlu Muhammed was raiding right up to his capital, Tabriz, with a force of 3,000 cavalry. The Venetian, Burgundian and Muscovite envoys, with two accompanying 'Turkish' ambassadors, were told to return to their countries and inform:

> their sovereigns and the Christian princes that he Uzun Hassan had intended fighting the Ottomans but because of his son's rebellion his forces were split, some against his son, some to 'annoy the Ottoman' but at a future time he would be ready to attack the Ottomans.

Barbaro had informed Contarini that Uzun Hassan had over 20,000 cavalry with 'good and handsome horses'. With the Muscovite ambassador, Contarini had a hazardous and lengthy journey home. Travelling via Georgia and Mingrelia they were robbed of their horses, money and arms, found Caffa taken by the Ottomans, and were forced to stay almost a year in Astrakhan, beset by money troubles and Tatars. It was not until 17 August 1476 that they resumed their journey in a caravan of about 300 riders and 200 led horses for consumption and sale in Russia. En route they saw 400 horses from the previous year's caravan roaming loose, escapees from Tatars who preyed on travellers, but once past Riazan safety improved as Ivan III of Moscow had a border patrol of Service Tatars. From Moscow Contarini travelled to Warsaw by horse-sled, then purchased horses for travel to Frankfurt.[37]

Venice also sent envoys into the Ottoman camps: Caterino Zeno and Giovan Maria Angiolello travelled to Anatolia and Persia and gave details of Ottoman and Persian armies from the time of Uzun Hassan to that of his grandson Ismail. Angiolello, no doubt trusting to diplomatic immunity, ranged between Ottoman and Ak Koyunlu military camps. Both envoys commented on the huge booty from engagements between Persian and Ottoman forces. Angiolello singled out the 1,000 horses the Ottomans acquired from the Persians after their defeat at the Battle of Tabeada in 1473.[38]

A century later Vicentio d'Allesandri was sent to Shah Tahmasp to pressure him to attack the Ottomans and so divert their forces away from their attack on Cyprus. Tahmasp refused, although in the event peace was concluded between the Ottomans and Venice, but Persia lost out with much of her territory, including Tabriz, falling to Murad, Selim II's son (1566–74).

D'Alessandri gives much information on Persian and other oriental horses. The Arabian was highly prized in the east and also well beyond the confines of its homeland, Persia having made extensive use of it in crossing with its own breeds for home and export use, especially to India via the Persian Gulf:

> the horses are so well trained and are so good and handsome since the arrival of Sultan Bayazeth who fled into Persia with some magnificent Caramanian (Cilician) and Arab horses, which were given away throughout the country . . . there were 1,000 horses and mares (Bayazeth's). On this account there has never been so fine a breed, and the Ottomans even have not got one like it.[39]

THE MERCENARIES

Some mercenaries plied their trade in tandem with curiosity about other lands. I am not talking about French *écorcheurs* or Italian *condottieri* bands, but individuals whose travels culminated in armed service. Some were leaders with sizeable retinues, others part of a lord's retinue, and some simply unfortunates forced to travel and making the best of it, with many leaving informative memoirs.

Johann Schiltburger was captured at Nicopolis and spent years in captivity. He wrote of his part in the battle, and, when out of Ottoman imprisonment, of an unusual aspect of armed conflict from his time spent with Zeggra Sadarmelickh, 'an infidel woman with 4,000 maidens'. She was Tchekre whose coins were struck *c.*1414–1416. Sadarmelickh, a corruption of Sadra Melyka, suggests a Persian background, 'Sadra' being a woman's name and 'melyka' an angel. Zeggra and her warrior maidens 'rode to battle and fought with the bow, as well as men . . .'. In one avenging encounter her husband's killer was captured. Brought before her, she decapitated him with one blow of her sword claiming, 'now am I revenged'. Schiltburger noted: 'I was present there and I also saw this.'[40] Schiltburger's eyewitness account confirms the Mongol and Persian practice of horse-women taking the field.

Marienburg, the Teutonic Knight's capital, was the new focus for crusading knights, drawing adventurers eastward from as early as 1232 when seven Polish dukes went, followed in 1233 by Margrave Henry of Meissen with 500 knights, and knights from Brandenburg, Austria and Bohemia. Between 1323 and 1344 contingents went there from the Rhineland, Bohemia, Alsace, England, Flanders, Austria, France, Bavaria, Holland, Hungary and Burgundy, and after 1350 there were Occitanians, Scots and Italians.[41] Two famous men were Henry Bolingbroke, Duke of Lancaster and Earl of Derby (later Henry IV) who came twice in 1390/1 and 1392/3, and Ghillebert de Lannoy who led a peripatetic life. Horses featured strongly in all crusading expeditions as no rich knight went without a *remuda* to fall back on. Prussian conditions were harsh, with swampy land, poor forage, devastating cold on a winter *reyza* and swarms of insects on a summer campaign. In spring and autumn the land was an impassable morass, only dry summer and frozen winter conditions being tolerable.

Bolingbroke's 1390 accounts show logistics and trading. His retinue of 100, with thirteen knights, eighteen squires, three heralds, ten miners and engineers, and about fifty volunteers, cost the huge sum of £4,360 to outfit and run. Periodically it was necessary to augment his string of horses, and he purchased a total of twenty-one en route at Danzig, Prak, Wene and Portgruer; his retinue members traded among themselves with stock already owned, which indicates some were well supplied with mounts. Booty yielded welcome additions, 200 saddled horses being captured in a battle with the Lithuanians.[42] In 1208 Henry of Livonia noted a battle between Lithuanians and Germans in which 'the Lithuanians flew around on their speedy horses':[43] that is, on nimble, fast, moderate sized indigenous animals still common to the area, unlike the heavy German destriers.

Lannoy spent a two-year spell as ambassador to Philip the Good of Burgundy and Henry V of England (1413–22), scouting prospects for a new crusade. Spain beckoned him on a crusade against the Moors, and the Teutonic Knights against 'pagans'. He travelled overland to Prussia but his retinue came by sea, landing at Danzig. It was probably the need to equip them that sent him on a side trip to Denmark to purchase mounts at a fair. When returning to Burgundy he went through Russia, travelling by horse-sled to Novgorod, transferring to horseback and continuing on through Poland, Bohemia and Austria. On an oriental foray he went by horse to Caffa, and en route to Akerman was beaten by robbers in 'the great tartar desert', his horses scattered and he and his party were isolated for seven days until his Tatar guides rounded up his horses. At Caffa he sold them, embarking on a Venetian galley for Constantinople. Later he toured Syria, Palestine and Egypt.[44]

It would seem the land route via the Crimea and the Black Sea shores was a danger zone as bandit attacks on European travellers were common, whereas Ibn Battuta had received a hospitable Crimean welcome.

THE INDEPENDENT TRAVELLER

Some with the wanderlust risked hazardous or uncomfortable independent travel. Wealthier folk sure of hospitality toured the courts of Europe, either on their own account, or as part of their overlord's retinue. Significantly, nearly all the secular accounts are from the fifteenth century onwards, when literacy expanded out of monastic confines. Several Europeans travelled widely; Bertrandon de la Brocquière from the Duchy of Guienne from 1432/3 to 1439; the Spaniard Pero Tafur from 1435 to 1439; the German Arnold von Harff from 1496 to 1499 and the Italian Ludovico Varthema from 1503 to 1508. All noted that in Mamlūk and Ottoman towns Jews and Christians were forbidden to ride a horse, so donkeys, asses and camels were town transport.

Von Harff and Varthema visited Mamlūk territory when there was internal dissension, uprisings and assassinations paving the way for the ascendant Ottomans. Von Harff gives few, but enlightening, equestrian details. Because of the prevalence of Arab bandits an armed Mamlūk guard accompanied the monthly caravan which crossed the Alhijset (the Hejaz) en route to Mecca. Although travelling only part of the route, for six ducats Von Harff joined the caravan which he estimated at 7,000, counting in excess of 3,000 people and the multitude of horses, camels and donkeys for riding and pack. Making the acquaintance of Conrad, a mercenary from Basle who had enlisted with the Mamlūks (earlier he had encountered a Danish mercenary in similar employ), he had an insight into their system. Each Mamlūk received 150 *ceraphtim* (nine ducats) for equipment of two handbows, quiver, arrows, sword, spear and an iron mace. He was required to have three horses, one to ride, one for his slave to ride and another to spell his horse when it tired. If sent to battle he received 'as much as when he was first chosen', which was 100 ducats. Monthly pay was six ducats (contradicting himself as he also said twelve), and 1 lb of meat and bread daily, and a quartern of barley for his horse(s) which were kept in the hot sand with no straw or hay. Von Harff much admired their entire chargers. The caravan must have encountered Arabs en route, whether bandits hovering or peaceable Bedu he does not say, but describes them as 'rough blackish hard people' who travelled with their tents, camels, asses, sheep, goats, wives and children, so they must have been a tribe, maybe on annual transhumance. 'They have beautiful little horses which they ride with bare legs and feet in the stirrups. They carry in their hands a javelin which is a long hollow tube having a long iron point, and ride in this manner.'[45]

Varthema concurs with much of Von Harff's notes but gives more details on Arab riding and raiding, having been in a caravan that was attacked. He singled out the main Arab family, which was based on El Mezarib. Its leader, Ez Zaabi, was reputed to have a total of 40,000 horses and 300,000 camels, of which 10,000 mares were with him at court and were used in raiding.[46] This is the first time I have come across a contemporary hint in European writings that it was the mare, not the stallion, that was the preferred saddle horse among the Arab tribes. The Arabs put a higher premium on mares than entires, tracing foals through the maternal line, and were very reluctant to part with a good mare.

In addition to constant tribal warfare, *razzias* took the Arabs as far as Damascus, Cairo and Jerusalem, and harvested grain was often targetted. Ez Zaabi's pace on a *razzia* was relentless:

> Sometimes he runs a whole day and night with his said mares without stopping . . . at the end of the journey they are given camels' milk to drink . . . they ride for the most part without saddles . . .

Caravans for Mecca could be enormous. Varthema gives statistics which are rather more believable than Ez Zaabi's herds of horses and camels. For the Mecca/Cairo gathering there were 64,000 camels and 100 Mamlūk guards. His Mecca caravan, also huge, had 40,000 people and sixty Mamlūk guards divided into vanguard, centre and rearguard. The Damascus/Mecca journey took forty days, and with waterholes eight days apart 16,000 of the 35,000 camels were needed to carry water. At one waterhole an army of Arabs attacked, demanding payment for water; given 12,000 ducats they demanded more so the Mamlūks and all those capable of bearing arms, around 300, fought back. The Arabs killed a man and a woman, but lost 1,600 of their own because riding bareback they 'had difficulty in turning our way'.[47]

Centuries later, Lady Anne Blunt visited many Arab tribes in her quest for the purebred desert-bred horse and commented on the horses' lean condition. It is infinitely harder, and vastly more uncomfortable, to stay aboard a razor-backed lean horse! De la Brocquière also commented on the Turkish habit of keeping their horses 'very low',[48] it being the custom in Europe, Spain apart with its Moorish heritage, to overstuff horses, many of which were cold-blooded and inclined to larger body mass.

Mamlūk equestrian and weapon expertise, gained in obligatory *Furusiyya* exercises, impressed: Varthema, shades of William Tell, saw a Mamlūk shoot a pomegranate from his slave's head at the second shot. Another, riding at the gallop, unsaddled his horse, placed the saddle on his head, and then returned it to the horse's back.[49]

De la Brocquière and Pero Tafur gave similar information on the Cairene and Meccan situation, but added much equestrian and incidental information on Europe. Both secured an audience with the Grand Turk, Murad II (1421–51), so must have been men of some consequence.

Tafur's travels come across as mostly a pleasure jaunt. He was awed by the glamorous and ostentatious side of oriental and European society. A black horse given to the Mamlūk sultan at Cairo excited his admiration. It was shod with gold, its saddle and bridle gold-garnished, the saddle bow (pommel) adorned with a ruby the size of a large orange and the cantle with three rubies the size of hen's eggs. Its trappers were of white damask bordered with valuable pearls. When the sultan hunted he was accompanied by 5,000–6,000 horsemen and many falcons and leopards (cheetahs). After the morning's hunt a hazardous game of polo was fought; with 1,000(!) on each side it appears to have resembled a grudge rugby match on horseback, all attacking the ball at once. One player tried to hinder the sultan's son, at which he drew his sword to kill him, only the sultan's intervention preventing a death.[50] At his audience with Murad II he was again bowled over by the huge mounted retinue, said to be 60,000: '. . . in good faith I am afraid to repeat all that was told me'. Tafur said no one walked but all rode on 'very small lank horses', and comparing the great number of horses among the Turks he boasted Spain 'could show as many. I would as lief ride to war or to tourney on one of our asses as on any of their horses'.[51] Continuing his itinerary he reported on the huge slave trade shipping out via Caffa. The Mamlūk sultan sent his agents there, and the Pope authorized Christians to purchase Christian slaves 'to prevent their falling into the hands of the Moors and renouncing the Faith . . .'[52]

Once back in Europe, Tafur crossed the Alps by the dangerous St Gothard Pass sitting on an ox-drawn sled and leading his horse behind him by the reins. Only the ox was at risk. In Germany and Belgium he went on a 'Cook's Tour' visiting fairs at Cologne, Antwerp and Frankfurt, having a go at a tournament at Schaffhausen, and visiting the armourers of Nuremberg. At Breslau (now Wrocław in Poland) the frozen roads were like glass, making it dangerous to ride for fear of the horses falling; instead, those who could afford it travelled in a horse-drawn sled, the 'horses shod with iron after the manner of the country', presumably with large calkins and heavy frost nails to give grip. Others, wealthier, rode in an eight- or ten-horse coach. In Italy he visited Rome and witnessed a Papal procession, with clergy, archbishops and bishops on foot, followed by mounted cardinals, then twelve crimson-trapped horses carrying religious regalia, the last horse covered in brocade with a silver saddle and carrying a casket with the Blessed Sacrament. The Pope rode a crimson-trapped horse led by the Marquis of Ferrara and the Count of Urbino. Tafur's horses which had given him excellent service over many hundreds of miles had been left to rest and regain flesh at Ferrara, and his journey being almost at an end he sold them[53] – no sentiment there, just a means of transport.

De la Brocquière, doing in part a similar journey, was far more concerned with equestrian and military customs, especially those of the Ottoman among whom he spent two years (see ch.11) He was far more knowledgeable about horses than Tafur, and on his return via Hungary assessed the Hungarian horse trade (see ch.2). He appreciated a good horse whatever its type, describing horses ridden by the Arabs as 'beautiful' and the small horse he bought in Damascus as 'turning out very well'. He kept it for the whole of his journey, eventually giving it to the Duke of Burgundy on his return, along with his Turkish dress, a copy of the *Koran* and a *Life of Mohammed* written in Latin, which the chaplain of the Venetian Consul at Damascus had given him. Shoeing among the Turks was very different from that practised in Europe – it still is. The little horse was shod at Damascus, the set lasting him for fifty days as far as Bursa. The shoes were light, thin, lengthened towards the heel, and thinner there than at the toe. They were not turned up (no calkins) and only had four heavy-headed square nails, two to each side. The horses were cold-shod, the metal workable because it was so thin. This tells us much about expertise in shoeing – a shoe always wears most at the toe, and the lengthening towards the heel gave the horse a better weight distribution, thus relieving some strain on tendons, and the lack of calkins meant he was not tipped forward, also resulting in less strain on tendons and suspensory ligaments.

> The horses of this country [that is Syria and Anatolia] only walk and gallop. Those which have the best walk are preferred, as in Europe those which trot the best. They have wide nostrils, gallop well, and are excellent, costing little on the road; for they eat only at night, and then but a small quantity of barley with chopped straw. They never drink but in the afternoon.

When stabled, their two hind hooves were hobbled. General riding horses were geldings; only a few stallions for breeding were kept

> but the Moors [here meaning Turks not Bedu] esteem only mares. In that country a great man is not ashamed to ride a mare with a foal running after its dam. I have seen some sold as high as two or three hundred ducats. They are accustomed to keep their horses very low, and never allow them to get fat.[54]

When de la Brocquière adopted the Turkish manner of riding with short stirrups he at first found it very uncomfortable, and stiffened so much he could not remount once having dismounted. But after a short time he found he preferred it to the European long-stirruped method.

Travelling back on his Damascene horse through Serbia, Bulgaria and Hungary he was made aware of how ground-down were the people, longing but not daring to throw off the Ottoman yoke.[55]

A FIFTEENTH-CENTURY 'GRAND TOUR'

The 1465–67 travels of the Catholic Czech Baron Leo of Rozmital encompassed all aspects of a leisurely Grand Tour. His travelogue, written by his squire Schasek and the German Gabriel Tetzel, gives no hint of any ambassadorial purpose for his visits to the courts of Germany, Flanders, England, France, Spain, Portugal and Italy, but he may have aimed at gaining help from European monarchs to lay the ground for a rapprochement with the Pope. Rozmital's sister had married the excommunicated Bohemian Hussite King George Podebrad.

Schasek and Tetzel describe the journey's hazards and highlights, including the lavish hospitality, sometimes at courts but more often at inns to which hosts sent sumptuous victuals, as well as offering entertainment at their residences, and usually settling the inn reckonings.

Rozmital left Prague on 26 November with a retinue of forty, composed of knights, attendants, jesters and a lute player, a cart for baggage and fifty-six horses. At Nuremberg he hired chronicler Tetzel. No expense was spared, even the servants were clad in red embroidered with gold and velvet, their sleeves garnished with pearls.

It was a punishing itinerary. From Nuremberg they went to Anspach, Feuchtwangen, Keylsam (Crailsheim), through the Hohenlohe country, Ohringen, Hall (Schwabish Hall),

Wimpfen, Heidelberg, Frankfurt, Mainz, Rudesheim, Coblenz, Cologne, Aachen and Neuss. Mostly they rode, but occasionally shipped their horses, as from Coblenz to Cologne.[56]

Tourneying was an addictive pastime; Rozmital's uncle Jan Zehrowsky was by far the most ardent, though not always very smart. Tiltings punctuated their journey at several stopovers, including Anspach, Cologne, the court of Duke Philip of Burgundy, and at Graz before Emperor Frederick III. In Duke Philip's hall one very peculiar form was undertaken. Burgundy ordered it 'in the manner of his country across a barrier' and Rozmital requested some part to be according to Czech customs *sans* barrier. After the normal courses were run Zehrowsky, for a bravura show of strength 'in honour of the illustrious ladies . . .', charged the wall of the hall, hitting it so hard his horse was thrown onto its haunches, at which some of the courtiers investigated to see if he was fastened to the saddle. Not satisfied with showing off, Zehrowsky charged again, drawing a comment from Duke Philip that punishing a parricide by forcing him to fight that way was too harsh, and that he was amazed the Bohemian considered it sport! To finish the exhibition Achatz Frodner, one of Rozmital's knights, leaped fully accoutred from his horse without touching his stirrups. At Graz Zehrowsky's opponent was the 'strong and valiant tilter' Lord Reinprecht Renburger who scored an own goal. Running his spear into Zehrowsky's borrowed horse's head he then impaled himself on it. (Tetzel) Schaseck saw it differently:

> . . . the German transfixed Lord John's horse under him, but with the force of the attack he was unhorsed, which caused much surprise to the Emperor and the others. John, however, remained unmoved in his saddle.[57]

It seems not only knights got punch drunk! Zehrowsky's well-battering horse must have been short of a few brain cells! At that period the Court of Burgundy was known for its glitz and glamour, and among the Burgundian treasures were horse furniture and armour coverings worth 10,000 crowns, and a chamfron worth over 30,000. Anticipating some reciprocal Burgundian splendour, Rozmital presented Charles of Burgundy (Charolais, later Charles the Bold) 'with a very fine horse, hoping for a better one in return . . .' Tetzel does not say if Rozmital lucked out, but comments on the white palfrey, superior to Rozmital's horse, given to Frodner by Charles.[58]

From the Burgundian court Rozmital headed for Calais and embarked for England with thirty-six horses, sending the rest home with some of his pages. The journey was rough. The ship sprang a leak and water rose to the horses' bellies, but eventually they arrived at Canterbury. Rozmital's hopes of tourneying at Windsor against the Earl of Warwick were dashed when Edward IV forbade it. Nevertheless, on leaving after a forty-day sojourn, several of his retinue made a gift to Edward IV of all their tourney horses and harness. They endured an even rougher passage back to France, holing up in Guernsey for twelve days on account of bad weather and pirates. They ran out of food and fodder and could buy none. When they sailed again, a great storm blew up so that the horses below deck 'fell against each other and at times lay on each other and were quite spent . . .' Docking at St Malo in Brittany the horses were so debilitated they had to be hoisted out and 'could neither stand nor go and were quite overcome'.[59]

After travelling without mishap through France they crossed into Spain and met trouble. Around Biscay the people were 'evil and murderous', the inns 'evil beyond measure', the country devoid of fodder for their horses, and, to cap it all, when they got hold of grain two of Tetzel's horses sickened – 'they fell away and became swollen and could not evacuate'. Rozmital lost a fine horse and ten of his horses were ill. The grain must have been mouldy or otherwise unfit to eat, and the two who became swollen most likely had grain fermented in the digestive tract, and this was compounded by a compacted gut. They were lucky to lose only one. As they headed south to Burgos the heat was intolerable. At a river crossing they at first refused to pay the toll, so the toll collectors impounded their baggage horses and attacked. Fearing for their lives they loaded crossbows, but Rozmital feared they would all be killed, so reluctantly they paid the toll and recovered their horses. It took thirteen days to cross the mountains, during which two more horses died, one of them Rozmital's favourite stallion. Once at Burgos they attended a wild bull hunt in which picadors on swift jennets (see below) surrounded the bull and shot darts into it. Maddened, it attacked wildly, killing one horse and injuring two more plus one of the men, then when it tired dogs were set on it. At Salamanca the baiting process was repeated in the marketplace after which the riders attacked each other with lances, either defending themselves with shields or catching the lances 'as the heathen do'.[60] Tetzel was describing the Spanish tourney with reed lances where the riders rode Andalusian-type horses *à la ginete* on a low saddle and with short stirrups, relying more on horsemanship than brute force – the latter they reserved for defenceless animals subjected to their baiting.

In Portugal they fared much better, remarking on the yearly slave-catching campaign undertaken in Africa in which '100,000 or more ethiopians (blacks)' were captured and 'sold like cattle'. On leaving Portugal the King gave Rozmital: 'two elegant horses called jennets, the like of which for speed and agility are scarcely to be found in any other christian country . . .' The jennets were Lusitanos, of similar genetic stock to the Andalusian.[61]

Although Rozmital's horses were reduced still further by death and gift-giving, he still had the Lusitanos when he reached Prague, and on a courtesy visit to Neustadt to visit the empress, sister of the king of Portugal, he gratefully described her brother's generous gift of the horses, two 'ethiopians' and an ape.[62]

Rozmital covered well over 4,600 miles (as the crow flies). He used his horses continuously and they suffered on many an occasion from rough seas, scant and/or bad fodder and hard usage. Overall the medieval traveller using his horse as transport put an inordinate amount of stress upon his mount. Feast or famine frequently alternated, and not all riders were horsemen, as shown by the comparisons between Tafur and de la Brocquière.

CHAPTER 11
Warhorse Territory:
The Geographical Canvas

The best way to plot the course of history's warhorses in a single chapter is to take a brief gallop over the medieval map of equestrian peoples drawn into cavalry conflict. It shows a substructure of breed and type infiltration, subsequent interbreeding, the emergence of new equid strains and a glimpse of how much of Europe was affected by the equine overspill from Asiatic and oriental stock. For a fuller appreciation of warhorses' decisive roles I should like to direct my readers to my *The Medieval Warhorse: from Byzantium to the Crusades* and *The Warhorse 1250–1600*, where the geographic, cultural and military aspects of medieval mounted warfare are covered.

The three elements in medieval cavalry were Asiatic, oriental, and occidental. The first two eventually blended to some degree, owing to Turkic elements in both human and equine resources. In turn some oriental patina rubbed off on to parts of European mounted warfare, especially where east met west in Russia and eastern Europe which suffered mightily from Asiatic and steppe nomad attacks on several occasions. The Balkans and much of eastern Europe bore the brunt of Ottoman aggression. In the occident cavalry was different, from the type of horse used to the tactics in which it was deployed. The western element floundered and blundered along, for the most part using massed horseflesh in a once-off total committal that either disintegrated into disorganized multiple mêlées, or, like a spent arrow, was impossible to retrieve: European destriers were not noted for their nimbleness, nor knights for working in the cohesion that was such a part of much of oriental warfare where the horse was used more intelligently, notably by their light horse archers in a sting, retreat, and hit-again manner which softened up the enemy with minimal danger to themselves. In the ninth century Al Jahiz wrote of the Turks as being as much to be feared in retreat as in attack:

> . . . and if they do turn their backs they are to be feared as much as deadly poison and sudden death; for their arrows hit the mark as much when they are retreating as when they are advancing. And one cannot be sure of not being caught by their lasso or having one's horse caught and their riders seized in the same motion . . .[1]

EQUESTRIAN HERITAGE

In the heavy cavalry and light horse divisions the orient had a rich inheritance. At the opening of the medieval era Europe had yet to (re)find its way aboard a warhorse, apart from the small mounted retinues serving the multitude of minor kings, especially in the Frankish sphere. This is strange for there was an equestrian legacy but it had fallen into desuetude.

Backtracking to the Roman era we can see how, at the beginning of their thrust for empire, Rome had little cavalry – only 300 per legion according to Polybius writing in the second century BC.[2] By Diocletian's day (284–305) approximately one-third of Roman forces were cavalry.[3] In the intervening period Rome had fought many nations noted for their cavalry, and/or had drafted into her orbit horsed warrior peoples who left their mark and their breeds of horses well into the medieval era. From North Africa came the Numidian horsemen of the Roman era, and the Berbers and Moors of later centuries; the Persians' cavalry expertise went back to antiquity and lasted beyond the medieval era. Many Asiatic and Turkic tribes, with whom the later Romans were plagued as their empire crumbled, had an enduring effect on the medieval period. Syrian horsed archers played their part in Rome's forces. Syria and Egypt were territories of the Mamlūks, the most renowned military horsemen of the era. Rome made extensive use of Gallic and Spanish horsemen, drawing in as auxiliary horse in the late first century AD a total of 17,500 from Lugdunensis (Lyon), Narbonensis (Narbonne) and Belgica, and 6,000 from Spain. From these provinces were also added 3,375 mounted men in the *Cohortes Equitatae*. The provinces of Thrace, Pannonia, Syria, Africa, Britain, Palestine and Moesia also added significantly to Roman cavalry.[4]

Considering that Gaul and Belgica had provided so many mounted units to Rome it poses a big question as to why, when Roman power waned so did the use of cavalry across these regions, so much so that its re-emergence was looked on as something new? That cavalry did reappear can in some measure be attributed to the need to combat Moorish mounted troops based in their newly conquered Spanish lands. The catalyst for the re-emergence of west European cavalry was the Frankish royal house. In the interim between Romans and Franks most cavalry in Europe was imported, either by warring people who came to stay, or by invaders whose hold was eventually reversed (although in some cases not till after a span of several centuries), but who left an equestrian legacy on which the medieval era could build.

On other fronts, within a spectacularly short time, much of the warhorse canvas was gathered into the clutches of the rapidly expanding Islamic phenomenon.

THE EARLY MEDIEVAL EQUESTRIAN MATRIX

Byzantium

The Eastern Roman Empire, which endured until its annihilation by the Ottomans with the fall of Constantinople in 1453, was still enlarging its territory and/or reimposing its authority over earlier holdings throughout the reign of Justinian (527–65). Procopius of Caesarea, the historian who recorded Justinian's wars, often accompanied the Byzantine army which fought against Persia, the Vandals in Africa and the Goths in Italy. Belisarius and Narses were the two most famous Byzantine generals, and cavalry the most important arm of their forces, with mounts from many sources. There were imperial herds in Thrace, Phrygia and Cappadocia,[5] some of which went back a long way; and horses were also drafted from other sources. During the war against the Vandals Belisarius received 'an exceedingly great number of horses from the royal pastures, which are kept for him (the emperor) in the territory of Thrace'. From Sicily Amalsuntha, the Gothic Queen Regent, provided 'a multitude of horses to which the final mastery of the enemy was chiefly due', and the beaten Vandals surrendered all the government post horses in Africa to Belisarius.[6] Steppe peoples and nomadic tribes provided much of the Byzantine horse, notably from the Eruli, Massagetae and Goths.[7] Booty from successful wars in Persia and Africa and the eighteen-year long Gothic wars would have swelled the remount lines. These areas had a long history of horsebreeding and utilizing the horse in military operations.

The best source for Byzantine cavalry detail is the *Strategikon of the Emperor Maurice*

(582–602) under whom cavalry was *the* arm. It contains sensible advice on management in the horse lines and in action. The bulk of Byzantine cavalry were archers trained to shoot rapidly on a fast-moving horse to front, rear, right and left. Deft handling of the spear was also to be practised at the gallop.[8] All cavalry horses were worked at speed in all types of terrain: open level country, hills, rough ground, up and down hills, and in thick, i.e. wooded and/or heavy going.[9] The rider was equipped with an ankle-length, hooded mailcoat; a gorget; a small, plumed helmet; a bow and bowcase; a quiver for 30–40 arrows; and two Avar-type lances and sword. An awl and file were carried for mending gear and sharpening weapons. He wore a roomy tunic, fixed at the knee when riding, and a large felt cloak to protect against rain and to hide the gleam of mail when on patrol. His horse's tack consisted of a saddle with stirrups, a thick saddle pad, a good quality bridle, a capacious saddle bag for iron rations, a lasso and hobbles.[10] At the least all officers' and front-rank horses wore iron chamfrons and peytrals of either iron or felt.[11] The allotment in formation of a space 3 ft wide by 8 ft long suggests cavalry mounts ranged from *c.*14.3 hh to 15.2 hh. The narrow width meant stirrup-to-stirrup formation, which would have presented an impressive shock force.

The Lombards

The Lombards were a fierce equestrian tribe which migrated into central Europe, reaching Pannonia in AD 165. Evicted by the Romans, they returned to settle in the Älfold. In 547 Justinian legalized their tenure to gain them as much-needed allies. When confronted by the Gepids, Justinian aided their cause with 10,000 Byzantine horse. In the wars against the Goths the Lombards provided 1,000 heavy cavalry for the Byzantine general, Germanus. Later Narses used them against Totila, the Gothic leader, dismounting them to ensure they stayed to fight. Subsequently he had them escorted out of Byzantine territory because they celebrated victory by a rampage of burning and looting. In 568 they returned in force to Italy, staying for a further two centuries.[12] Paul the Deacon described Lombard heavy cavalrymen as wearing cuirass, greaves and helmet, and bearing a heavy *contus* and *spatha*. Horsebreeding and dealing were regulated by Lombard law, with horse values set high: the Lombard king's royal stud produced a superior type of warhorse.[13]

The Avars

In the mid-sixth century the Juan Juan, who fought almost exclusively on horseback and are credited with introducing the stirrup to Europe, were driven from their Altaic and Siberian territories by a Turkic revolt and appeared in the Caucasus in 557. They became known as the Avars, a Turkic word meaning 'exiles'. In 558 they sent an embassy to Constantinople requesting gifts, money and land to settle on, agreeing to ally with Justinian against his enemies. But they used their new alliance to carve out their own territory, rapidly subjugating the peoples of the lower Danube. On the accession of Justin II in 565 the Avars sent another embassy to Constantinople requesting tribute. It was denied. They next allied with the Lombards to defeat the Gepids and seize the latter's Dacian and Pannonian lands, then turned on the Lombards and forced them out of Pannonia. By 568 they had overrun the Älfold grazing grounds. There they settled, being a constant threat to their former Byzantine allies, who nevertheless still used them on occasion, notably in 578 when 60,000 Avar horsemen crossed the Danube, repulsed the Slavs, then freed thousands of Byzantine prisoners. They next went repeatedly against Byzantium until a treaty was brokered between Emperor Maurice and the Avars, an annual tribute being paid to keep them away. Subsequently their raids resumed, until in the reign of Heraclius in 626 they finally withdrew into Pannonia,[14] where we meet them again in the reign of Charlemagne, who with his son Pepin, conducted a long campaign against them. It was not successfully completed until its eighth year according to Einhard; in fact it lasted from 791 to 803.[15]

The Magyars

Less than a century later Hungary suffered another invasion of nomadic horsemen who left their imprint on the country's horsemanship. The Magyars were of Finno-Ugrian and Turkic stock, and came into the Byzantine sphere, as had the Avars, due to nomadic pressure movements. They were then driven from the Russian steppes in 889 by the Pechenegs (Patzinaks), taking up their unwanted residence in the Hungarian plains in 892. By 895/6 it was clear they had come to stay. The horses of the massed archers were mostly small, but their leaders rode larger, better-bred animals.[16] The 1966 report by V.I. Calkin on Russian research into the animal husbandry of Central Asia in the Scythian period indicated the taller, better-bred horse, similar to a modern Akhal Teke, was the mount of the ruling classes, and the shorter-statured, heavier-boned animal, around 13.3 hh, the mount of the masses.[17] These types continue today in Russia and in territories over which much of the early medieval nomadic peoples warred.

The Arabs and the Moors

While the Avars were settling into the Älfold, the tribes of the Arabian Peninsula were being suborned by the charismatic leader Mohammed, who combined his religious fanaticism with a call to arms. Arabia could then only field about 300 heavy Meccan cavalry, but within an astonishingly short period the Arabs, by conquest and loot, had acquired sufficient horses to become a formidable horsed people. Initially there was strife within the Peninsula tribes, but externally Byzantium and Persia were the first major targets against which the camel-borne, soon to be horsed, Arabs scored significant victories: at Ajnadain against Byzantium and at Babylon on the Euphrates against the Persians, both in 634, with another victory over the Persians at Qadisiya in 637. Once masters in Persian territory, the Arabs had access to both the best horses and the best armourers. In the next few decades the Arab whirlwind drew into its vortex Byzantine territory in Syria, Palestine and Egypt, and Kufa and Basra in Iraq. In 711 the first waves of Islamic warriors crossed to Spain, followed by larger incursions, the cavalry mostly mounted on tough Berber (Barb) horses. By 750 the forces of Islam had added North Africa and the Maghreb, Afghanistan, Baluchistan, Turkestan, Khorassan and Uzbekistan to its conquests.

Within these Arab conquests were the breeding grounds of many fine oriental breeds of horse, noted in preceding chapters. In addition to the Byzantine imperial herds, and many horses taken from Qadisiya, remount depots were set up, notably at Kufa in Iraq, and in northern Syria. Pillaging went on unabated, the Malagina Byzantine depot losing its horses to an Arab *Razzia* in 789. The Arabs could now draw on stock suitable for war in almost every part of their territories.[18] Spain provided larger horses than the African Berber mounts. The Arab historian Tarif ibn Taric says these were quickly requisitioned, enabling Moorish foot to become cavalry. Al Mansur, who ruled Moorish Spain from 978 to 1002, in place of the titular but weak Umayyad Caliph, Al Hisham (976–1002), imported much Berber stock, setting up stud farms around the Córdoban area.[19]

Persia

The *Strategikon* said Persians were cunning and servile, but had foresight, skill, bravery and resourcefulness. Persia was a recurring enemy against Byzantium (and later against the Ottomans), with wars from Justinian through to Heraclius (610–41), who with the aid of the Turkic Khazars fought his last and decisive campaign against them in 627. In 628 they sued for peace.[20]

In antiquity Persia was known for its quality horses, especially the Nisaean bred on the lush plains of Media. It was of considerable size and bulk, judging by the Apadana Frieze at Persepolis and from later carvings at Firuzabad in the third century AD, and at Tāq-i-Bōstān in the seventh. The late second-century Roman poet Oppian commented on several breeds then found in Persia. The Parthian was 'eminently handsome, and the only one to stand up to a lion; the Nisaean the best, most beautiful, gentle to ride, obedient to the bit (and had a) small head'. In that era Armenia and Cappadocia produced superb horses and paid yearly tribute to Persia in horses.[21]

Persian and Parthian chargers had long been armoured. A second-century AD rock drawing, and a third-century mail bard were discovered at Dura Europus,[22] and the Firuzabad rock carvings show the horses of Parthian King Ardashir I (224–41), his son Shapur and other warriors riding fully barded chargers; on the Tāq-i-Bōstān rock, Shabdiz, the mount of Persian King Chosroes II (591–628) wears head, neck and forequarters' protection. In the thirteenth century, Friar John de Plano Carpini described the Persian armours made for Mongol conquerors (see p. 68), and in the fifteenth, when Venice sent ambassadors to Uzun Hassan, the Ak Koyunlu ruler of Persia, and to his successors, Caterino Zeno, Josefa Barbaro, M. Ambrogio Contarini, and Giovan Maria Angiolello all commented on the superb cavalry horses and armour of the Persians. Zeno, sent to Persia in 1471, said, 'finer cavalry were never seen in any army'; Contarini commented on the Persians' 'good and handsome horses'; and Barbaro, with more exactitude than normal in medieval arithmetic, dropped a bean into his pocket for every fifty head at a Persian muster: of the 20,000 'horses of service' 2,000 were covered:

> with armour of iron, made in little squares and wrought with gold and silver, tacked together with small mail which hanged down in maner to the ground, and under the gold it had a fringe. The rest were covered some with leather after our manner, some with silk, and some with quilted work so thick that an arrow could not have passed through it. The horsemen's armour was of the same sort . . .[22]

Angiolello noted that Shiraz was the major centre for arms and armour manufacture, equipping both men and horses with full panoply and supplying not only Persia but Syria, Constantinople and all the east.[23] Persian armourers were, as we have seen, also to be found plying their craft in India.

Europe

Under the Frankish kings cavalry made a fresh start. In 755 Pepin I (741–68) changed the traditional muster of troops from March to May,[24] a time when grazing is lush, thus indicating the army was now largely mounted. By that date clashes with the mounted Moors had already taken place. In 758 after Pepin defeated the Saxons he set their annual tribute at 300 horses.[25] Now land tenure and cavalry service went hand in hand, the acreage a man held determining his liability. Under Charlemagne it was considered that four manses (100–148 acres) supplied the wherewithal for one cavalryman and mount,[26] but it took twelve manses to provide the full panoply of trooper, horse, weapons, armour, baggage beasts, horse for squire, and fodder and food for horses and men for three months, the usual term demanded.[27] Between the years 800–840 it is estimated the Carolingians could field some 35,000 cavalry based on an average retinue of twenty for each of the king's 1,800 tenurial vassals.[28]

The battle of Anghiari by Pierre Paul Rubens, copy of a fresco painted by Leonardo da Vinci for the Palazzo Vecchio, Florence.

During the tenth century the Magyars terrorized western Europe and the Balkan territories of the Byzantines using their Turkic tactics of swarming horse archers. But in 955 they suffered a catastrophic defeat in the Battle of the Lech at the hands of the 8,000-strong army of Otto the Great. This battle stands out for reversing the flow of nomadic incursions into Europe (for the present), and because it was one of the earliest, if not the first, purely cavalry engagement in western Europe.[29]

Coming from Scandinavia in the mid-ninth century the Norsemen probed the mouths of the Rhine, Meuse, Scheldt, Seine and Loire: across the channel, England suffered their plundering visitations. At first purely foot and marine warriors, they quickly became *au fait* with the horse, appropriating them on landing in France and England. The *Anglo-Saxon Chronicles* often refer to the 'force' being horsed on landing, as in 866 when they lifted horses from East Anglia. In 892, using a fleet of 250 ships, the 'force' landed in Kent with horses purloined from Frankland.[30]

Giving their name to Normandy and integrating with the locals, as well as taking over their land and stud farms, the Normans evolved into first-class cavalry, bringing a renewed assault on England in 1066 when Bastard William's cavalry was the decisive arm in his victory at Hastings. From then on the importance of cavalry in Europe escalated, and breeding the right type of horse for war got under way as the knight became more heavily armed and armoured, and the horse began to wear bards of mail, leather, and eventually plate.

The battle of Pavia as recreated by Leeds Armoury.

The Normans also hired themselves out as mercenaries. Their cavalry affected warfare in England, Italy, Byzantium, Syria and France. Aimo of Salerno, an eleventh-century monk, recorded the 1016 Muslim siege of Salerno. Normans were asked to help and, equipped by Salerno, because of their success they were invited to stay, but declined and returned to Normandy laden with gifts. They were soon back to serve as mercenaries, rapidly introducing Norman warfare to southern Italy. German cavalry also regularly crossed the Alps into Italy with a show of force from the German king who also wore the crown of Lombardy and the imperial crown of the Holy Roman Empire. To aid Christians regain lost territories from Moorish invaders a stream of Frankish knights crossed into Spain, and in 1035 Castile was added to the Christian kingdoms of Leon and Navarre.[31]

WEST MEETS EAST

1095 heralded the Crusading era and a massive exodus of fighting men from Europe. At the Council of Clermont Pope Urban II called for armed aid to be given to the Christians of the east, in response to an appeal from Emperor Alexius Commenus I for aid in his wars against the Seljuks. Alexius' daughter Anna Comnena wrote of her father's concern over the size of the Frankish armies, in place of the mercenaries he had asked for. She deplored the hooliganism of the troops of Godfrey de Bouillon. She reported on the first cavalry engagement where, to break the force of the Norman charge, the Byzantines shot at the Franks' horses, but although disgusted by the Normans, she was awed by the charge of Frankish heavy horse,[32] but as we have seen (above) Abou Bekr ibn Bedr saw it as a mass of ill-trained horses lacking manoeuvrability.

Horses going to the Crusades had only a small chance of returning to Europe. Most died from starvation, dehydration, endemic diseases and wounds. They were ill suited to the intense heat of crusading territory, to which the lighter framed oriental horse is well adapted. Of the many monastic chroniclers who accompanied crusading armies, Raymond of Aguiliers seems most sympathetic to the horses' plight. He speaks many times of Arabian horses, and the Crusaders replenishing their stocks by gift, purchase, theft and booty. He graphically describes their sufferings. For two days after the Crusaders' victory at the Battle of Dorylaeum on 1 July 1097 the ground was littered with dead horses and men; at the siege of Antioch, horses were dying of hunger. In the Provençal camp there were hardly 100 left, and they were scrawny and feeble. After Antioch city fell more than 100 Christians and a greater number of horses died at one city entrance alone; on the journey to Jerusalem such was the scarcity of horses that many men turned back. Those that arrived at the Pool of Siloam, at the foot of Mount Zion outside Jerusalem, were met with the sight of 'horses, mules, cattle, sheep, and many other animals too weak to take another step. There they shrivelled, died from thirst and rotted in their tracks.'[33]

The Seljuks

The Seljuks were one of the twenty-four tribes of the Ghuzz (Oghuz) federation. Under their leader Alp Arslan almost yearly incursions were made into Byzantine territory, culminating in 1071 with the Turkish victory at the Battle of Manzikert which gave them access to the whole of Asia Minor. Turkic tribes were superb equestrians, their horses mainly those bred by the Turcoman tribes as described by Ibn Battuta (see above). It was due to tribal inroads that the Turcoman horse, in its many strains, spread into Asia Minor, and eventually became well enough known to Europe to be a worthwhile buy in the markets of Aleppo, but that was many centuries ahead.

Turks and Franks used different fighting methods; the Frankish charge which the Turks could not withstand, and the Turkic hovering archers who brought horses down in droves. The Sultan of Rum, Kilij Arslan, employed these tactics against the army of Bohemund as he marched for Antioch via Dorylaeum in June 1097 after his capital, Nicaea, had surrendered to the Franks on 18 June 1097. A week later when the army under Bohemund and Raymond of St Gilles were en route to Antioch via Dorylaeum, the opposing sides met. The two Christian leaders had split their forces; William of Tyre says this was possibly accidental, but considering the Turks had stripped the countryside it was likely to have been the need to search for fodder and water. On 1 July Kilij Arslan, at the head of allegedly 200,000 horse, appeared against Raymond. The Turks dealt with repeated Frankish charges by opening their ranks, raking them with arrow fire, then closing in with swords for the kill and driving the Franks back to their camp. At this point what looked like a Turkish victory was reversed by the arrival of Bohemund. The combined forces turned on the Turks, harrying them for three or four miles and slaughtering many. A huge booty in pack animals, asses, camels and horses was taken.[34]

The Mongols

A different type of invader now came out of the east: the Mongols – superlative, disciplined warriors and horsemen. At the start they rode only their steppe ponies, rugged small-statured and hardly beautiful animals, but soon they had access to the best horses that Turkestan, India, Persia, the whole of Asia Minor and the Levant could supply.

After victories in China, Genghis Khan had set his sights westwards, extending his empire to the Pamirs and the Syr Daria (Jaxartes) by 1217. In 1219 he moved against the

Two Mamuk horsemen whose lance-heads are between each other's shoulder blades.

Khwarazmians; Otrar fell in 1219; and by March 1220 Senjar, Khojend and Jena, Bokhara and Samarkand had followed suit.

And again Europe felt the terror of nomadic invaders as they rampaged through Russia in the 1230s, and Hungary and the Balkans in the early 1240s. Unusually for nomadic invaders they did not stay in Hungary – possibly the Älfold had insufficient grazing for their huge herds of horses and meat on the hoof that followed their armies. In Russia they left a legacy of centuries of oppression. In the orient they ravaged India, Asia Minor and the Levant, but in 1260 at Ayn Jalūt they suffered one of their few defeats at the hands of the Mamlūks.

The Mamlūks

In 1259 Hulegu, the first of the Mongol Il Khans of Persia, marched on Syria. Aleppo was sacked in January 1260. Homs, Hama and Damascus yielded, and in April Hulegu returned to Iran, leaving General Kitbugha to hold Syria.

At Ayn Jālūt on 3 September 1260, 20,000 Mongol horse met 12,000 Mamlūk cavalry under Sultan Qutuz. Kitbugha drew first blood, sweeping away the Mamlūk left flank. Risking all, Qutuz, surrounded by his Mamlūk guard and backed by the rest of his army, plunged in with General Baibars at his side. Mamlūk discipline and superior weight, riding larger mounts, broke the Mongols. Kitbugha's horse was killed and he was captured; faced with decapitation he boasted that one year's increase in men and horses from Mongolia would repair the day's losses.

A Mamluk horseman with a small shield round his neck and a sword in his hand which he brandishes to left and right.

Mamlūk is a word meaning 'slave'. Recruits were drawn mostly from Turkic tribes, notably the Kipchak, who as youngsters were sold into willing military slavery, a career in the Mamlūk army offering large prospects. A royal Mamlūk underwent intensive military and equestrian training at the Cairene barracks. Amirs' Mamlūks underwent similar preparation and, once trained, the young Mamlūk was manumitted and served in the retinue of his respective erstwhile owner.

The Mamlūk phenomenon started in 1250 (although there had long been Mamlūk slaves) with the assassination of the Ayyubid Sultan Turanshah by his Mamlūk guard. Its commander, Aibek, married Turanshah's widow and ruled as Malik al Muizz Aibek (1250–57). The sultanate's rise was rapid. Under Baibars (1260–77), Al Mansur Qalaoon (1279–90) and al Nasir (el Nacer) Muhammed (1298–1308 and 1309–41) the Mamlūks became the most sophisticated equestrians and superb warriors. In part their supremacy was due to the Arabian and other oriental horses of their cavalry (see ch.2). Their power spread until they governed all of Egypt and Syria, but in the late fourteenth and early fifteenth centuries their power waned as sultan rapidly succeeded sultan due to weak leadership, internecine strife and assassinations. Timur, another Turkic/Mongol invader, sacked all of Syria in 1400/01, then came conflict with the rapidly rising Ottoman Turks. The end came in Egypt at the Battle of Ridanieh on 22 January 1517. The long struggle with the Ottomans was over. For the next four centuries the Ottomans travelled a similar course, at first militarily aggressive and strong, then inevitably weakening.[36]

A Mamluk horseman with a sword in his hand.

The Ottomans

Bertrandon de la Brocquière, who lived among the Ottomans for two years, vividly described man and mount:

> Their horses are good, cost little in food, gallop well and for a long time . . . All their horses are geldings, they keep some others for stallions, but so few, I have never seen a single one . . . Their saddles are hollow having pummels before and behind, with short stirrup leathers and wide stirrups.

On the Turkish soldier:

> They wear very handsome coats of armour like to ours, except that the links of the mail are smaller, the vambraces are the same . . . on their head they wear a round white cap, half a foot high, terminated in a point. It is ornamented with plates of iron on all sides to ward off from the face, neck and cheeks blows of the sword . . . the arms of those who have any fortune are a bow, a tarquais (shield), sword, heavy mace with short handle, the thick end of which is cut into many angles. This is a dangerous weapon when struck on the shoulders, or on an unguarded arm. A blow given with it on a head armed with a salade could stun a man. Several have small wooden bucklers with which they cover themselves well on horseback when they draw the bow . . . *having seen it myself.*

De la Brocquière was impressed with their discipline and training:

> 10,000 Turks will make less noise than 100 men in the christian armies. In their
> ordinary marches they only walk, but in these (advance guard going ahead to lay an
> ambush) they always gallop, and as they are besides lightly armed they will thus
> advance further from evening to daybreak than in three other days . . . They choose also
> no horses but such as walk fast, and gallop for a long time, while we select only those
> who gallop well and with ease. It is by these forced marches that they have succeeded in
> surprising and completely defeating the christians.[37]

This they did on 28 September 1396 at the Battle of Nicopolis where oriental discipline
and horse met the ill-disciplined, multi-national European host vying for first thrust at
the enemy, with the French refusing to listen to the Hungarian king Sigismund's tactical
advice and blundering in. The outcome was a decisive Ottoman victory with many men
and horses slaughtered, the horses riddled with arrows or impaled on lances. Thousands
of Europeans were led into slavery and thousands more executed.[38]

The Ottomans warred successfully on several fronts – in Hungary and the Balkans; and
in Asia Minor where they retook land they had lost to Timur, and were the major enemy
of the Ak Koyunlu rulers of Persia throughout the late fifteenth century. In Europe they
had their reverses, notably at Belgrade in 1456 when defeated by John Hunyadi, but at
Mohacs in 1526 their victory initiated 150 years of Turkish overlordship.[39] It is in these
regions that Turcoman stock mixed with native breeds, and Turkic methods of warfare
influenced the Hungarians who had westernized after the Magyar era had waned.

EUROPE AGAIN

At the time of Nicopolis, European heavy cavalry had advanced to its maximum
importance and was on the brink of a reappraisal. As the use of firearms and artillery
began to improve in the fifteenth century, these were effective against the enemy instead
of being more of a threat to the cavalrymen themselves. Nevertheless cavalry was still the
elite arm. Only the wealthy could afford the price of a decent destrier which was always
expensive: the best could cost over £100.

In England royal warhorse breeding peaked under Edward III, wardrobe and *equitia*
accounts have many entries concerning the king's purchases. In 1330 John Brocas bought
for Edward three destriers: Pomers, a grey, cost £120; dappled grey Lebryt £70; and
bright-brown bay Bayard £50. In 1332/33 Arnold Garsy de St John went to Spain and
twenty-three horses were purchased for £715 13s 4d, averaging over £31 each, which was
a considerable price. The highest price paid by Edward was £150 for a destrier given to
the Earl of Salisbury. Moderate, but still high, prices were paid to German dealer
Landuch who sold Edward four horses ranging from £22 10s to £40 10s.[40]

The warhorse of Europe had come a long way since the chunky cob type of the
Norman era. Selective breeding markedly increased the size, but never to draughthorse
bulk. Various horse armours in the Royal Armouries, which I measured, prove the size
was closer to a 1,200–1,300 lb horse. Further proof was that the horse from which the
measurements for the models which wear the plate armour of the High Medieval Period,
and later dates, were taken was itself of this stamp. Fleur is a 15.2 hh Lithuanian draught
mare, far closer to a middleweight cob/hunter than a modern shire.

In England the Plantagenets built their mounted force using the law to implement
recruitment. In 1278 Edward I issued a distraint of knighthood on every landholder with a
yearly income of £20 or more. In May 1282 this was amended; any man with thirty
librates of land (i.e. income of £30 per annum) should have one warhorse with proper

armour to serve at need. Shortage of warhorses forced Edward to allow anyone owing service to compound for cash. In November 1282 the screw was tightened. Landholders with less land but skilled in arms were obliged to serve as cavalrymen. In 1298, when Edward was embroiled in Scotland, all parcels of land worth £3 or more were to be grouped into units of £30 to provide a barbed horse and trooper.[41] Edward could raise a total of about 8,000 cavalry, of which approximately 2,750 were knights, the rest men-at-arms.[42]

Under Edward III, and successive warrior Plantagenets, mounted archers, who dismounted to shoot, were used extensively, thus giving the armies tremendous mobility.[43] It was largely due to this firepower that much of the carnage was caused on the battlefields of Crécy (1346), Poitiers (1356), and Agincourt (1415), when the French galloped their heavy horse into blistering steel-tipped barrages. By this period the warhorse was still king, but usually not on the battlefield, it becoming more and more the norm for knights to dismount to fight.[44]

That cavalry was still considered essential is shown by the huge numbers raised by the various Italian city and ducal states. In the early fifteenth century Milan was reliably reputed to have 20,000 cavalry, and the same of foot. Venice fielded 9,000 horse in 1404 against Verona and Padua, and in 1439 the Venetian chronicler Sanuto estimated Italy had a total of 70,000 cavalry.[45] Much of this cavalry was of mercenary bands of *condottieri* who hired their services out to the highest bidder for a specified term. In France these bands were known as *écorcheurs*. Germany had its infantry of Landsknechts and Switzerland her famous pikemen, all for hire. When out of work as various phases of European war subsided, notably the 100 Years War in France, these bands were a menace in any countryside 'at peace'. The rulers may have agreed terms, but the countryfolk suffered from the depredations of rootless, unpaid bands who now pillaged for a living.

One band of mercenary horse known for their ferocity was the Albanian stradiots, mostly in the pay of Venice, but hiring out as far afield as England in the army of Henry VIII. Philippe de Commynes compared them to Spanish jinetes:

> Stradiots dress as Turks except for the head . . . they are hardy people, sleep in the open year round as do their horses. They are all Greek and they come from the places which Venetians own in Greece, some from Nauplia in Argolis, in the Morea, and others from Albania around Durazzo, and their horses are strong and are all Turkish horses.[46]

They fought unarmoured, except for a shield, breastplate and Turkish-style helmet. They were armed with a double-ended lance, shorter javelin, sword, mace or club; some used crossbows. They were used for reconnaissance, harrying after battle, and attacking the enemy's rear and baggage train during a march, when the desire to pillage often overrode military orders.[47]

In all these theatres of war the warhorse suffered. The Norman horse from Byzantine arrows; Crusaders' horses died in droves, far more from natural than military hazards, their constitutions weakened. In the wars that raged between Spain and southern Italy in the thirteenth century Spanish Almugavars had a habit of disembowelling the enemy's horses. Stradiots stabbed them. At Falkirk in 1298, out of 2,500 horse, 110 horses valued for service were killed. As there were probably two or three times as many unpaid as paid cavalry the toll must have been hideous, rocketing to 300–400, plus those injured.[48] At Caravaggio on 24 September 1448 the battlefield was littered with the corpses of 10,000 horses.[49]

Conclusion

As the fifteenth century drew to a close many changes in equestrian life were on the horizon. The horse began to figure more as a sentient animal than a costing in accounts or in a muster roll. Royal records had greater descriptive sections: for example the Mantuan horses sent to Henry VIII; and Henry's preferences from among the select group of stallions and mares that arrived with Giovanni Ratto in 1514 of two called Altobello and Gobernatore particularly pleased him. A bright bay ridden by Ratto in the Spanish fashion was reputably worth its weight in silver.[1] Illustrations became truer to a horse's conformation and individual characteristics. The changes were heralded by a group of superb animal artists – da Vinci, Pisanello, Dürer and Titian – all of them either close to the end of the medieval era, or bridging the transition to the Renaissance.

Throughout the medieval era the warhorse at the top end of the money market evolved into the ponderous destrier only suitable for delivering a battering to the enemy in a massed cavalry charge. By the end of the era he was *passé*. Artillery put paid to his perceived usefulness, except in the tournament which also changed as the martial element gave way to pure spectacle in its successor, the carousel.

Equestrian manuals proliferated, usually following a strict format. All had a short *de rigueur* section on the warhorse, but were more concerned with the art of *haute école*. Pleasure riding increased. With the end of the feudal age more people rode to hounds from choice and not only because they had the right, providing of course they had the cash to indulge in the sport. Racing became very popular under the Stuarts. These trends led to a change in breeding policies. Europe began to catch up on oriental expertise; indeed it was the oriental horse that put such vigour into the English racehorse, an animal that in time became the most renowned horse worldwide – the English Thoroughbred.

Other great changes took place. The legacy we inherited of many specialized breeds, especially during the nineteenth and twentieth centuries, had their impetus for specialization thrust upon them as the carriage age arrived, and as the horse superseded the ox on the farm.

But the horse in all its guises – for war, as a hunter, as a carriage horse, pleasure mount, farm and draught animal – had a history stretching over several millennia, and the medieval era had so many aspects that when drawn together they made a platform for the advances of the later Renaissance riding and studmasters.

Glossary

The following may help equestrians with some historical terms and historians with equestrian terms. Many are obvious from their textual placement.

à la brida	Spanish method of riding as in France, England, etc., with a long stirrup and a deep saddle with high pommel and thigh and hip encasing cantle
à la ginete (jinete)	Spanish method of riding with lower saddle and using shorter stirrups, similar to the Moorish method
azoturia	build-up of lactic acid in the horse causing swelling of the muscle fibres, followed by degenerative changes, locomotor inability, passage of myoglobin into blood plasma and its excretion into the urine
to *bere*	Middle English meaning to carry
Blood(ed) cold	horses of heavy conformation, mostly from the Occident as represented in Medieval Europe by the Germanic type of horse; the bone is heavier and more porous than that of hot-blooded horses
hot	horses with Oriental ancestry with a lighter framed conformation, thinner skin with blood vessels nearer the surface and usually with bone of a lighter and denser composition, e.g. Arabian, Turcoman, Caspian
warm	mix of the hot and cold bloods
carectarius	carthorse, but not to be confused with modern heavy breeds such as Shire, Suffolk Punch, etc.
dam	term used for foal's mother
dry type	horse, usually of Oriental breeding, whose head in particular seems sculpted, with no excess of flesh thereon; usually denotes high-class horses
an entire	a stallion
at farm	nearest equivalent in modern times would be subletting of land and its produce (i.e. overlord took a flat rate, lessee recouped costs from those using mill, smithy, etc.)
flapper racing	races held on an ad hoc basis and not under Jockey Club or National Hunt rules
flying change	exercise in which a horse changes his leads at canter without going into a trot; movement appears to be done in momentary suspension
hand (hh)	unit of 4 inches, the average width of a man's hand, used in measuring horses from wither to ground
hastilude	a kind of joust or tournament
hercarius	equid used for harrowing

hundred	a subdivision of a county or shire, having its own court
imping	mending a broken flight feather on the tail or wing, using perfect moulted flight feathers cut to required length and sealed into hollow of broken shaft of damaged feather
knights to spell themselves	to have a rest/breathing space
laminitis	congestion affecting vascular system within the hoof causing increased pressure within the unyielding horn of the hoof; a painful condition rendering horse very lame
at livery	in medieval times meant stabling and feed provided; today a horse at livery is one kept by a stableowner for a fee-paying client
livres tournois	French pound, of which there were four to the pound sterling
nerge	the Mongolian system of hunting
passador de cavalls	route used over Pyrenees for exporting Spanish horses into France
remuda	string of spare horses and/or group of spare horses used to spell those being ridden
restauro/restor	replacing dead and/or injured horses
scutifer	shield bearer: in medieval times knight's page, usually
tenant	challenger at a tournament
venant	tourneyer going to a tournament to accept challenge
at wages	knight being paid for his services; he had then to find his own and horses' accommodation and feed (and those of retinue); usually a knight had a combination of livery and wages according to whether he was on war duty or not

Notes

ABBREVIATIONS USED

Archaeologia:	*Arch.*
Anglo-Saxon Chronicles, The:	*ASC*
Anglo-Saxon Wills:	*ASW*
Bain, J., *Documents Relating to Scotland*:	Bain, *Scot.*
Boke of Marchalsi:	*BOM*
de Villis, *Capitularies*:	De V.
English Historical Review:	*EHR*
Hyland, A., *Medieval Warhorse*:	*Warhorse* I
Hyland, A., *Warhorse 1250–1600*:	*Warhorse* II
A Narrative of Italian Travels in Persia in the Fifteenth and Sixteenth Centuries:	*Persian Travels*
Byerly, B.F. and Byerly, C.F. eds, *Records of the Wardrobe and Household 1285–6*:	*Wardrobe 1285–6*
Byerly, B.F. and Byerly, C.F. eds, *Records of the Wardrobe and Household, 1286–9*:	*Wardrobe 1286–9*
The Register of the Black Prince:	*BPR*
Royal Frankish Annals:	*RFA*
Usāmah ibn Munqidh:	Usāmah

Introduction

1. *Wardrobe 1285–6* (1977), no. 460
2. Notker, The Stammerer (henceforth Notker), 'Charlemagne' in *Two Lives of Charlemagne*, tr. and intro. Lewis Thorpe (Harmondsworth, Penguin Books, 1969), Bk. II. 9
3. J. Hewitt, *Ancient Armour and Weapons in Europe* (1855), quoting Wace. II. 12, 673f. on p. 173

1. Domesday and Before

1. J.G. Speed MRCVS and M.G. Speed, *The Exmoor Pony* (1977), pp. 1–3 and ch. 5 part 1 passim
2. A. Dent and D.M. Goodall, *A History of British Native Ponies* (1988), p. 10
3. ibid., pp. 13f.
4. Speed, *Exmoor Pony*, p. 57

5. J. Caesar, *The Gallic Wars* (1955), Bk. 4.1 & 4.2
6. Tacitus, *Germania*, ch. 32
7. A. Hyland, *Equus* (1990), p. 183f. *Warhorse* I (1994), pp. 67f.
8. G. Fleming, *Horseshoes and Horseshoeing* (1869), pp. 277–8, quoted from Cotton MSS Cleopatra B.5 (Department of Manuscripts, British Museum, London)
9. *ASC* (1982)
10. Speed, *Exmoor Pony*, p. 56f.
11. *ASW* (1930): No. I. Theodred; II. Alfgar; III. Wynflaed; IX Ealdorman Alfheah; X. Ealdorman Aethelmaer; XI Brihtric and Aelsfwith; XII Aethelwold; XIII Aelfhelm; XIV Aethelflead; XVI Aethelric; XVII Wulfric; XIV Wulgeat; XV Aethling Aethelstan; XXVII Wulfsige; XXXI Thurston; and XXIV Ketel
12. Bede, *Bede's Ecclesiastical History of the English People* (1969), p. 259

13. Hywel Dda, *Welsh Medieval Law* (1909), p. XXI
14. ibid., V. 1a1, V. 1b3, V.29.18
15. ibid., V. 29b 10
16. ibid., V. 29b 15
17. ibid., V. 30a7
18. ibid., V. 90b13
19. *Warhorse* I (1994), pp. 84f.
20. Notes taken (passim) from the translations of the Domesday Book published by Phillimore, gen. ed. J. Morris: Huntingdonshire, no. 19, 1995; Northamptonshire, no. 21, 1979; Cambridgeshire, no. 18, 1981; and Norfolk, parts I & II, no. 33, 1984. For references see under respective village/town name.
Also translation of *Inquisitio Comitatus Cantabrigiensis* (1938), pp. 400–27

2. Supply and Demand

1. *RFA* (1972), 60–70
2. P. Contamine, *War in the Middle Ages*, tr. M. Jones (Oxford, Basil Blackwell, 1984) p. 25
3. Prince A.M. Kurbsky, *History of Ivan IV* (1965), ch. 4. passim
4. M.M. Reese, *The Royal Office of Master of the Horse* (1976), p. 54
H. Harrod. 'Some details of a Murrain of the Fourteenth Century', *Archaeologia*, Vol. XLI (1867), 1–14
Bain, *Scot.*, Vol. II. 1116/Exchq. Q.R. Misc. (army) no. 34/40
5. J.L. Bolton, *The Medieval English Economy 1150–1500* (1980), pp. 181ff.
6. ibid., p. 182
7. L. Brehier, *Les Instituts de L'Empire Byzantin* (1949), p. 330f.
Procopius, *The History of the Wars*, 1914–28: Vol. LI. b.iii. ch. xii. p. 6
A. Hyland, *Warhorse* I (1994), pp. 21, 27
8. Gregory of Tours, *The History of the Franks* (1974), Bk. III.15, V. 48, VII. 37
9. De V. in *The Reign of Charlemagne* (1975), nos 10, 13, 14, 15, 23, 24, 27, 34, 37, 41, 46, 48, 50, 62, 69
10. H.P.R. Finberg, *The Formation of England, 550–1042* (1974), p. 77
11. G. Fleming, *Horseshoes and Horseshoeing* (1869), p. 27
12. Ingulph, *Chronicle of the Abbey of Croyland* (1893), p. 182
13. *ASW* (1930), p. 13ff., no. 111; p. 47, no. XVII; p. 55, no. XIX note p. 166. I. 19f.
14. G. Webster, *The Roman Army* (1973), p. 5
15. G. Cambrensis, 'The Journey through Wales' in *Gerald of Wales*, tr. and intro. L. Thorpe (Harmondsworth, Penguin, 1978), Bk. I. ch. 9 & 12
16. Hywel Dda, *Welsh Medieval Law* (1909), V41a2; V30a7; p. 301.1794 W92b.13–15; W 88b21; V 29a3; W105b13; V32b11; W65b21; V44.b.15; p. 314 15.1744
17. R.H.C. Davis, 'The Medieval Warhorse' in *Horses in European Economic History* (1983), p. 7
18. R.H.C. Davis, 'The Warhorses of the Normans', *Anglo-Norman Studies* (1987), 67–82
19. S. Loch, *The Royal Horse of Europe* (1986), p. 59
20. *The Plantagenet Chronicles*, ed. El Hallam (1986), John of Marmoutier, p. 48
21. W. Malmesbury, 'Historia Novella' or 'History of his own Times' in *Contemporary Chronicles of the Middle Ages* (Llanerch Enterprises), B.III. nos 57 and 72
22. R. de Monte, *The Chronicles of Robert de Monte* (1991), pp. 66–9
23. Sir W. Gilbey, *The Great Horse* (1899), p. 16f.
24. W. Childs, *Anglo-Castilian Trade in the Later Middle Ages* (1978), p. 120f.
25. Y. Renouard, 'L'exportation de chevaux de la Péninsule Ibérique en France et en Angleterre au moyen âge' in *Maluquer de Motes Nicolaus* (1965), Vol. I, pp. 571–7
26. W. Childs, *Anglo-Castilian Trade* (1978), p. 120f.
27. R.H.C. Davis, 'The Medieval Warhorse' in *Horses in European Economic History* (1983), p. 11
28. W. Childs, *Anglo-Castilian Trade* (1978), p. 120f.
29. Y. Renouard, 'L'exportation de chevaux', in *Maluquer* (1965)
30. ibid.
31. W. Norwell, *The Wardrobe book of Wm. de Norwell* (1983), p. 268, f. 108v (216) 262f. 106 v (212), 230f. 95 v (190)
Warhorse I (1994), p. 30f.
H.J. Hewitt, *The Horse in Medieval England* (1983), p. 25f.
32. *Warhorse* II (1998), pp. 17f.
33. Langlois, *Le Règne de Philippe III Le Hardi* (1887), p. 371f.
34. R.H.C. Davis, 'The Medieval Warhorse' in *Horses in European Economic History* (1983), p. 11
35. Langlois, *Le Règne de Philippe II Le Hardi* (1887), pp. 371–2

36. *Warhorse* II (1998), p. 19
37. R.H.C. Davis, 'Warhorses of the Normans' *Anglo-Norman Studies* (1987), 67–82
38. ibid.
39. A. Dent and D.M. Goodall, *A History of British Native Ponies* (1988), p. 103f.
40. M.M. Reese, *The Royal Office of Master of Horse* (1976), p. 42
41. R.H.C. Davis, 'The Medieval Warhorse' in *Horses in European Economic History* (1983), p. 11
42. V. Chomel, 'Chevaux de Bataille et Roncins en Dauphiné au XIV siècle', pp. 5–23
43. Y. Renouard, 'L'exportation de chevaux' in *Maluquer* (1965), p. 576
44. *La Règle du Temple* (1886), nos 181, 115, 52
45. Y. Renouard, 'L'exportation de chevaux' in *Maluquer* (1965), p. 577
46. J.H. Pryor, 'Transportation of Horses by Sea during the Era of the Crusades, eighth century to AD 1285. Parts I & II', *Mariner's Mirror*, no. 68 (1982), 9–27, 103ff.
47. M. Burleigh, *Prussian Society and the German Order* (1984), p. 28
48. *Warhorse* II (1998), pp. 72–9 *passim*
49. Bain, *Scot.* V.II. no. 1144. Chancery misc. portfolio. 41/92
50. M.W. Labarge, *A Baronial Household of the Thirteenth Century* (1965), pp. 133.m.151, 163f., 194ff.
51. K. Chivers, *The Shire Horse* (1976), p. 4f.
52. Lady Wentworth, *Thoroughbred Racing Stock* (1939), p. 247f.
    Warhorse II (1998), p. 95
53. Abou Bekr ibn Bedr, *Le Naceri* (3 vols, 1860), Vol. III, pp. 67–70
54. S. Loch, *Royal Horse of Europe* (1936), p. 28f.
55. The Showmen's Guild of Great Britain, *All the Fun of the Fair* (1987), p. 1
56. J.L. Bolton, *The Medieval English Economy 1150–1500* (1980), p. 132ff.
57. *The Laws of the Earliest English Kings* (1922), p. 55, cap. 56, p. 101, cap. 4, p. 115, cap. 1, p. 157, cap. 16
    The Laws of the Kings of England from Edmund to Henry I (1925), p. 15, cap. III, cap. 5, p. 55, cap. 3
58. F. Braudel, *The Wheels of Commerce* (1983), p. 90f.
59. P. Tafur, *Travels and Adventures 1435–39* (1926), pp. 192–205 *passim*
60. *Plantagenet Chronicles* (1986), p. 98f.
61. *BPR* (1930–33) Vol. IV, p. 67ff., p. 326
62. C. Walford, *Fairs Past and Present* (1883), pp. 250–69

63. V. Chomel, 'Chevaux de Bataille'
64. F. Braudel, *The Structures of Everyday Life* (1981), p. 349
65. R. Muntaner, *The Chronicles of Muntaner* (1920), Vol. 1, p. 208
66. B. de la Brocquière, 'Travels of Bertrandon la Brocquière' in *Early Travels in Palestine* (1848), p. 370ff.
67. M.E. Mallet and J.R. Hale, *Military Organization in a Renaissance State: Venice1400–1617* (1984), p. 138f.
68. *Warhorse* II (1998), p. 67: East European Chapter
69. R.H.A. Merlen, 'Horses in Old Russia', *Horse World* (1972), 13–15
70. Ibn Battuta, *The Travels of Ibn Battuta 1325–1354*, Vol. I, 1956; Vol. II, 1962; Vol. III, 1971; Vol. IV, 1994; Vol. II (1962), p. 478f.
71. ibid., Vol. III (1971), p. 746
72. K.D. Swaminathan, 'The Horsetraders of Malai-Mandalam', *Journal of Indian History* (1954–5), 139–43
73. S. Digby, *Warhorse and Elephant in the Delhi Sultanate* (1971), p. 45ff.
74. A. Nikitin, 'The Travels of Athanasius Nikitin of Tver' in *India in the Fifteenth Century* (1857), pp. 10–15 *passim*, p. 26f.
75. *Warhorse* II (1998). For detailed account of Indian horsetrade, especially on Arabians, see ch. 8
76. J. Barbaro, 'Travels to Tana and Persia' in *Persian Travels* (1873), Bk. II, pp. 20, 67
77. A. Hanham, *The Celys and Their World* (1985), letters on pp. 48f., 63, 65, 69f., 72ff., 78, 215, 276ff.

3. Everyman's Horse

1. G. Chaucer, *The Canterbury Tales* (1977), Prologue 21–36 *passim*
2. A. Hyland, *Equus* (1990), pp. 73, 171f., 178, map. pp. 12f.
3. H.J. Hewitt, *Horse in Medieval England* (1983), p. 44
4. Bain, *Scot.*, Vol. IV, nos 406, 312, 469
5. Practical experiments conducted with Katchina, one of my horses that racks.
6. G. Fleming, *Horseshoes and Horseshoeing* (1869), p. 425
7. Bede, *Bede's Ecclesiastical History* (1969), p. 466
8. G.G. Coulton, *Medieval Village, Manor, and Monastery* (1960), pp. 215f., 508, 511
9. W. Langland, *Piers Plowman* (1959), pp. 55, 46, 65, 121

10. G.G. Coulton, *Medieval Village* (1960), p. 296
11. ibid., p. 511
12. *Laws of the Kings of England from Edmund to Henry I* (1925), p. 37
13. *Laws of the Earliest English Kings* (1922), p. 69, cap. 9.2
14. ibid., p. 73, cap. 16
15. *Laws of the Kings of England from Edmund to Henry I* (1925), p. 257, n.9(1)
16. *Laws of the Earliest English Kings* (1922), p. 159, VI Athelstan, cap. 5, n.6
17. ibid., p. 159, cap. 5, nos 4 & 5
18. G.G. Coulton, *Medieval Village* (1960), p. 75, merchet; p. 79f.
    H.S. Bennet, *Life on the English Manor 1150–1400* (1939), p. 143ff., tallage, p. 281
    Laws of the Kings of England from Edmund to Henry I (1925), p. 263, cap. 20.3
19. G.G. Coulton, *Medieval Village* (1960), p. 85
20. ibid., p. 489ff.
21. ibid., p. 85
22. ibid., p. 447
23. ibid., p. 176
24. ibid., p. 85
25. Ingulph, *Chronicle of the Abbey of Croyland* (1893), p. 142
26. *ASC* under year 1127
27. W. Malmesbury, *The Kings Before the Norman Conquest* (1989), ch. 204, p. 197
28. *A Cambridgeshire Gaol Delivery Roll 1332–1334* (1978), p. 33, nos 2 & 3; p. 39, no. 8; p. 41, no. 12; p. 44, no. 16; p. 41, no. 13
29. Bain, *Scot.*, Vol. II, no. 183 Inq. p. m. 8 Edw. I. no. 81.3
30. ibid., no. 1317. Excheq. Q.R. Misc. (Army) 26.14
31. ibid., Vol. III, no. 948 (patent 2 Edw. III. p. 1. m. 29 dorso)
32. ibid., Vol. II, no. 822. 1295/6.10th May section. Chapter House Scots Documents, box 93, no. 15.m.3, 5, 5d, 8, 9d
33. ibid., Vol. II, no. 168, Assize roll (Northumberland)
34. J. Strutt, *The Sports and Pastimes of the People of England* (1969), p. 197f., dog baiting. Roy. lib., no. 2. b. vii; dancing. Roy. lib. 20. D. iv; others from Bodleian MS no. 264
35. ibid., p. 197f.
36. *Warhorse* II (1998), p. 123
37. *Plantagenet Chronicles* (1986), p. 100
38. *Wardrobe 1286–9* (1986), no. 1922
39. T. Gray, *Scalacronica* (1907), p. 4
40. J. Strutt, *Sports and Pastimes* (1969), p. 33
41. R. Barber and J. Barker, *Tournaments* (1989), p. 77
42. Lady Wentworth, *Thoroughbred Racing Stock* (1939), p. 247f.

4. Farming and Commerce

1. Bain, *Scot.*, Vol. II, no. 1084. Excheq. Q.R. Misc. (Army) 23.8
2. ibid., no. 1075 and 1076 Chancery misc. portfolios nos 11 & 41
3. J. Spruytte, *Early Harness Systems* (1983)
4. ibid., pp. 10–11
5. A.C. Leighton, *Transport and Communication in Early Medieval Europe AD 500–1100* (1972), pp. 112–16 *passim*
6. G.M. Trevelyan, *English Social History* (1972)
7. P. d'Osma, in *The Royal Studs of the Sixteenth and Seventeenth Centuries* (1935), pp. 26f.
8. Bain, *Scot.*, Vol. II, no. 1805. Exchq. Q.R. Misc. (Army) 32/19
9. ibid., no. 1115. Exchq. Q.R. Misc. (Army) 23.4.
10. ibid., no. 1439, Exchq. Q.R. Memoranda
11. ibid., no. 79 Patent Ed. I. m. 11 Seleburne
12. ibid., no. 591. Tower Misc. rolls 450. 16
13. E. Miller (ed.), *The Agrarian History of England and Wales Vol. III 1348–1500* (1991), p. 456f.
14. Lennard, 'Composition of Demesne Plough Teams in 12th Century England', *EHR*, no. CCXCV (April 1960), 193–206
15. A.C. Leighton, *Transport and Communication* (1972), p. 69
16. J. Langdon, *Horses, Oxen and Technological Innovation* (1986), p. 53
17. G.G. Coulton, *Medieval Village* (1960), p. 256f.
18. J. Langdon, *Horses, Oxen and Technological Innovation* (1986), p. 50
19. R. Lennard, 'Composition of Demesne Plough Teams', *EHR*, no. CCXV (April 1960), 193–206
20. R.D. Connor, *The Weights and Measures of England* (1987), p. 154
21. Walter of Henley, *Seneschauchie* (1971), p. 319, 36–41, 160ff., 423.10, 439, 49 & 51
22. J. Langdon, *Horses, Oxen and Technological Innovation* (1986), p. 250
23. ibid., p. 20
24. *The Bayeux Tapestry and the Norman Invasion* (1973), plates 10, 11, 48, 49
25. J. Langdon, *Horses, Oxen and Technological Innovation* (1986), p. 24
26. ibid., p. 62

27. J. Ravensdale, *The Domesday Inheritance* (1986), p. 147f.
28. M.M. Reese, *The Royal Office of Master of Horse* (1976), p. 54
29. H. Harrod, 'Some details of a Murrain of the Fourteenth Century from Court Rolls of a Norfolk Manor', *Archaeologia*, Vol. XLI (1867), 1–14
30. J. Ravensdale, *The Domesday Inheritance* (1986), p. 56
31. S. Lysons, 'Copy of a Roll of Expenses of King Edward I at Rhuddlan Castle in the 10th and 11th years of his Reign', *Arch.*, Vol. XVI (1812), 32–89
32. *Plantagenet Chronicles* (1986), p. 264
33. C. Richardson, *The Fell Pony* (1990), p. 17ff.
34. A. Dent, *Cleveland Bay Horses* (1978), pp. 23, 37f.
35. *Wardrobe 1286–9* (1986), nos 8, 33, 169, 426, 137, 140
36. M. Prestwich, *The Three Edwards* (1980), p. 67
37. I. Origo, *The Merchant of Prato* (1986), part I, chapters 2 & 3 *passim*
38. ibid., pp. 92–4
39. ibid., p. 93f.
40. ibid., p. 36
41. ibid., pp. 71 & 108
42. ibid., pp. 93, 259–61

5. Trades and Crafts

1. Gregory of Tours, *The History of the Franks* (1974), Bk V. ch. 48
   G. Fleming, *Horseshoes and Horseshoeing* (1869), p. 370
2. ibid., p. 372f.
3. *Wardrobe 1285–6* (1977), pp. xxxv–xxxvii
4. R.H.C. Davis, 'The Medieval Warhorse' in *Horses in European Economic History* (1983), p. 9
5. G. Fleming, *Horseshoes and Horseshoeing* (1869), pp. 377, 379, 376
6. Bain, *Scot.*, Vol. II, no. 1132 Chapter House (Scots Docs box 93, no. 18)
7. J.G. Sparkes, *Discovering Old Horseshoes* (Discovering Series, no. 19, Shire Publications 1983 (1976)), p. 4
8. S. Bökönyi, *History of Domesticated Mammals in Central and Eastern Europe* (1974), p. 271
9. J. Clark, *Medieval Horseshoes*, datasheet 4: p. 4
10. J.G. Sparkes, *Discovering Old Horseshoes*, p. 10
11. R.E. Walker, *Ars Veterinaria* (1991), pp. 52, 54
12. A. Hyland, *Equus* (1990), p. 49f.
13. R.E. Walker, *Ars Veterinaria* (1991), p. 49
14. *Warhorse* I (1994), p. 40
15. R.E. Walker, *Ars Veterinaria* (1991), p. 50
16. ibid.
17. *BOM* (1972), iii
18. ibid., xxxii
19. ibid., xxxi
20. ibid., xxxixf.
21. ibid., pp. 14–20 *passim*
22. *Warhorse* I (1994), pp. 2f., 20, 22f., 54f., 57 R. Aguiliers, *Historia Francorum Qui Ceperent Iherusalem* (1968), note. Aguiliers Ch.XI, p. 83f., 91f. The translators put 'Thoroughbred' for 'Arabian'. Thoroughbreds were not even bred and recorded until Wetherby's started registering bloodstock in the late eighteenth century.
23. *BOM* (1972), pp. 1–8 *passim*
24. ibid., XL, pp. 31–5 *passim* H.M. Hayes, *Veterinary Notes for Horseowners* (1976), pp. 229–36 *passim*
25. *BOM* (1972), xxxii
26. ibid., XL
27. ibid., xxxiv
28. ibid., pp. 29f.
30. ibid., ff. 41b19
31. ibid., xxxiii
32. ibid., p. 35
33. ibid., xxxiii f. 41a20
34. G.R. Vernam, *Man on Horseback* (1964), pp. 141ff.
35. J. Clark (ed.), *The Medieval Horse and its Equipment* (1995), p. 46
36. ibid., p. 127
37. ibid., p. 125
38. G.R. Vernam, *Man on Horseback* (1969), p. 143f.
39. E. Oakeshott, *A Knight and His Horse* (1962), pp. 36f.
40. P. Martin, *Armour and Weapons* (1968), p. 210
41. S. Lysons, 'Copy for purchases for Tournament at Windsor Park 6 Edward I', *Arch.*, Vol. XVII (1814), 297–310
42. A. Hyland, *Equus* (1990), p. 22, 131–4 *Warhorse* I (1994), p. 5
43. R Muntaner, *The Chronicles of Muntaner*, Vol. II (1921), pp. 337–43
44. T. Astle, 'Ceremonial of Funeral of King Edward IV', *Arch.*, Vol. I (1770), 350ff.
45. Dr. Milles, 'Observations on the Wardrobe A/C for 1483 wherein are contained the liveries made for the Coronation of King Richard III', *Arch.*, Vol. I (1770), 363–82
46. P.M. Kendall, *Richard III* (1952, 1972), p. 230

47. R. Robinson, *Oriental Armour* (1967), pp. 17, 83
48. *Warhorse* I (1994), p. 109
49. *Warhorse* II (1998), p. 177
50. R. Robinson, *Oriental Armour* (1967), p. 51
51. ibid., p. 168
52. Behā ed-Dīn Abu el Mehāsan Yūsuf, *Saladin, or What Befell Sultan Yusuf, Salāh ed-Dīn* (Library of the Palestine Pilgrims Text Society, Vol. XIII, 1897), LXXVIII
53. *Warhorse* I (1994), p. 153
54. *Warhorse* II (1998), p. 54
55. J.G. Mann, 'The Sanctuary of the Madonna delle Grazie with notes on the evolution of armour during the 15th century', *Arch.*, Vol. 80 (1930), 117–42

6. *The Black Prince's* Register: *The Horse in Estate Management*

1. Froissart, *Chronicles*, tr. & ed. G. Brereton (Penguin Books, 1983 edn), pp. 177f.
2. T.B. Costain, *The Pageant of England 1272–1377: The Three Edwards* (Universal Tandem Publishing Co. Ltd., 1973 edn), p. 395
3. *BPR*, 4 Vols (1930–33)
4. ibid., Vol. II (18 July 1352, 19 Sept 1353)
5. ibid., Vol. IV, pp. 67ff. (28 Nov 1352)
6. ibid., Vol. IV, p. 254, f. 145 (1358)
7. ibid., Vol. IV, pp. 87, f. 51d; 162 f. 95d (1353)
8. ibid., Vol. IV, p. 376 (10 Feb 1361)
9. ibid., Vol. IV, p. 252, f. 144 (1358)
10. ibid., Vol. IV, p. 289, f. 165 (1359)
11. ibid., Vol. IV, p. 67ff., f. 43 (1352)
12. ibid., *passim* Vol. IV
13. H.J. Hewitt, *The Horse in Medieval England* (1983), p. 27
14. *BPR*, Vol. I, p. 72 (1347)
15. ibid., Vol. IV, p. 15 (18 May 1351)
16. ibid., Vol. IV, p. 253f., f. 145 (20 June 1358)
17. ibid., Vol. IV, p. 269 (11 Dec 1358)
18. ibid., Vol. IV, p. 286 (10 March 1359)
19. ibid., Vol. IV, p. 268 (10 Dec 1358), Baldwin sale, p. 67ff., f. 43 (28 Nov 1352), gifts
20. ibid., Vol. I, p. 56 (12 March 1347)
21. ibid., Vol. IV, p. 15 (18 May 1358), p. 269 (11 Dec 1358), p. 502 (23 June 1363), p. 512 (13 Nov 1363), p. 532 (12 July 1364)
22. ibid., Vol. III (11 Jan 1354), f. 75d; (1354), f. 101, no. 3
23. ibid., Vol. III, f. 238 (26 Aug 1362)
24. ibid., Vol. IV, p. 269 (11 Dec 1358)
25. *Warhorse* I (1994), p. 92
    Warhorse II (1998), pp. 91, 184
26. ibid., p. 91
27. *BPR*, Vol. IV, p. 124 (5 Feb 1355)
28. ibid., Vol. IV, p. 176 (1 Dec 1355)
29. ibid., Vol. IV, p. 113 (13 March 1354)
30. ibid., Vol. I (1347), p. 79 (19 May) Brunham – 40 carthorses; (13 June) Brunham 50 carthorses
    Vol. II (1357), p. 110, (27 Feb) John de Kendale purchases
    Vol. II (1357), p. 205, (22 Nov) Dabernoun – 80 for Aquitaine
    Vol. III (1357), f. 130., (27 Feb) John de Brunham
    Vol. IV (1363), p. 488, (23 Feb) f. 256 to order to John Prynne
    (where numbers unstated a general order went out)
31. ibid., Vol. IV (1359), p. 326
32. *Warhorse* II (1998), pp. 23f. and 30
33. *BPR*, Vol. I, p. 56 (12 March 1347), p. 152 (22 Nov 1347)
34. ibid., p. 269 (11 Dec 1358)
35. ibid., Vol. IV, p. 34 (30 Nov 1351), p. 330 (27 Oct 1359)
36. ibid., Vol. IV, p. 15 (18 May 1351)
37. ibid., Vol. IV, p. 34 (30 Nov 1351)
38. ibid., p. 502 (23 June 1363)
39. ibid., Vol. IV (all 1364), p. 526 (17 April), p. 530 (2 July), p. 532 (12 July)
40. ibid., Vol. IV, p. 176 (3 Dec 1355)
41. ibid., Vol. IV, p. 330 (7 Oct 1359)
42. ibid., Vol. IV, p. 269 (11 Dec 1358)
43. ibid., Vol. IV, p. 290 (May 1359)
43. ibid., Vol. IV, p. 290 (1 May 1359)
44. ibid., Vol. IV, p. 357 (4 Aug 1360)
45. ibid., Vol. III, f. 238 (26 Aug 1362)
46. ibid., Vol. IV, p. 466 (26 Aug 1362), p. 517 (5 Dec 1363)
47. ibid., Vol. IV, p. 49 (25 Apr 1352)
48. ibid., Vol. IV, p. 17 (13 June 1351), p. 24 (29 Aug 1351)
49. ibid., Vol. I, p. 68 (6 Apr 1347)
50. ibid., Vol. IV, p. 296 (3 July 1359)
51. ibid., Vol. II, p. 94 (27 March 1356), p. 105 (8 Dec 1356), p. 107 (8 Feb 1357)
52. ibid., Vol. IV, p. 488 (23 Feb 1363), p. 512 (23 Nov 1363), p. 523 (7 Feb 1364)
53. ibid., Vol. II, p. 205 (22 Nov 1363)
54. ibid., Vol. III, p. 458 (2 June 1363)
55. ibid., Vol. II, p. 204 (1 July 1363), p. 202 (29 May 1363)
56. ibid., Vol. IV, p. 268 (10 Dec 1358), p. 326 (1359) (Little Watte), p. 355 (14 July 1360), p. 428 (26 March 1362)

57. ibid., Vol. IV, p. 67ff. (horse gifts – list of) (1352)
58. ibid., Vol. I, p. 79 (19 May 1347), p. 88 (13 June 1347)
59. ibid., Vol. IV, p. 99 (24 Sept 1353)
60. ibid., Vol. IV, p. 253f. (20 June 1358)
61. ibid., Vol. IV, p. 475 (8 Nov 1362)
62. ibid., Vol. I, p. 108 (5 Aug 1347)
63. ibid., Vol. I, p. 82 (26 May 1347)
64. ibid., Vol. I, p. 158 (26 Dec 1347)
65. ibid., Vol. III, p. 265 (16 July 1357)
66. ibid., Vol. IV, p. 220 (20 Sept 1357)
67. ibid., Vol. III, p. 383 (12 Sept 1360)
68. ibid., Vol. III, p. 356f. (16 Aug 1357)
69. ibid., Vol. II, p. 45 (10 Mar 1353)
70. ibid., Vol. I, p. 69 (11 Apr 1347)
71. ibid., Vol. IV, p. 253f. (20 June 1358), p. 318 (1 Oct 1359)
72. ibid., p. 321 (22 Oct 1359), p. 364 (7 Nov 1360)
73. ibid., Vol. IV (19 Apr 1352)
74. ibid., Vol. II, p. 71 (6 Oct 1354)
75. ibid., Vol. IV, p. 174f. (28 Nov 1355)
76. ibid., Vol. III, p. 430f., f. 231A (1361)
77. ibid., Vol. I (13 June 1347)
78. ibid., Vol. IV, p. 202 (18 Feb 1357)
79. ibid., Vol. IV, p. 434 (15 May 1362)
80. ibid., Vol. III, f. 28d, nos 16 & 17 (1351)
81. ibid., Vol. III, f. 36 (12 Feb 1352)
82. ibid., Vol. IV, p. 84 (16 Mar 1353)
83. ibid., Vol. IV, p. 67ff. (1352)

7. Hunting

1. J. Cummings, *The Hound and the Hawk, The Art of Medieval Hunting* (1988), pp. 173–7 *passim*
2. J.M. Gilbert, *Hunting and Hunting Preserves in Medieval Scotland* (1979), p. 72
3. Ammianus Marcellinus, *The Later Roman Empire AD 354–378* (1986), Bk. 24.5
4. Maurice (Emperor), *Maurice's Strategikon* (1984), BK. XII.D. *passim*
5. D. Martin, 'The Mongol Army', *Journal of the Royal Asiatic Soc.* (April 1943), 46–85
6. M. Polo, *The Travels of Marco Polo* (1984), pp. 82–5 *passim*
7. J. Masson Smith, 'Ayn Jalut. Mamlūk success or Mongol Failure?', *Harvard Journal of the Asiatic Soc.* (1984), 307–45
8. *Warhorse* I (1994), p. 137
9. M. Polo, *Travels* (1984), pp. 82–5 *Warhorse* I (1994), p. 137
10. D. Ayalon, '*Furusiyya* Exercises and Games in the Mamlūk Sultanate', *Scripta Hierosolymitana*, Vol. IX (1961), pp. 31–62

11. Abou Bekr ibn Bedr, *Le Naceri* (3 vols, 1860) Vol. I, section IV, Ch. III. ii, p. 112
12. A.N. Polliak, 'The Influence of Chingis Khan's Yasa upon the General Organization of the Mamlūk State', *Bulletin of the School of Oriental and African Studies*, no. 10 (1942), 862–76; *Warhorse* II (1998), p. 120
13. Jahiz of the Basra (Amr. b. Bahr b. Mahbub Abu Othman al Jahiz), 'Exploits of the Turks and the Army of the Khalifate in General', *Journal of the Royal Asiatic Soc.* (1915), 631–97
14. Kai Ka'us ibn Iskander, *Qabus Nama; A Mirror for Princes* (1951), pp. IXf., 83
15. ibid., p. X
16. Usāmah ibn Munqidh, *Memoirs of Usāmah ibn Munqidh (Kitab al-l'Tibār)* (1929), p. 254
17. ibid., pp. 222–31 *passim*
18. ibid., p. 236f.
19. ibid., pp. 243f.
20. ibid., pp. 251f.
21. S.A.H.A.A. Imam, *The Centaur* (1987), pp. 173f.
22. ibid., p. 186
23. *Bābur Nāma* (1922), pp. 108–14ff. (year AH.905/AD 1499/1500)
24. ibid. (year AH.925/AD 1519, 3 Jan–23 Dec)
25. J.M. Gilbert, *Hunting and Hunting Preserves in Medieval Scotland* (1979), pp. 5, 10
26. *RFA*, under years: 804, 805, 819–21
26. *RFA*, under years: 804, 805, 819–21, 823, 826, 829
27. Einhard, 'Life of Charlemagne' in *Two Lives of Charlemagne* (1969), Bk. IV. 30
28. Notker, as above, Bk. II.8 & 9
29. De V. in *The Reign of Charlemagne* (1875), no. 36
30. ibid., no. 45
31. ibid., no. 46
32. ibid., no. 47
33. ibid., no. 58
34. ibid., no. 62
35. ibid., no. 69
36. ibid., pp. 98, 102f.
37. J.M. Gilbert, *Hunting and Hunting Preserves in Medieval Scotland* (1979), p. 108
38. *The Laws of the Kings of England from Edmund to Henry I* (1925), pp. 80f.
39. ibid., p. 243.10.1
40. *ASC*, under year 1087
41. Henry of Huntingdon, *The Chronicle of Henry of Huntingdon* (1991), p. 217

42. W.L. Warren, *Henry II* (1991), pp. 390f.
43. *BPR*, Vol. II, p. 15 (16 Aug 1351), p. 197 (10 Oct 1362)
44. F. Barlow, *William Rufus* (1983), p. 122
45. J.M. Gilbert, *Hunting and Hunting Preserves in Medieval Scotland* (1979), p. 27
46. *BPR*, Vol. III, p. 15 (24 March 1351)
47. J.M. Gilbert, *Hunting and Hunting Preserves in Medieval Scotland* (1979), p. 191
48. ibid., p. 249
49. *BPR*, Vol. III, f. 75d. (11 Jan 1354)
50. *The Reign of Henry VII*, from Original Documents preserved in the PRO, ed. Revd W. Campbell (London, Longman & Co., 1857), pp. 6, 10
51. F. Barlow, *William Rufus* (1983), p. 123
52. J. Cummings, *The Hound and The Hawk* (1988), p. 48f.
53. *Wardrobe 1285–6* (1977), nos 10 and 13
54. J.F. Willard and W.A. Morris (eds), *The English Government at Work, 1327–36* (1940), chapter V, by J.M. Johnson, p. 436
55. J. Cummings, *The Hound and The Hawk* (1988), p. 14
56. *Wardrobe 1285–6* (1977), nos 2044, 48
57. ibid., V and E101/351/24, nos 2044 to 2238
    Wardrobe 1286–9 (1986) IV and E101/252/20, nos 2782–2895
58. ibid., nos 2161, 2094, 2206, 2155, 2235, 2238
59. *Wardrobe 1285–6* (1977), no. 460
    Wardrobe 1286–9 (1986), no. 1890
60. *Wardrobe 1285–6* (1977), no. 177
61. *Wardrobe 1286–9* (1986), nos 720, 892, 913
    Wardrobe 1285–6 (1977), no. 677
62. *BPR*, Vol. III, p. 66, f. 40 (18 July 1352)
63. ibid., p. 9, f.5 (1351); p. 13, f. 7 (1351); f. 10 (11 April 1351)
64. ibid., p. 429, f. 231 (4 Dec 1361)
65. ibid., f. 430f., f. 231A (1361)
66. N. Saul, *Medieval England* (1983), p. 99f.
67. *BPR*, Vol. IV, p. 82 (19 Feb 1353)
68. *BPR*, Vol. III, p. 466, f. 245d (15 April 1365)

8. Tournaments

1. Nithard, 'Nithard's Histories' in *Carolingian Chronicles* (1972), B.III.6
2. G. Fleming, *Horseshoes and Horseshoeing* (1969), p. 117
3. J. Strutt, *Sports and Pastimes* (1969), p. 117
4. *Plantagenet Chronicles* (1986), p. 22
5. ibid., pp. 48–52
6. R. Barber and J. Barker, *Tournaments* (1989), p. 8
7. ibid., p. 139f.
8. ibid., p. 140
9. J. Strutt, *Sports and Pastimes* (1969), p. 117f.
10. J. Barker, *The Tournament in England 1110–1400* (1986), p. 145
11. ibid., pp. 11, 64
12. ibid., p. 28f., 20
13. ibid., p. 68
14. *BPR*, Vol. IV, p. 165 (1365)
15. R. Barber and J. Barker, *Tournaments* (1989), pp. 3f.
16. ibid., pp. 125f., 164
    J. Barker, *The Tournament in England* (1986), pp. 13ff., 144ff., 115
17. *La Règle du Temple* (1886), Rules. 128 and 315
18. G. Nielsen, *Trial by Combat* (1890), pp. 189, 191f., 227
    J. Barker, *The Tournament in England* (1986), p. 160
19. Bain, *Scot.*, Vol. IV (1888), no. 468. Issue Roll (pells) Easter 18 Richard II
20. ibid., Vol. II (8 Nov 1303), Exchq. Treasury of receipt misc. no. 42/19
21. G.D. de Games, *The Unconquered Knight* (1928), p. 10f.
22. M. Jankovich, *They Rode into Europe* (1971), p. 156
23. *Warhorse* II (1998), Tudor chapter
24. ibid., pp. 9f.
25. E. Oakeshott, *A Knight and His Horse* (1962), p. 19
26. Abou Bekr ibn Bedr, *Le Naceri* (1860), Vol. II, p. 183
27. ibn Hodeil (Aly Ben Abderrahman Ben Hodeil El Andalusy), *La Parure des cavaliers et l'insigne des preux* (1924), pp. 294, 298
28. *RFA*, year 801
    W. von Eschenbach, *Willehalm* (1977), p. 12f.
29. ibid., 1.118, 1.128, 1.405
30. ibid., 1.58, and p. 380 note on Puzzat
31. *Warhorse* I (1994), pp. 44–6, and p. 57
32. W. von Eschenbach, *Willehalm* (1977), p. 331
33. *Warhorse* I (1994), p. 42
34. W. von Eschenbach, *Parsival* (1961), p. 215
35. ibid., pp. 69, 87, 114, 156 (twice), 169, 243
36. ibid., p. 89
37. ibid., pp. 320, 169, 193
38. G.D. de Games, *The Unconquered Knight* (1928), p. 41

39. ibid., pp. 146f., 165
40. J. Martorell and M.J. de Galba, *Tirant lo Blanc* (1984), p. 92, LXXII
41. ibid., p. 100, LXXII
42. ibid., p. 167f., CX
43. ibid., p. 198, CXXII
44. W. von Eschenbach, *Parsival* (1961), p. 209
45. R. Barber and J. Barker, *Tournaments* (1989), p. 192
46. ibid., p. 21
47. Froissart, *Chronicles* (1983), pp. 373–81 *passim*
48. R. Barber and J. Barker, *Tournaments* (1989), p. 43
49. Froissart, *Chronicles* (1983), p. 379
50. R. Barber and J. Barker, *Tournaments* (1989), p. 135
51. H.T. Leodius, 'Biography of Palatine Frederick II' in *Gentlemen Errant: The Journeys of Four Noblemen in Europe during 15th & 16th C.*, tr. Mrs. Henry Cust (London, John Murray, 1909), p. 283
52. T. Gray, *Scalacronica* (1907), p. 148
53. J.F. Michaud and J.J. Poujoulat (eds), *Les Livre des faicts du bon messire Jean le Maingre, dit Boucicaut, marechal de France et Gouverneur de Gennes*, Paris (1836), pp. 219–20
54. Personal discussion with James Russel, PE teacher, Marshland High School, West Walton, Norfolk
55. M. Prestwich, *Edward I* (1990), pp. 7, 28, 34, 38, 120
56. S. Lysons, 'Windsor Tournament Roll' in *Arch.*, Vol. XVII (1814), 297–310
57. M. Prestwich, *The Three Edwards* (1980), p. 205
58. 'Roll of the Arms of the Knights at the Tournament at Dunstable 7. Edward III' in *Collectanea Topographica et Genealogica*, Vol. IV (1837)
59. *Wardrobe 1285–6* (1977), p. xvi
60. ibid., nos 50, 60, 210, 247, 321, 418
61. *Wardrobe 1286–9* (1986), nos 361, 356, 262
62. R. Barber and J. Barker, *Tournaments*, p. 192
63. Froissart, *Chronicles*, pp. 373–81 *passim*
64. *The High History of the Holy Grail* (post 1909), pp. 8, 93, 128, 157, 100, 257, 110, 45, 160, 328, 286/7
66. Duarte of Portugal, notes printed in R. Barber and J. Barker, *Tournaments* (1989), p. 201f. Analysis from experience of horse's mentality gained from training many animals. Loan of horses, p. 162
67. von Eyb, the younger, biographer of Wilwolt of Scaumberg Kt, in *Gentlemen Errant* (1909), pp. 161ff.
68. Leodius in *Gentlemen Errant* (1909), p. 285ff.

9. Medieval Postal Services

1. A.C. Leighton, *Transport and Communication* (1992), pp. 21f.
2. R.H.C. Davis, 'The Warhorses of the Normans' in *Anglo-Norman Studies* (1987), 67–82
3. A.C. Leighton, *Transport and Communication* (1992), p. 22
4. J. Crofts, *Packhorse, Wagon and Post* (1967), pp. 59, 62
5. Zeissmer, W. (ed.), *Das Grosse Anterbuch des Deutschen Ordens* (1921, 1968), 103f.
6. M.C. Hill, *The King's Messengers 1199–1377* (1994), p. 27
7. ibid., p. 98 Swyn, p. 131 Robert
8. ibid., p. 2
9. ibid., p. 3
10. ibid., p. 78
11. ibid., p. 93
12. ibid., p. 101
13. ibid., pp. 26, 39f., 32, 53
14. ibid., pp. 43ff.
15. ibid., pp. 15, 18, 24, 95
16. ibid., pp. 15ff.
17. A. Hyland, *The Endurance Horse* (1988), pp. 49f. A. Hyland, *Equus* (1990), p. 254, 262. Procopius, *Secret History* (1987 edn), p. 188. Herodotus, *The Histories* (1974), pp. 359f., 556. J.M. Cook, *The Persian Empire* (1983), p. 108.
18. J.N. Sarkar, *The Art of War in Medieval India* (1984), p. 99.
19. I.L. Pfalser, 'Ancient Asian Pony Express' in *Western Horseman* (December 1973)
20. Rashid al-Din, *The Successors of Genghis Khan* (1971), pp. 55, 62f.
21. Marco Polo, *The Travels of Marco Polo* (1818), pp. 364–6
22. R.G. de Clavijo, *Narrative of the Embassy of Ruy Gonzalez de Clavijo to the Court of Timur at Samarkand 1403–6* (1859), pp. 105f.
23. Taghri Birdi Abu l-Mahasin ibn, *History of Egypt*, in series on Semitic Philology, Vol. 14–16 (1954), Part I, 1382–1469. Part II, 1300–1411. Vol. XV, pp. 45ff.
24. J.N. Sarkar, *The Art of War in Medieval India* (1984), p. 177
25. *Bābur Nāma* (1969): p. 629

10. Travel

1. S. de Chair, *The Legend of the Yellow River* (1979), *passim*.
   A. Hyland, *Endurance Horse* (1988), pp. 31ff.
2. P. Jackson, *Early Missions to the Mongols. Carpini and his Contemporaries* (1994), pp. 15–32
3. *Warhorse* I (1994), p. 137
4. Rubruck, W. *The Journey of William Rubruck to the Western Parts of the World, 1253–55, with two accounts of the earlier journey of John of Plano Carpini* (1900), pp. 4–8, 18–24, 261
5. ibid., pp. 63f., 59, 241, 81
6. ibid., pp. 74f.
7. *Warhorse* I (1994), p. 127
8. Rubruck, W., *Journey of William Rubruck* (1900), p. 175
9. Abou Bekr ibn Bedr, *Le Naceri*, Vol. I, third exposition, ch. 7. iii, pp. 388f., 164, 18, 183
10. M. Polo, *Travels* (1984), pp. 22ff.
11. Rashid al-Din, *The Successors of Genghis Khan* (1971), p. 78
12. Ibn Hodeil, *La Parure* (1924), pp. 309–12
13. M. Polo, *Travels* Waugh/Bellonci ed. (1984), 30–42 *passim*
14. *Warhorse* II (1998), Indian chapters 8, 146, and 9, 159
15. M. Polo, *Travels*, Waugh/Bellonci edn (1984), 58
    Ibn Battuta, *Travels* (1962), Vol. II, 474
16. E.W. Safford, 'An Account of the Expenses of Eleanor Sister of Edward III on the Occasion of her Marriage to Reynald, Count of Guelders', *Arch.* (1927), pp. 111–40
17. M.W. Labarge, *A Baronial Household of the Thirteenth Century* (1965), 109, 156f., 163f., 194ff.
18. M.W. Labarge, *Medieval Travellers* (1982), 56f.
19. ibid.
20. W.L. Warren, *Henry II* (1991), 71f. quoting Fitzstephen, bk. 110/20–30
21. Ibn Battuta, *Travels* (1956), Vol. I, p. 71f.
22. ibid., Vol. II, p. 472ff, V.III.586
23. ibid., Vol. II, p. 478
24. ibid., Vol. II, pp. 497–503
25. ibid., Vol. III, pp. 546 & 549
26. ibid., Vol. IV, pp. 773ff.
27. ibid., Vol. IV, p. 799
28. R.G. de Clavijo, *Embassy of Clavijo to Timour at Samarcand*, 1859: pp. 90f, 97f.
29. ibid., p. 100
30. ibid., p. 111
31. ibid., p. 122
32. ibid., pp. 134f., 150
33. ibid., p. 174
34. E.R. Chamberlain, *The World of the Italian Renaissance* (1982), p. 121f.
35. ibid., p. 133
36. J. Barbaro, in *Persian Travels* (1873), Bk. II, pp. 55–67 *passim*
37. A. Contarini, in *Persian Travels* (1873), Bk. II, pp. 143–73 *passim*
38. C. Zeno in *Persian Travels* (1873), Bk. I, pp. 18–27
    G.M. Angiolello in *Persian Travels* (1873), Bk. I, pp. 77–90
39. V. d'Allesandri, in *Persian Travels* (1873), pp. xi–xvi, 227
40. J. Schiltberger, *The Bondage and Travels of Johann Schiltberger*, tr. Commander J. Buchan Telfer, RN, with notes by Professor P. Brunn (London, The Hakluyt Society, 1879), pp. 1f., 37, and note 27
41. E. Christiansen, *The Northern Crusades* (1960), pp. 80, 149ff.
42. Derby, Earl of, accounts quoted in *Expeditions to Prussia and The Holy Land* (Camden Society, Vol. XXX, 1874), pp. 262f.
43. Henry of Livonia, *Chronicle of Henry of Livonia* (1961), under year 1208
44. M.W. Labarge, 'Ghillebert de Lannoy, Burgundian Traveller', *History Today*, Vol. 26 (1976), 154–63
45. A. von Harff, *The Pilgrimage of Arnold von Harff 1496–1499* (1946), pp. 181, 122, 136
46. L. Varthema, *The Travels of Ludovico Varthema 1503–1508*, tr. J.W. Jones, Hakluyt Society (1863), p. 16f.
47. ibid., 16f, 37, 24, 20f.
48. B. de la Brocquière, in *Early Travels in Palestine* (1846), p. 305
49. L. Varthema, *Travels* (1863), p. 19
50. P. Tafur, *Travels and Adventures 1435–39* (1926), pp. 75, 80
51. ibid., p. 51
52. ibid., p. 52
53. ibid., pp. 182, 191, 204f., 208f., 211, 217, 225, 230
54. B. de la Brocquière, in *Early Travels in Palestine* (1848), p. 304f.
55. ibid., pp. 356–62 *passim*
56. G. Tetzel and Schaseck, *The Travels of Leo of Rozmital* (1955), pp. 2–20 *passim*
57. ibid., on tourneying pp. 24f., 30, 37f., 162, 165
58. ibid., pp. 28, 30
59. ibid., pp. 32, 48, 59f.

60. ibid., pp. 76, 78, 83, 85f., 94
61. ibid., pp. 106f.
62. ibid., p. 162

11. Warhorse Territory – The Geographical Canvas

1. Jahiz of Basra, 'Exploits of the Turks', *Journal of the Royal Asiatic Society* (1915), 631–97
2. Polybius, *The Rise of the Roman Empire* (1979), B. VI. 20
3. A.H.M. Jones, *The Later Roman Empire 284–602* (1964), pp. 679f.
4. G.L. Cheesman, *The Auxilia of the Roman Imperial Army* (1914), *passim*
   A. Hyland, *Equus* (1990), p. 188, 194, 77 and ch. 14 *passim*
5. *Warhorse* I (1994), p. 28
6. Procopius, *The History of the Wars* (1914–28), Vols I–V: Vol. II. b. iii. ch. xii, p. 6f.; Vol. III b. V. ch. iii, p. 22f.; and Vol. II. b. iii. ch. xvi, p. 12
7. *Warhorse* I (1994), p. 23
8. Maurice (Emperor), *Maurice's Strategikon* (1984), Bk. 1, ch. 1
9. ibid., Bk. VII, ch. 17
10. ibid., Bk. I, ch. 2
11. ibid., Bk. IX, ch. 5
12. *Warhorse* I (1994), pp. 54f.
13. C. Oman, *A History of the Art of War in the Middle Ages* (1924), Vols I & II; VI & II, pp. 48f.
14. *Warhorse* I (1994), pp. 31ff.
15. Einhard, Life of Charlemagne in *Two Lives of Charlemagne* (1969), p. 67 and note 28, p. 183
16. *Warhorse* I (1994), pp. 50f.
17. M. Jankovich, *They Rode into Europe* (1971), p. 94
18. *Warhorse* I (1994), pp. 40–7
19. S. Loch, *The Royal Horse of Europe* (1986), p. 59
20. Maurice (Emperor), *Maurice's Strategikon* (1984), Bk. XI, ch. 1
    Warhorse I (1994), pp. 29, 39
21. A. Hyland, *Equus* (1990), p. 15
    Oppian, *Cynegetica* (1928), under breed
22. A. Hyland, *Equus* (1990), pp. 152f.
23. *Persian Travels*, Bk. I, Zeno, pp. 15–18; Anglilello, p. 95; Bk. II, Barbaro, pp. 66f.; Contarini, p. 137
24. L.White, Jr, *Medieval Technology and Social Change* (1962), pp. 3f.
25. *RFA*, under year 758
26. P. Contamine, *War in the Middle Ages* (1984), p. 24
27. F. Lot, *L'Art militaire et les armées au moyen âge en Europe et dans la proche orient*, Vol. I (1946), p. 93
28. P. Contamine, *War in the Middle Ages* (1984), p. 25
29. *Warhorse* I (1994), p. 51
30. ibid., pp. 66, 73
    ASC, respective years
31. P. Contamine, *War in the Middle Ages* (1984), pp. 54, 35f., 56
32. A. Comnena, *The Alexiad* (1987), Bk. X, ch. viii, p. 313, ch. ix, p. 321; Bk. V, ch. iv *passim*
33. R. de Aguiliers, *Historia Francorum*: gifts, pp. 87, 92, 105; purchases, 36, 84; theft, 46; plundering, 91 (2,000 from pasture); spoils, 79, 84ff.; dead horses, 28, fifty dying outside Antioch; hunger, 34; turning back, 79; at Siloam, 118
34. *Warhorse* I (1994), pp. 109, 111ff.
35. ibid., ch. 7; *Warhorse* II (1998), ch. 4 *passim*
36. *Warhorse* II (1998), ch. 6 *passim*, and p. 136f.
37. B. de la Brocquière, *Travels* (1848), pp. 363–7 *passim*
38. *Warhorse* II (1998), p. 134
39. ibid., p. 70
40. ibid., pp. 22f.
41. ibid., p. 25
42. ibid., p. 31
43. ibid., pp. 40, 42, 44
44. ibid., ch. 2 *passim*
45. ibid., p. 53
46. P. de Commynes, *Memoirs de Philippe de Commynes*, 2 vols, Vol. II (1973), p. 520
47. *Warhorse* II (1998), p. 53
48. ibid., p. 36
49. ibid., p. 57

Bibliography

PRIMARY SOURCES

Abou Bekr ibn Bedr, *Le Naceri*, tr. M. Perron, 3 vols, Paris, Ministry of Agriculture, 1860

Aguiliers, Raymond of, *Historia Francorum Qui Ceperunt Iherusalem*, tr. and annotated J. H. Hill and L. Hill, Philadelphia, American Philosophical Society, 1968

d'Allesandri, Vincentio, quoted in *A Narrative of Italian Travels in Persia in the Fifteenth and Sixteenth Centuries*, Bk. I, ed. and tr. C. Grey, London, Hakluyt Society, 1873; Bk. II, tr. W. Thomas and S.A. Roy, London, Hakluyt Society, 1873 (Henceforth *Persian Travels*)

Ammianus, Marcellinus, *The Later Roman Empire AD 354–378*, tr. W. Hamilton, Harmondsworth, Penguin, 1986

Angiolello, Giovan Maria, quoted in *Persian Travels*

Anglo-Saxon Chronicles, tr. and collated A. Savage, London, William Heinemann, 1982

Anglo-Saxon Wills, ed. and tr. D. Whitlock, Oxford, Oxford University Press, 1930

Bābur Nāma, tr. A.S. Beveridge, London, Luzac, 1922 (reprinted 1969)

Bain, Joseph, *Calendar of Documents Relating to Scotland, Preserved in HM PRO*, Vols 2–4, Edinburgh, General Register House, 1884–8

Barbaro, Josefa, quoted in *Persian Travels*

Barbosa, D., *The Book of Duarte Barbosa*, tr. M. Longworth Dames, Vol. I, London, Hakluyt Society (second series, no. XLIV), 1918

The Bayeux Tapestry and the Norman Invasion, intr. and tr. by Lewis Thorpe from the contemporary account of William of Poitiers, London, Folio Society, 1973

Bede, *Bede's Ecclesiastical History of the English People*, ed. Bertram Colgrave and R.A.B. Mynors, Oxford University Press, 1969

Behā ed-Dīn Abu el Mehasan Yusuf, *Saladin, or What Befell Sultun Yusuf, Salāh ed-Dīn*, Library of the Palestine Pilgrims Text Society, Vol. XIII, *The Life of Saladin (1137–1193)*, Committee of the Palestine Exploration Fund, 1897

Boke of Marchalsi (a fifteenth-century treatise on horsebreeding and veterinary medicine), ed. Bengt Odenstedt from MS. Harley 6398, Uppsala, Stockholm University, 1972

Caesar, Julius, *The Gallic Wars*, tr. J.J. Edwards, London, Heinemann, 1955

A Cambridgeshire Gaol Delivery Roll 1332–1334, ed. Elizabeth G. Kimball, Cambridge Antiquarian Record Society, 1978

Carolingian Chronicles, tr. B.W. Scholz with B. Rogers, Ann Arbor, University of Michigan Press, 1972

Carpini, John de Plano, see Rubruck

Cely Letters in *The Celys and Their World*, A. Hanham, Cambridge University Press, 1985

Ceremonial of Funeral of King Edward IV, from a MS of the late Mr Anstis now in possession of Thomas Astle, Esq, *Archaeologia* I (1770), 350ff

Chaucer, Geoffrey, *The Canterbury Tales*, tr. Nevill Coghill, Harmondsworth, Penguin Books, 1951 (this edition, 1977)

Clavijo, R.G. de, *Narrative of the Embassy of Ruy Gonzalez de Clavijo to the Court of Timour at Samarcand 1403–6*, tr. C.R. Markham, New York, B. Franklin, originally published by the Hakluyt Society (first series no. XXVI), 1859

Commynes, P. de, *Memoirs of Philippe de Commynes*, ed. S. Kinser, tr. I. Casseaux, 2 vols, Columbia University of South Carolina Press, 1969 and 1973

Comnena, Anna, *The Alexiad*, tr. E.R.A. Sewter, Harmondsworth, Penguin, 1969 (this edition, 1987)

Contarini, A., quoted in *Persian Travels*

Derby, Earl of, accounts quoted in *Expedition to Prussia and the Holy Land*, ed. L. Toulmin-Smith, London, Camden Society Vol. XXX, 1894

Domesday Book, ed. J. Morris, Huntingdonshire, no. 19, Phillimore, 1975

——, ed. J. Morris, Northamptonshire, no. 21, Phillimore, 1979

——, ed. J. Morris, Cambridgeshire, no. 18, Phillimore, 1981

——, ed. J. Morris, Norfolk parts I and II, no. 33, Phillimore, 1984

Einhard, Life of Charlemagne in *Two Lives of Charlemagne*, tr. and intro. L. Thorpe, Harmondsworth, Penguin, 1969

Eschenbach, Wolfram von, *Parsival*, tr. H.M. Mustard and C.E. Passage, New York, Random House, 1961

——, *Willehalm*, tr. C.E. Passage, New York, Frederick Unger, 1977

Eyb von, the younger, in *Gentlemen Errant, The journeys of four noblemen in Europe during the fifteenth and sixteenth centuries*, tr. Mrs. Henry Cust, London, John Murray, 1909

Froissart, J., *Chronicles*, ed. and tr. G. Brereton, Harmondsworth, Penguin, 1969 (reprinted 1983)

Games, Gutierre Diaz de, *The Unconquered Knight*, tr. J. Evans, London, George Routledge & Sons Ltd., 1928

Giraldus Cambrensis, 'Description of Wales' in *Gerald of Wales*, tr. and intro. L. Thorpe, Harmondsworth, Penguin, 1978

Gray, Sir Thomas, *Scalacronica*, tr. Sir Herbert Maxwell, Glasgow, James Maclehose and Sons, 1907

Gregory of Tours, *The History of the Franks*, tr. L. Thorpe, Harmondsworth, Penguin, 1974

Harff, A. von, *The Pilgrimage of Arnold von Harff 1496–1499*, tr. M. Letts, London, Hakluyt Society (second series, no. XCIV), 1946

Harrod, H, 'Some details of a murrain of the fourteenth century', *Archaeologia* XLI (1867), 1–14

Hayes, H.M., *Veterinary Notes for Horseowners*, London, Stanley Paul, 1976

Henry VII, *The Reign of Henry VII* from Original Documents preserved in the PRO, ed. Revd W. Campbell, London, Longman and Co., 1857

Herodotus, *The Histories*, tr. A. de Selincourt, Harmondsworth, Penguin, 1974

The High History of the Holy Grail, ed. Ernest Rhys, tr. Sebastian Evans, Everyman's Library, London, J.M. Dent & Sons, no date but after 1909

Hill, M.C., *The King's Messengers 1199–1377*, Stroud, Alan Sutton Publishing Ltd, 1994

Huntingdon, Henry of, *The Chronicle of Henry of Huntingdon*, ed. and tr. T. Forester, Llanerch Press, first published 1853, facsimile reprint, 1991

Hywel, Dda, *Welsh Medieval Law*, tr. A.W. Wade-Evans from Harleian MS 4353 in The British Museum, Oxford, Clarendon Press, 1909

Ibn Battuta, *The Travels of Ibn Battuta 1325–1354*, tr. H.A.A. Gibb, Vol. I, London, Hakluyt Society (second series, no. CX), 1956, and 3 vols, Cambridge University Press, 1958–94

Ibn Hodeil (Aly Ben Abderrahman Ben Hodeil El Andalusy), *La Parure des cavaliers et l'insigne des preux*, tr. L. Mercier, Paris, Librairie Orientaliste/Paul Geuthner, 1924

Ibn Munqidh, Usāmah, Memoirs of, *Usāmah ibn Munqidh*, tr. P.L. Hitti, Cairo, Princeton University at the Cairo Press, 1961

Ingulph, *Chronicle of the Abbey of Croyland*, tr. H.T. Riley, London, Bell, 1893

Inquisitio Comitatus Cantabrigiensis in *History of Cambridgeshire and the Isle of Ely*, ed. L.E. Salzman, Vol. I, Victoria History of the Counties of England, Oxford, OED, 1938

Jahiz of Basra (Amr. b. Mahr b. Mahbub Abu Othman al-Jahiz), 'Exploits of the Turks and the Army of the Khalifate in General', tr. C.T. Harley-Walker, *Journal of the Royal Asiatic Society* (1915), 631–97

Kai Ka'us ibn Iskander, *Qabus Nama: a Mirror for Princes*, tr. R. Levy, Cresset Press, 1951

Kurbsky, Prince A.M., *History of Ivan IV*, ed. and tr. J.L.I. Fennell, Cambridge University Press, 1965

La Brocquière, Bertrandon de, from The Travels of Bertrandon de la Brocquière in *Early Travels in Palestine*, ed. and annotated Thomas Wright, London, Henry G. Bohn, 1848

Langland, W., *Piers Plowman*, tr. J.F. Goodridge, Harmondsworth, Penguin Classics, 1959

The Laws of the Earliest English Kings, ed. and tr. F.L. Attenborough, Cambridge University Press, 1922

The Laws of the Kings of England from Edmund to Henry I, ed. and tr. A.J. Robertson, Cambridge University Press, 1925

Leodius, H.T., in *Gentlemen Errant*, London, John Murray, 1909

Livonia, Henry of, *Chronicle of Henry of Livonia*, tr. J.A. Brundage, Madison, University of Wisconsin Press, 1961

Lysons, S., 'Copy of a Roll of Expenses of King Edward I at Rhuddlan Castle in the 10th and 11th Years of his Reign', *Archaeologia* XVI (1812), 32–89

——, 'Copy of Purchases for Tournament at Windsor Park 6 Edward I', *Archaeologia* XVII (1914), 297–310

Malmesbury, W., *The Kings Before the Norman Conquest*, tr. J. Stephenson, Llanerch Enterprises, 1989

Mann, J.G., 'The Sanctuary of the Madonna delle Grazie with notes on the evolution of armour during the fifteenth century', *Archaeologia* 80 (1930), 117–42

Martorell, J. and de Gabla, M.J., *Tirant lo Blanc*, tr. D. Rosenthal, London, Macmillan, 1984

Maurice, The Emperor, *Maurice's Strategikon*, tr. G.T. Dennis, Philadelphia, University of Pennsylvania Press, 1984

Michaud, J.F. and Poujoulat, J.J., *Les Livres des Faicts du bon Messire Jean le Maingre, dit Boucicaut, Marechal de France et Gouverneur de Gennes*, Paris, 1836

Milles, Dr., Dean of Exeter, 'Observations on the Wardrobe account for 1483 wherein are contained the liveries made for the Coronation of King Richard III', *Archaeologia* I (1770), 263–382

Monte, Robert de, *The Chronicles of Robert de Monte*, tr. J. Stevenson, first published in 1856 by Seeleys in the series The Church Historians of England, facsimile reprint, Llanerch Publishers, 1991

Muntaner, R., *The Chronicles of Muntaner*, tr. Lady Goodenough, 2 vols, London, Hakluyt Society, 1920–21

Nikitin, A., 'The Travels of A. Nikitin of Tver', in *India in the Fifteenth Century*, ed., tr., and intr. R.H. Major, London, Hakluyt Society, 1857

Nithard, 'Nithard's Histories', in *Carolingian Chronicles*, tr. B.W. Scholz with B. Rogers, Ann Arbor, University of Michigan Press, 1972

Norwell, W., *The Wardrobe Book of Wm. de Norwell* (12 July 1338–27, May 1340), ed. Mary Lyon, Bruce Lyon and Henry S. Lucas with Jean de Sturler, Brussels, 1983

Notker, the Stammerer, 'Charlemagne', in *Two Lives of Charlemagne*, tr. and intro. L. Thorpe, Harmondsworth, Penguin, 1969

Oppian, *Cynegetica*, tr. A.W. Mair, Loeb Classical Library, Heinemann, 1928

d'Osma, Prospero, Report quoted in C.M. Prior, *The Royal Studs of the Sixteenth and Seventeenth Centuries*, London, Horse and Hound, 1935

Pires, T., *The Suma Oriental of Tome Pires*, tr. Armando Coresao, Vol. I, London, Hakluyt Society, 1944

The Plantagenet Chronicles, ed. E. Hallam, London, Guild Publishing, 1986

Polo, Marco, *The Travels of Marco Polo*, tr. W. Marsden (from the Italian edition by Remusio), London, Cox & Bayliss, 1818

——, *The Travels of Marco Polo*, tr. T. Waugh (from the Italian edition by M. Bellonci), London, Book Club Associates, 1984

Polybius, *The Rise of the Roman Empire*, tr. Ian Scott-Kilvert, Harmondsworth, Penguin, 1979

Procopius, *Secret History*, tr. G.A. Williamson, Harmondsworth, Penguin, 1966

——, *The History of the Wars*, tr. H.B. Dewing, Loeb Classical Library, 5 vols, Heinemann, 1914–28

Rashid al Din, *The Successors of Genghis Khan*, tr. J.A. Boyle, New York and London, Columbia University Press, 1971

Records of the Wardrobe and Household 1285–6, ed. B.F. Byerly and C.F. Byerly, London, HMSO, 1977

Records of the Wardrobe and Household 1286–7, ed. B.F. Byerly and C.F. Byerly, London, HMSO, 1986

The Register of the Black Prince, 4 vols, HMSO, 1930–33: Vol. I 1346–1348, 1930; Vol. II 1351–65 Duchy of Cornwall, 1931; Vol. III 1351–65, Palatinate of Chester, 1932; Vol. IV 1351–65, England, 1933

La Règle du Temple, Henri de Curzon, Paris, Librairie Renouard, for the Société de l'histoire de France, 1886

Royal Frankish Annals, in *Carolingian Chronicles* (see above)

'Roll of the Arms of the Knights at the Tournament at Dunstable 7 Edward III', in *Collectanea Topographica et Genealogica*, Vol. IV, London, 1837

Rubruck, William, *The Journey of William Rubruck to the Western Parts of the World, 1253–55 with two accounts of the earlier journey of John of Plano Carpini*, ed. and tr. W.W. Rockhill, London, Hakluyt Society (second series, no. IV), 1900

Safford, E.W., 'An account of the Expenses of Eleonor Sister of Edward III on the occasion of her marriage to Reynald, Count of Guelders', *Archaeologia* 77 (1927), 111–40

Speed, J.G., MRCVS and Speed, M.G., *The Exmoor Pony*, Droitwich, Countrywide Livestock Ltd, 1977

Tacitus, *Agricola and Germania*, Harmondsworth, Penguin, 1970

Tafur, P., *Travels and Adventures 1435–39*, ed. and tr. M. Letts, London, Routledge, 1926

Taghri Birdi, Abu l-Mahasin ibn, *The History of Egypt*, tr. W. Popper, series on Semitic Philology (Vols 14–16, Part I 1382–1469 and Part II 1399–1411), Berkeley and Los Angeles, University of California Press, 1954

Tetzel, G. and Schaseck, *The Travels of Leo of Rozmital*, tr. M. Letts, Hakluyt Society (second series, no. CVIII), Cambridge University Press, 1955

Villis, de (*Capitularies of Charlemagne*), in *The Reign of Charlemagne*, ed. H.R. Loyn and J. Percival, Edward Arnold, 1975

Walter of Henley, *Seneschaucie* in *Walter of Henley and other treatises on estate management and accounting*, ed. Dorothea Oschinsky, Oxford, Clarendon Press, 1971

Zeissmer, W. (ed.), *Das Grosse Änterbuch des Deutschen Ordens*, Wiesbaden, 1921 (reprinted 1968)

SECONDARY SOURCES

Ayalon, David, '*Furusiyya* Exercises and Games in the Mamlūk Sultanate' in *Scripta Hierosolymitana*, Vol. IX, Jerusalem, Magnus Press and the Hebrew University, 1961, pp. 31–62

Barber, R. and Barker, J., *Tournaments*, Woodbridge, Boydell Press, 1989

Barker, J., *The Tournament in England 1100–1400*, Woodbridge, Boydell Press, 1986

Barlow, F., *William Rufus*, London, Methuen, 1983

Bennett, H.S., *Life on the English Manor 1150–1400*, Cambridge University Press, 1939 (reprinted 1965)

Bökönyi, S., *History of Domesticated Mammals in Central and Eastern Europe*, Budapest, Akadémiai Kiadó, 1974

Bolton, J.L., *The Medieval English Economy 1150–1500*, London, Dent, 1980

Braudel, F., *The Structures of Everyday Life*, tr. Sian Reynolds, London, Collins, 1981

——, *The Wheels of Commerce*, tr. Sian Reynolds, London, Book Club Associates, 1983

Brehier, L., *Les Institutes de L'Empire Byzantin*, ed. Albin Michel, Paris, 1949

Burleigh, M., *Prussian Society and the German Order*, Cambridge University Press, 1984

Chair, Somerset de, *The Legend of the Yellow River*, London, Constable, 1979

Chamberlain, E.R., *The World of the Italian Renaissance*, London, Book Club Associates, 1982

Cheesman, G.L., *The Auxilia of the Roman Imperial Army*, Oxford, Clarendon Press, 1914

Childs, W., *Anglo-Castilian Trade in the Later Middle Ages*, Manchester University Press, 1978

Chivers, K., *The Shire Horse*, London, J.A. Allen, 1976

Chomel, V., 'Chevaux de Bataille at Roncins en Dauphine, au XIV siècle'

Christiansen, E., *The Northern Crusades*, London, Macmillan, 1960

Clark, J., *Medieval Horseshoes*, Department of Medieval Antiquities, Museum of London, Finds Research Group 700–1700, datasheet 4, reproduced and distributed by Coventry Museums

Clark, J. (ed.), *The Medieval Horse and its Equipment 1150–1450*, London, HMSO, 1995

Connor, R.D., *The Weights and Measures of England*, London, HMSO, 1987

Contamine, P., *War in the Middle Ages*, tr. Michael Jones, Oxford, Basil Blackwell, 1984

Cook, J.M., *The Persian Empire*, London, Book Club Associates, 1983

Costain, T.B., *The Pageant of England 1272–1377: The Three Edwards*, Universal Tandem Publishing Co. Ltd, 1973

Coulton, G.G., *Medieval Village, Manor, and Monastery*, New York and London, Harper & Row, 1960 (first published by Cambridge University Press as *The Medieval Village*, 1925)

Crofts, J., *Packhorse Wagon and Post*, London, Routledge & Kegan Paul, 1967

Cummings, J., *The Hound and The Hawk, The Art of Medieval Hunting*, London, Weidenfeld and Nicolson, 1988

Davis, R.H.C., 'The Medieval Warhorse', in F.M.L. Thomson (ed.), *Horses in European Economic History*, Reading, 1983

Davis, R.H.C., 'The Warhorses of the Normans', *Anglo-Norman Studies* X (1987), 67–82

Dent, A. and Goodall, D.M., *A History of British Native Ponies*, London, J.A. Allen, 1988

Digby, S., *Warhorse and Elephant in the Delhi Sultanate*, Oxford University Press, 1971

Finberg, H.P.R., *The Formation of England 550–1042*, Hart Davis Macgibbon, 1974

Fleming, G., *Horseshoes and Horseshoeing*, London, Chapman and Hall, 1869

Gilbert, J.M., *Hunting and Hunting Preserves in Medieval Scotland*, Edinburgh, John Donald, 1979

Gilbey, Sir W., *The Great Horse*, London, Vinton, 1899

Hewitt, H.J., *The Horse in Medieval England*, London, J.A. Allen, 1983

Hewitt, J., *Ancient Armour and Weapons in Europe*, Oxford and London, John Henry and James Parker, 1855

Hore, J.P., *The History of Newmarket*, Vol. I, London, A.H. Bailey, 1886

Hyland, A., *The Endurance Horse*, London, J.A. Allen, 1988

——, *Equus, The Horse in the Roman World*, London, Batsford, 1990

——, *The Medieval Warhorse from Byzantium to the Crusades*, Stroud, Alan Sutton Publishing Ltd, 1994

——, *The Warhorse 1250–1600*, Stroud, Sutton Publishing Ltd, 1998

Imam, S.A.H.A.A., *The Centaur*, Bihar, Indian Heritage, 1987

Jackson, P., 'Early Missions to the Mongols – Carpini and his Contemporaries', in Hakluyt Society Annual Report, 1994

Jankovich, M., *They Rode into Europe*, tr. A. Dent, London, Harrap, 1971

Jones, A.H.M., *The Later Roman Empire, 284–602*, London, Basil Blackwell, 1964

Kendall, P.M., *Richard III*, London, George Allen & Unwin, 1955 (Sphere edition, 1972)

Labarge, M.W., *A Baronial Household of the Thirteenth Century*, London, Eyre and Spottiswoode, 1965

——, *Medieval Travellers, The Rich and the Restless*, London, Hamish Hamilton, 1982

——, 'Ghillebert de Lannoy, Burgundian Traveller', *History Today* 26 (1976), 154–63

Langdon, J., *Horses, Oxen and Technological Innovation*, Cambridge University Press, 1986

Langlois, *Le Règne de Philippe III Le Hardi*, Paris, 1887

Leighton, A.C., *Transport and Communication in Early Medieval Europe AD 500–1100*, Newton Abbot, David and Charles, 1972

Lennard, R., 'Composition of Demesne Plough Teams in 12th century England', *English Historical Review* CCXCV (April 1960), 193–206

Loch, S., *The Royal Horse of Europe*, London, J.A. Allen, 1986

Lot, F., *L'Art militaire et les armées au moyen âge en Europe et dans la proche orient*, Vol. I, Paris, Payot, 1946

Mallet, M.E. and Hale, J.R., *Military Organization in a Renaissance State: Venice 1400–1617*, Cambridge University Press, 1984

Martin, H.D., 'The Mongol Army', *Journal of the Royal Asiatic Society* (April 1943), 46–85

Martin, P., *Armour and Weapons*, tr. R. North, Herbert Jenkins, 1968

Masson-Smith, J., 'Ayn Jālūt. Mamlūk Success or Mongol Failure?', *Harvard Journal of the Asiatic Society* 44 (1984), 307–45

Merlen, R.H.A., 'Horses in Old Russia', *Horse World* 7 (July 1972), 13–15

Miller, Edward (ed.), *The Agrarian History of England and Wales, Vol. III. 1348–1500*, Cambridge University Press, 1991

Nielsen, G., *Trial by Combat*, Glasgow, Wm. Houge & Co., 1890

Oakeshott, E., *A Knight and His Horse*, London, Lutterworth Press, 1962

Oman, C., *A History of the Art of War in the Middle Ages*, Vols I & II, revised edition, New York, Burt Franklin, 1924

Origo, I., *The Merchant of Prato*, Harmondsworth, Penguin Books, 1986

Ormrod, W.M., *The Reign of Edward III*, London, Guild Publishing, 1990

Pfalser, I.L., 'Ancient Asian Pony Express', *Western Horseman* (December 1973), 66–7, 149–50

Polliak, A.N., 'The Influence of Chingis Khan's Yasa upon the General Organization of the Mamelūk State', *Bulletin of the School of Oriental and African Studies* 10 (1942), 862–76

Prestwich, M., *Edward I*, London, Methuen, 1990

——, *The Three Edwards*, London, Book Club Associates, 1980

Pryor, J.H., 'Transportation of Horses by Sea during the Era of the Crusades, eighth century to AD 1285, Parts I & II', *Mariners Mirror* 68 (1982), 9–27, 103ff

Ravensdale, J., *The Domesday Inheritance*, Landbeach, Souvenir Press Ltd, 1986

Reese, M.M., *The Royal Office of Master of the Horse*, London, Threshold Books, 1976

Renouard, Y., 'L'exportation de chevaux de la Péninsule Ibérique en France et en Angleterre au moyen âge', *Maluquer de Motes Nicolaus*, ed. *Homenaje a Jaime Vicens Vives*, Barcelona, 1965, Vol. I, 571–77

Richardson, C., *The Fell Pony*, London, J.A. Allen, 1990

Robinson, R., *Oriental Armour*, London, Herbert Jenkins, 1967

Sarkar, J.N., *The Art of War in Medieval India*, Munshiram Mancharlal Ltd, 1984

Saul, N., *Medieval England*, London, Batsford Academic and Educational Ltd, 1983

The Showmen's Guild of Great Britain, *All the Fun of the Fair*, 1987

Spruytte, J., *Early Harness Systems*, tr. M.A. Littauer (from *Etudes Experimentales sur l'Attelage*, 1977), London, J.A. Allen Ltd, 1983

Strutt, J., *The Sports and Pastimes of the People of England*, Firecrest Publishing, 1969 (reprint of 1801 publication)

Swaminathan, K.D., 'The Horsetraders of Malai-Mandalam', *Journal of Indian History* 32–3 (1954–5), 139–43

Trevelyan, G.M., *English Social History*, Longmans Green, 1942 (reprinted Pelican, 1967)

Vernam, G.R., *Man on Horseback*, New York, Harper and Row, 1964

Walford, C., *Fairs Past and Present*, London, Elliot Stock, 1883

Walker, R.E., *Ars Veterinaria*, Kenilworth, New Jersey, Schering-Plough Animal Health, 1991

Warren, W.L., *Henry II*, London, Methuen, 1973 (new edition, 1991)

Webster, G., *The Roman Army*, Chester, Grosvenor Museum, revised edition 1973

Wentworth, Lady, *Thoroughbred Racing Stock*, London, Allen & Unwin, 1938

White, L., Jr, *Medieval Technology and Social Change*, Oxford, Clarendon Press, 1962

Willard, J.F. and Morris, W.A. (eds), *The English Government at Work, 1327–36*, Cambridge, Massachussetts, Medieval Academy of America, 1940

Index of Horse-related Subjects

General

anthrax, 11

bitting, 64ff
Boke of Marchalsi, 53–9; on
  ailments:
    broken wind, 58; canker of
    the tongue, 58; colic
    (trenchelouns), 57; of the
    legs, 58; worms, 57
  on choice of horse, 55; on
  conformation, 55; on training, 56
branding, 73, 118, 128
Bucephalus, 126

carthire, 46
cavalry, 139f: *Ala(e)*, 4; *Ala I
  Asturum*, 4; *Ala II Asturum*, 4;
  Ala Hispanorum Vettonum, 4; *Ala
  I Pannoniorum Sabiniana*, 4;
  Avar, 141f; Byzantine, 141;
  English, 150; European, 150f;
  Frankish, 143f; Italian, 151;
  Lombard, 141; Magyar, 142;
  Mamlūk, 140, 148; Mongol,
  146f; Moorish, 142; Norman,
  145; Ottoman, 143; Persian, 140,
  142f; Roman, 140
    *Coh. I Aelia Hispanorum
    Milliaria Equitata*, 4; *Cuneus
    Frisiorum*, 4; *Cuneus Sarmatorum
    Brementenraco*, 4
cavalry equipment, Persian, 126
caveat emptor, 6
chariotry, 4
collar, 39
Count of the Stable, 12
cursibus equorum, 36
customs relating to horses, 31f,
  34f

dealing, 21f; Hungarian, 22;
  Hindustani, 126; Indian, 23f;
  Oriental, 23f
docking, 32

ear cropping, 32
ecclesiastical equestrianism, 17

encephalitis, 6
epidemics, 11
equestrian matrix, 140f
equipment of Black Prince's studs,
  73

fairs: Antwerp, 22; Brie, 22;
  Champagne, 22; Cologne, 22;
  Frankfurt, 22; Geneva, 22;
  Medina del Campo, 22;
  Smithfield, 22
farcy, 6, 57
farrier/ferrator, 51
farrier, King's, 51

gaits, 28–30
glanders, 6

hippiatrika, 4
hipposandals, 51
horse baiting, 35
horse breeds, *see* list
horse provenance, *see* list
horse management, 53f
horse racing, 36, 86; in Egypt, 36;
  in England, 36; in Italy, 36; in
  Syria, 36
horse types, *see* list
horse wealh, 13
horse weard, 13

Isik, 125

lassoing, 89, 139
laws: governing sales, 22; relating
  to horses, 31
licences, for export, 22
Livro da Montaria, 83
Loriner's Guild, 59

Marshalsea, 51
mareschal, marshal, mariskalk,
  51
Master of Horse, 15, 51
murrain, 11f, 45

pfeifferella mallei, 57
polo, 86
prices, 41f

remount depots, 142
requisitioning, 41f
restauro, 76ff

Saddler's Guild, 59
Saddler's Guild of Limoges, 60
saddlery, 59ff
saddles of: Henry V, 61; Pazyryk,
  61; Roman, 61; de Tournemine,
  61
Shabdiz, 143
shoeing, 51ff
shoeing damascene, 135
sizes of horses, 21
spurs, 60
staggers, 6
stealing horses, 31, 33, 126
stirrups, 62f
strangles, 7
studs, *see* list

tack, Oriental, 64
trappers, 66f
trenchelouns (colic), 57

veterinary care, 53–9 *passim*
veterinary treatises, 53f

warbles (lowe), 57
warhorse: breeding of, 150;
  purchase, 150; shortage of, 151
war saddle, 62
weightbearing capacity (of horse),
  104f
whippletree, 62

Breeds – Specific

Akhal Teke, 142
Altai, 124
Andalusian, 1, 3, 105, 137
Apulian, 27
Arabian, 1, 3, 14, 17, 21, 87ff, 126,
  135f, 145; strains of, 20, 21, 131
Barb (Berber), 14, 19, 125, 142
Barqa, 125f
Caramanian, 131
Caspian, 1, 3
Castilian, 15, 22, 106

Chahri, 125f, 129
Chapman, 47, 123
Cleveland Bay, 47
Dales, 1, 4, 46
Exmoor, 1, 3
Faras (purebred Arabian), 17, 125
Fell, 1, 3f, 46
Flanders, 14f, 18
Friesian, 4, 19
Galloway, 46
Garron, 5
Kazakh, 124
Khorassanian, 125
Kirghiz, 125
Lombard, 14f, 18, 27, 141
Lusitano, 105, 137
Margonara, 36
Mongol pony/horse, 3, 23f, 126, 146f
Nisaean, 143
Orkney pony, 5
Persian, 1, 126, 131
Shetland, 5
Steppe pony (several breeds), 120, 150, ch. 10 passim
Trans Baikal, 126
Turcoman/Turkmene, 1, 3, 21, 23f, 125, 129, 146; Brocquiere on, 135
Yakut, 124

Exports

Castilian exports to: Bordeaux, 22; Gascony, 22; Navarre, 22; Toulouse, 22
Egypt(ian), 125
Ferghana, 129
Frisia, 4, 19
Haca, 21
Hejaz, 21
Hisar, 126
Hungary, 4, 18, 22f, 142
Ireland, 1, 15, 19
Kandahar, 126
Kashgar, 126
Katif, 21
Kufa, Iraq, 142
Levant, 1, 18, 21
Liège, 15
Lombardy, 14f, 18, 27
Luxembourg, 15
Moldavia, 23
Narbonne, 15
Navarre, 14f, 22
Normandy, 5, 8, 14, 144
North Africa, 1, 3
Pannonia(n), 4, 11
Persian Gulf, 21
Sardinia, 19
Scotland, 1
Sicily(ian), 14, 21, 120
Spain/Spanish, 1, 3ff, 15, 18

Spanish exports of warhorses and rouncies to: Avignon, 15; Foix, 15; Genes, 15; Montpellier, 15; Narbonne, 15; Perpignan, 15; Portugal, 15; Rodez, 15

Herds of/Horsebreeding Areas

Arabia, 120
Armenia, 120
Bactria, 120
Bellême, 17
Byzantium, 120
Cappadocia, 140
La Perche, 17
Lombardy, 141
Malagina, 12, 142
Media, 143
Normandy, 17
Persia, 120
Phrygia, 12, 120, 140
Samarkand, 125
Syria, 120
Tabrix, 125
Thrace, 4, 12, 125
Transylvania, 125
Turkmenia, 120
Upper Oxus (Amu Darya), 120

Horses from/National Provenance

Afghanistan (Badakshan), 126
Anatolia, 1, 126
Apulia(n), 27
Arabia, see breed list
Aragon(ese), 15
Auvergne, 14
Bactria, 120, 126
Baghdad, 126
Bahrein, 21
Balkh, 126
Belgium, 15
Bukhara, 126
Campania, 27
Cappadocia, 12, 120, 143
Tabriz, 121
Turkestan/Turkmenia, see breed list
Valenica, 14
Wales, 1
Wallachia, 23

Horse Types (not indicating breed or provenance)

affer (aver), 1, 12, 32
berdhun, 89, 125
carthorse, 1, 39, 41f; prices of, 42
courser, 1

destrier, 1 and passim
draught, 39
Frankish, 126
Germanic, 4
Great Horse, 1
Greek (blood), 27
Hackney (Hakenei), 1, 39; hire of, 118
Hedjin, 125
hercarius, 9, 12, 44
hobby, 1, 79
oriental, 27
pad, 1
pack, 3, 39, 44, 46f
palfrey, 1
plough, 42f; feed costs, 43; prices of, 42; speed of, 43
rouncy, 1, 9
stot, 1, 12, 32
sumpter, 1, 39
wilde weorf, 6

Studs/Stables of

Aelfhelm, 6
Austin Canons, 47
Benedictines, 47
Black Prince: breeding policies, 74f; locations, 71ff; staffing of, 72; stud keepers, 73
Burton Monastery, 13, 18
Caersws, 73
Cistercians, 18, 47
Cleythorpe, 9
Clipstone, 15
Cordoban, 14, 142
Domfront, 127
Easby Abbey, 18
English Royal (Plantagenet), 15
Fitzalans, 19
Frankish, 91
Gonzagan, 19
Haras du Pin, 17
Holland, 15
Jedburgh, Abbot of, 35
Malmesbury, 41
Monastic: of England, 47; of Normandy, 17
Monastic, military orders, 18f, 118
Odiham, 19, 127
Oriental, 3, 21
Scottish, 92
Sheen, 16
Thurstan, 6
Tutbury, 41
Wake, John of Liddell, 19
Warenne's, Earl of, 18
Wereham, 9
Whitby Abbey, 46f
Wynflaed, 6
Wulfric, 6
Wulfgeat, 6

General Index

Abbalava (Burgh by Sands), 4
Abou Bekr Ibn Bedr, 17, 21, 54, 105, 125
Acre, 18
Aelfhelm, 6
Aelfmaer (seneschal), 6
Aelfsige (bishop), 6
Aelfwine (Chaplain), 6
Aelfwold, 13
Aelfric, Godricson, 8
Aelthflaed, 6
Aethelbert, 13
Aethling, Aethelstan, 6
Agincourt, battle of, 151
Aibek, 148
Aidan, Bishop, 6
aide de la venerie, 83
Ailsworth, 7
Ajnadain, battle of, 142
Ak Koyunlu, 130f, 150
Alan, Count of Brittany, 8
Alauddin, Khilji, 121
Al Barid, 121
Alexander the Great, 126
Alexius, Comnenus I, 145
Alfold, 141
Al Hisham, 14
d'Allesandri Vicento, 131
Al Mansur, 14, 142
Al Mansur Qaloon, 148
Alp Arslan, 146
Aly Ben Abderrahman Ben Hodeil El Andalusy, 54, 105
Amalsuntha, 140
Amat Shurri, 120
Ambassadors' travels, 128–31
Ammianus Marcellinus on hunting, 84
Anazeh, 21
Angaros, 120
Angiolello, Giovan Maria, 131, 143
Anglo Saxon Chronicles, 4f
Anglo Saxon wills, 5f
Anjou, 14, 100
Ankara, battle of, 129
Anna Comnena, 145
Antioch, siege of, 146
Apadana Frieze, 143
Apsyrtus, 53
Aquitaine, 14f; campaign of Black Prince, 75

Arabian bandits, 133
Arabian peninsula, 142
Arabs, 142
armour, 67ff, 124
Arnold of Echaffour, 19
Arrian on hunting, 84
Asia, 3
Asian Steppes, 123
Asiatic Lion, 84
Assize of Tanners, 60
Athelstan, King, 4
Attalus, 12
Avars, 11, 141f
Avignon, 15, 22
Ayn Jālūt, battle of, 147

Babur, 90, 121
Bābur Nāma, 90
Babylon on the Euphrates, 142
Baibars, 147f
Barbaro, Josefa, 130, 143
Barid-i-Mamalik, 121
Barrington (Mendips), 3
Battiniya (Assassins), 87
Batu Khan, 86, 123, 125
Bayazid I, 129
Bayeux Tapestry, 44
Beaulieu Abbey, 18
Bede, Venerable, 6, 30, 36
Bedu, 21
Beha-ed-Din, 68
Belisarius, 140
Bellême, 17
Bellême, Robert de, 13
Bentivoglio, Hermes, 23
Benwell, 4
Black Hunt, 33
Black Prince, 11, 22, 92, 96, ch. 6 passim; Register of, ch. 6 passim, 95ff
    acquisitions of horses, 71f, 75f; imports of horses in, 72; purveyance of horses in, 74f
blacksmith, 51
Blunt, Lady Ann, 133
Bohemund, 146
Bolingbroke, 132
border infractions, 34f
Border Papers, 27
Borough Green, 8
Botetourt, Sir Baldwin de, 72f

Boucicaut, Jean de, 107f
Bouillon, Godfrey, 145
Brabant, John of, 110
Brecon Gaer, 4, 13
Bretigny, Treaty of, 27
Brevium Exempla, 91
Britain, 3
British, 4
Briton, Thomas, 15
Britons, 4
Brittany, John of, 110
Brocquière, Bertrandon de la, 22, 132ff, 149f
Brun, 13
Burgundian Court, 136
Bythorn, 7
Byzantine Empire, 12
Byzantium, 126, 140f, 144

Caballari, 117
Caen, 8
Cambridge(shire), 8
Cambridgeshire Gaol Delivery Roll, 31, 33
Canterbury, Archbishop of, 18
Canute, King, 91
Caravaggio, battle of, 151
Carlisle Fair, 34
Carpini, John of Plano, 68, 124
carrying duties, 45
Caster, 7
Castile, 15
Celys, as horse traders, 25
Charibert, King, 12
Charlemagne, 1, 11, 90f, 99, 117, 142f
Charles I of Anjou, 18
Charles II of Anjou, 18
Charolais (later Duke of Burgundy), 136
Chaucer, 27f
Chester, 4; Hugh, Earl of, 17; Palatinate of, 95f
Chevely Hundred, 8
China, 129f, 146
Chingis Khan, 125, 146
Chiron, 53
Chosroes II, 143
Cistercians, 18, 46f
Clavijo, Ruy Gonzalez de, 129f
Clermont, Council of, 100, 145

Cluny, Abbot of, 30
Coeur, Jacques, 22
Cokini, 118
Colonsay Island, 5
commerce, ch. 4 *passim*
Commynes, Philippe de, 151
Constantine, Porphyrogenitus, 54
Constantinople, 12
Contarini, Ambrogio, 48
Cordoba, 142
Costessy, 8
Courtrai, battle of, 127
crafts, ch. 5 *passim*
Crècy, battle of, 71, 151
Crimean Tartars, 11, 128
crop failure, 118
Crusades, 146
Cumberland, 7
Cursor, 118
Cursus Publicus, 120
Customs of Darnel and Over, 32
Cynlefu, 13

Dalileye, James de, 41
Damascus, Caliphate, 14
Danes, 5
Dartmoor, 9, 75
Datini, Francisco, 48f; businesses
   of, 49; commodities of, 48f;
   horses of, 49; mule of, 40
Dauphiné, 18
Delhi Sultanate, 121
Deodand, 32, 76
De Villis Capitulary, 12, 91
Dio Cassius, 4
Diocletian, 140
distaff travel, 126
distraint of knighthood, 150f
Domesday Book, 5–9 *passim*
Dorylaeum, battle of, 146
Duarte, King of Portugal, 105,
   112f
Dumfries Castle, 11
Dura Europus, 143
Durer, Albrecht, 153
Durham, 6; Manor and Prior of, 32

Eadwold, 13
Earl Marshal, 51
Easby Abbey, 18
East Anglia, 7, 144
Eastern Roman Empire, 140f
Edeva the Fair, 8
Edmaer, 13
Edmund, King, 6
Edward I, 1, 11, 15, 17 and *passim*
Edward II, 15; Prince of Wales, 18
Edward III, 11, 15, 21, 69, 74, 96,
   151
Edward IV, 136
Egypt, 1, 21
Elbe river, 15
Elizabeth I, 1, 41

Ellis of Rochester, King's Farrier, 51
Eleonor of Aquitaine, 126
Eleonor, Countess of Leicester, 127
Eleonor, sister of Edward III, 126f
El Nacer, 21, 54, 148
Engelnulf de l'Aigle, 17
Epona, 4
Eschenbach, Wolfram, 104f
estate management, 78f
Ethelred II, King, 6
Europe, 3
Evroul, St, Abbey of, 17
Exmoor, 9

fairs, 21f, 35
falconry, 78, 95
Falkirk, battle of, 151
farming, ch. 4 *passim*
Fauberti, 22
Fécamp Priory, 8, 17
Figuera, Domingo de, 22
fines, 32
Firuzabad, 143
Fitzalans, 19
Fitzosbern, William, 17
Fitzstephen, William, 22, 36
Flete, Richard of, 32
Foix, 15
Forest of Ardennes, 90
forest law, 92
forest rights, 96
Fotheringhay, 8
Fountains Abbey, 17, 46
France, 1, 3, 14f, 17ff
Frederick II, Emperor, 54, 124
Frederick III, Emperor, 136
Freemantle, 15
Frodner, 136
Fulbourn, 8f
Furusiyya, 86, 134

Gallic cult, 4
Games, Gutierre Diaz de, 104
Gascony, 14, 17f, 22
Gauls, 4
Geneats, 117
Genes, 15
Geoffrey Plantagenet, Count of
   Anjou, 14
Germany, 15, 18, 23
Ghuzz (Oghuz) Turks, 146
Giffard, Walter, 1
Gilanshah, 87
Giraldus Cambrensis, 13
Gir Forest, Gujarat, 84
Glinton, 7
Glos la Ferrière, 17
Gloucester, Earl of, 14
Gonzagas, 36
Gonzaga, Luigi, 36
Grand Tour, 123
Gray, Sir Thomas, 36
Great Bellingham, 9

Great Stour, 13
Gregory of Tours, 12
Grunwald (Tannenberg), battle of,
   19
Guntram, King, 12
Gwestwa, 6
Gwillim, Sir Walter ap, 30

Hanyes, Sir William, 30
Haroun Al Raschid, 1, 90
Hasan-i-Sabah, 87
hastiludes, 103
Hastings, battle of, 1, 144
Hawkwood, Sir John, 49
haymaking, 46
Heacham Manor, 11
Hemingford Grey, 7
Henley, Walter of, 43
Henry I, 14
Henry II, 14, 36, 74
Henry III, 15, 124, 127
Henry V, 132
Henry VII, 92, 103, 151, 153
Henry VIII, 104, 151, 153
Henry, Abbot of Poitou, 33
Heraclius, Emperor, 143
Herebald, 30, 36
heriot, 6, 13, 31f, 43f, 76
Hockham, 9
Hospitallers, 18
hound types, 94f
Hugh of France, 4
Hulegu, first Il Khan, 126, 147
hunting, 30f, 36, 78f, ch. 7 *passim*;
   Byzantine, 85; Indian, 90;
   Mamluk, 86; Moghul, 85f;
   Occidental, 84; Oriental, 84;
   Persian, 84; Syrian, 87ff;
   Turkish, 86f, 134
hunting: abuses in, 96; laws
   governing, 91f; reserves, 90, 92;
   types of, 93; as war training, 84;
   with raptors, 88
Huntingdonshire, 7
Hunyadi, John, 150
Hurstingstone, 8

Iazyges, 4
Ibn Battuta, 23f, 125f, 128, 132,
   146; travels of, 28f
Ice Age, 3
indentures, 76ff, 103f
independent traveller, 132f, 135
India, 23, 129, 131
Ine, King, 13
Inland Revenue, 7
Innocent III, Pope, 30
Innocent IV, Pope, 124
*Inquisitio Comitatus
   Cantabrigiensis*, 9
Invasion of Europe, 123
Iran, 3
Iraq, 21

Isabella, Queen, 126
Italian bankers, 74
Italy, 18f
Ivan III, 131

Jahiz of Basra, 86, 139
James II of Aragon, 15
Jerusalem, 18
Jervaulx Abbey, 18, 46
John, King of England, 15, 18, 46
John of Portugal, 83
jousting, *see* tournaments
Juan Juan, 141, 143
Judith, Countess, 8
Julius Caesar, 4
Jumièges Monastery, 8, 17
Jusjaini (chronicler), 24
Justin II, 141
Justinian, Emperor, 141

Kai Ka'us Ibn Iskander, 87
Kallay family, 73
Karakorum, 123
Kenstutis of Lithuania, 18
Khazars, 143
Kilij Arslan, 146
Kimbolton, 8
King's Hussar Regiment, 104
Kipchak Turks, 148
Kirtling, 8
Kitbugha, 147
Korea, 120
Kubilai Khan, 85f
Kuderai-Chettis, 24
Kumiss, 125
Kuyuk Khan, 124f
Kyukchi, 86

Lake District, 46
Lambkyn, saddler, 72
Landa, Thomas, 15
Landuch, dealer, 5, 150
Langland, William, 30
Lannoy, Ghillebert de, 132
lawing of dogs, 92
laws governing travel, 28
Laws of the March of Scotland, 34
Lech, battle of, 144
Leicester, Countess of, 19
Leighton, 7
Leightonstone, 8
Leo VI, Byzantine Emperor, 52
Leofwine, 6
Leudast, 12, 51
Leudesgisel, 12
Levantine Tatars, 120
Liagre, Albert de, 22
Lincoln, Bishop of, 7
Lincolnshire, 7
Lindesey, Simon de, 19
Lithuania, 18
Little Watte (Petit Watte), dealer, 22, 73

Livre de l'Ordre de Chevalrie, 84
Logothete of the Herds, 12
Lombards, 141
London, 15
Louis IX of France, 15, 124
Louis of France, 14
Louis the Pious, 90
Lyre Abbey, 17

Maclodio, battle of, 69
mae-pae, 120
Magna Carta, 123
Magyars, 142, 144
Mahaut, daughter of Robert of Artois, 127
Mainz Tournament, 99
Makrisi, 21
Malatesta, Pandolfo, 23
Mantua, 19
Manzikert, battle of, 146
Mamlūk, 132ff, 140, 147f
Mamlūk Sultanate, 21
Marcowefa, 12, 51
Marienburg, 132
markets, 21, 35
Marseilles, Bishop of, 18
Marshal, Walter, Earl of Pembroke, 51
Marshall, William, 107
Master of Game, 94
Matilda, Queen, 14
Maurice, Emperor, 85, 140f;
   Strategicon of, 85, 140f
Mecca, 133f, 142
Mediterranean, 3
mêlée, *see* tournament
Mendips, 3
mercenaries, 131f
merchet, 31
Milanese armourers, 69
Milton, 7
Missi Dominici, 117
Mohacs, battle of, 150
Mohammed, 142
Molecester, Sir William, 41
monastic pleasure riding, 30f
Mongke Khan, 124f
Mongol Invasion of Europe, 123
Montfort, Sir Simon de, 19, 127
Montpellier, 15
Montsaunes, 18
Moors, 14, 142, 145
mortuary, 31
Mouhanna, Beni, 21
Murad II, Grand Turk, 134
Murad III, 131
Museum of Electoral Hesse, 104

Najera, battle of, 71
Narses, 140
North America, 3
Neville, Hugh de, King's Forester, 46
New Forest, 91

Nicopolis, battle of, 131, 150
Nogays, 11
Norfolk, 7ff
Norman(s), 7, 14, 144f
Normancross, 8
Norsemen, 144
Northamptonshire, 7
Northumberland, 6
Numidian horsemen, 140
nuncii regis, 117f; careers of, 120;
   distances ridden, 118ff; horses of
   and values of, 118f; overseas
   journeys of, 119

Odenstedt, Bengt, 54
Oghurlu, Mohammed, 130
Ogodei, Khan, 120, 126
Oppian on hunting, 84
d'Osma, Prospero, 1, 41
Oswine, King, 6
Otto the Great, 144
Ottoman Empire, 19, 132f
Ottomans, 130f, 143, 148f
oxen prices, 41f

Paleolithic, 3
Palfreyman, Ragaz, 71, 74
Palfreyman, Rocelyn, 71
para veredarii, 117
Paris, Matthew, 123
Parsival, 106f
Patzinaks (Pechenegs), 142
Pazyryk burials, 61
Pepin I, 143
Pero, Niño, 104
Persepolis, 143
Persia, 142
Persian Ambassador, 130
Pest, 22
Peterborough Abbey, 33
Peterborough, Abbot of, 7
Philip III of France, 17
Philip the Bold, 127; equestrian
   establishment of, 127
Philip of Burgundy, 136
Philip the Good, 132
Phoebus, Gaston, 94
Picot, sheriff, 7
Picot de Lascelles, 8
pilgrimages, 27
Pisanello, 153
*Placita Roll of the English Army in
   Scotland*, 34f
Plantagenet(s), 14f and *passim*
poaching, 92
Podebrad, George, 135
Poitiers, battle of, 71, 77, 151
Polybius, 140
pomp and circumstance, 127
Portugal, 137
postal services, ch. 9 *passim*; Al
   Barid (Mamlūk), 121; Barid-i-
   Mamalik (Indian), 121;

Frankish, 117; Korean, 120;
    Nuncii Regis, 118–20
    circuits of, 118f; Oriental,
    120; Persian, 120; Roman,
    120; Turkic, 121
Prato, Merchant of, 48; mercantile
    contacts of, 48
Procopius, 140

Qabus Nama, 87
Qadisiya, battle of, 142
Qutuz, Sultan, 147

Ramsey, Abbot of, 7
Ratto, Giovanni, 153
Raymond of Aguiliers, 146
Raymond of St Gilles, 146
Raymond V of Toulouse, 14
recreation, 35
Register of the Black Prince, 27
    and ch. 6 *passim*
Regnault de Roye, 107
Reinprecht Renburger, 136
reiving, 34f
Raynald, Count of Guelders, 126
Reynold, 9
Rhuddlan Account Roll, 45f
Rhuddlan Castle, 45f
Ribchester, 4
Richard I, 100
Richard II, 11, 16, 27
Ridanieh, battle of, 148
Rievaulx Abbey, 18, 46
Robert II, Count of Artois, 127
Robert of France, 4
Robert I of Montgomery, 8
Rochester, 14
Rodez, 15
Rome, 4
Roxolani, 4
Rozmital, Count Leo, 135ff
Rubruck, William, 124
Rufus, Jordanus, 54
Rufus, William, 91
Russia, 23

Saladin, 68
Sailsbury, Earl of, 21
Salzburg, Archbishop of, 18
Samarkand, 2, 121, 126
Saone et Loire, 3
Sarhad, 13
Sarmatian, 4
Scararii, 117
Schaseck, 135ff
Schiltberger, Johann, 131
Scythian, 142
Selim II, 131
Seljuks, 145
Sempy, Jean de, 107
Seneschaucie, 43
Service Tartars, 131
Shaizar, Amir of, 87

Shapur, 143
Shiraz, 143
Siberia(n), 3
Sifirth, 6
Sigbert, King of Franks, 90
Silla Dynasty, 120
Silk Route, 125
Sindmanni, 117
slave catchers, 130
So Chi, King, 120
Solutre, 3
Song Jong, King, 120
Southorpe, 7
Spanish, 13, 15, 27
Speed, Prof. J.G., 3, 5
splinter bar (Swingletree), 41
Spofford, Bishop of Hereford, 30
sport, 35
St Inglevert Tournament, 107
St Neots, 7
Statutes of the Synod of Clermont, 42
Stephen, King, 14
Stodmarsh, 13
Stradiots, 151
Stukely, 7
Subudei, 123
Suebi, 4
superstitions, 32f

Tabeada, battle of, 131
Tacitus, 4
Tafur Pero, 22, 132ff
tallage, 32
Tallboys (Taillebois), Ivo, 9, 32
Tancarville, Raoul, 17
Tāq-i-Bōstān, 143
Teithi, 13
Templars, Knights, 18
Templars, Rule of, 18, 69
Tencteri, 4
Tetzel, Gabriel, 135ff
Teutonic Knights, 18f, 132; postal
    services of, 118; recruits to, 132
Thomas à Becket, 127f
Thurbrand, 6
Thurstan, 6
Timur, 68, 120, 129f, 148
Tirant lo Blanc, 106f
tithes, 74
Titian, 153
Toseland, 8
tournament, 78, ch. 8 *passim*; costs
    of, 108f; dangers of, 107f;
    injuries in, 111; localities, 100;
    Papal ban, 100; political aspect,
    101; rules, 101
    horses in: armour for, 103f;
        behaviour of, 111f; injuries to,
        111; mental and physical
        capabilities 110f; role, 103f
    types of: à outrance, 101f; à
        plaisance, 101f; behourd, 103;
        feat of arms, 101f; hastilude,

103; joust, 101, 113ff; mêlée,
    101; trial by combat, 103
tourneying Czech style, 136
tourneying of Rozmital and
    retinue, 136
tourneying at Windsor, 136
trades, ch. 5 *passim*
travel, ch. 10 *passim*
Turanshah, Sultan, 148
Turks, 139

Urban II, Pope, 145
Usamāh Ibn Munqidh, 87–90
    passim
Uzun Hassan, 130f, 143

Vandals, 140
varlet des chiens, 83
Varthema, Ludovico, 132ff
Vaureal, Abbot of, 96
Vegetius Publius Renatus, 53f
Venetian Ambassadors, travels of,
    130f
Venice and possessions, 130
Vikings, 5
Vinci, Leonardo da, 153
Visconti, Gian Galeazzo, Duke of
    Milan, 49
Vitalis, Orderic, 17
Von Harff, Arnold, 132f

Wace, 1
Wandrille Abbey, 17
Wallace Collection, 60
wardrobe accounts, 93, 95; on
    hunting, 93, 95
warhorse territory, ch. 11 *passim*
Welsh medieval law, 105f
Welsh war(s), 17
wergild, 31
Werrington, 7
Westmorland, 7
Willehalm, 105f
William Bastard/the Conqueror,
    1, 4, 6f, 14, 91
William of Poitiers, 14
William of Tyre, 146
Winchester, 7
Windsor Behourd, 109f
Wulfgeat, 6, 13
Wulfric, 6, 13
Wynflaed, 6, 13

Xenophon on hunting, 84

Yam (Mongol postal system):
    Morin Yam, 120; Tayan Yam,
    120; Tergen Yam, 120

Zaragoza, 22
Zegedin, 22
Zehrowsky, Jan, 136
Zeno, Caterino, 131, 143